Diachronic Settlement Studies in the Metal Ages

Diachronic Settlement Studies in the Metal Ages

Report on the ESF workshop
Moesgård, Denmark, 14-18 October 2000

Edited by Henrik Thrane

Jutland Archaeological Society

Diachronic Settlement Studies in the Metal Ages
Report on the ESF workshop at Moesgård, Denmark, 14-18 October 2000

Editor: HenrikThrane

© The authors 2003

Jutland Archaeological Society Publications Vol. 45

Layout & prepress: Jens Kirkeby
Cover: Jens Kirkeby
Type: Adobe Garmond
Paper: 130 Arctic Silk
Printed in Denmark by Narayana Press, Gylling

ISBN 87-88415-24-4

ISSN 0107-2854

Published by:

Jutland Archaeological Society
Moesgaard Museum
DK-8270 Højbjerg

Distributed by:

Aarhus University Press
Langelandsgade 177
DK-8200 Århus N
www.unipress.dk

Published with the financial support of:

The European Science Foundation, and
The Aarhus University Research Fund

Content

Preface

The idea of European collaboration over the study of Prehistoric settlements is not new. The opportunity to make a start came with the announcement of exploratory workshops from the European Science Foundation. We prepared an application for a workshop on: *Diachronic Settlement Studies in the Metal Ages in Europe before the Roman Empire* in the spring of 1999 and we were fortunate in obtaining the approval of the ESF. The workshop was held at Moesgård outside Århus in October 2000 and this report presents the results.

The idea was to present studies from a wide range of European countries in order to illustrate the different approaches to problems which really have a lot in common. The hope was that in this way it might be possible to discover how different research traditions and administrative practices – and, of course, financial restrictions – influence the archaeological practices, and to find levels for new common approaches. The intention was that the workshop should explore these aspects within the frame of settlement studies – in the widest sense, i.e. not only individual settlements but even more the patterns and structures of the settlement in given areas or regions of varying sizes. The emphasis was put on a specific approach to settlement studies, namely those with a chronological horizon long enough to make them properly diachronic. This varies from periods of a few hundred to thousands of years. We have, however, kept close to the Bronze Age as the main period of study, in order

not to make the workshop too diffuse. The Neolithic, not to mention the earlier Stone Ages, has its own problems just as the later Iron Age has. There is then a certain coherence in the contributions to the workshop which should make it useful for further studies and, we hope, inspiring.

We regret that misunderstandings at several levels prevented too many of the invited participants from coming. As a result the geographical coverage was not as full as intended.

The participants have been very helpful in producing their manuscripts in an easily accessible manner, for which we are grateful. There are two deviations from the actual workshop programme. The lecture by John Moreland could not be presented in person at Moesgård, while Dr. Blazek has been unable to produce a manuscript for this volume.

The workshop

The participants were taken through Jutland and Funen on an excursion on Sunday 14 October. We visited Ejer Bavnehøj – a Bronze Age mound on the highest point in Denmark; the Viking period royal site at Jelling – a Unesco World Heritage Site; the "ox road" – the main Prehistoric and historic trunk road down to Hamburg, and the Egtved mound where the famous oak coffin burial was found in 1921. From

Jutland we crossed over to Funen via the new bridge over Lillebælt. Lunch was taken at Hollufgård, followed by inspection of the collections of the archaeological museum with its "open store" displaying all the finds from the island. The afternoon was spent on southwest Funen, where one of the latest diachronic settlement projects was carried out in 1973-86. The causewayed Neolithic camp of Sarup, dolmens and the Late Bronze Age centre at Voldtofte with the Kirkebjerg settlement and the "princely" graves in Lusehøj as well as coastal settlements at Enemærket and Brydegård were inspected, the tour being conducted by the excavator. The manor of Frederiksgave, at one time summer residence of the royal amateur archaeologist Frederik VII, and the medieval castle ruin were also visited before we headed back to Århus via the old bridge and some devious roads in order to show more of the East Danish landscape.

On Monday 15 October the workshop began with an *introduction* to the 18th century manor house of Moesgård, which now houses a unique combination of an archaeological museum with institutes for Ethnography and Prehistoric as well as Medieval Archaeology.

Henrik Thrane opened the session stating the purposes of the workshop and deploring the absence of so many invitees.

He also gave the first lecture on "Diachronic Settlement Studies in the South Scandinavian Lowland Zone, The Danish Experience", outlining the Danish tradition for what is is worth. The historical development and research background of the projects were sketched. He stressed the interplay with the neighbouring countries and with humanistic disciplines, and, alas, less so with the sciences. The major problems were identified and presented, e.g. how insight gained elsewhere may change the priorities in a long term project; good and bad experiences were mentioned and proposals for future work were made as well.

Jens-Henrik Bech took the focus to the latest regional project in Denmark in his lecture "The Thy Archaeological Project – Results and Experiences from a Multinational Archaeological project". This international project from Late Neolithic to Bronze Age (in Central European terms "Frühe & mittlere Bronzezeit") has tried to solve methodological problems by a combination of the traditional survey (field walking) and trial pits. The relevance of sea level fluctuations, deforestation, sand drifts etc., was illustrated, the distribution of special products such as flint sickles out of the region was assessed, and the development of the settlement system was of course indicated.

Nils Björhem lectured on "Settlement Structure in southwestern Scania – a local perspective" which introduced Scandinavia's largest area excavation – 1 million m^2. Over ten years of city development, including the construction of the Øresund bridge and connected roads and railways have occasioned these enormous excavations which have given insight into otherwise neglected elements in the cultural landscape such as roads, borders, single burials etc. He demonstrated the advantage of working continuously in an area during two main periods of field work with study and publication of the first phase as the platform for the second and much larger phase which is only now finishing. The size of the project has necessitated a strict selection of sites according to a research based priority using a two tier model of intensive (total) excavation in selected areas combined with extensive work (survey and trial excavations) in other areas. It has been a very impressive piece of organisation with a wide range of results, including the development of the settlement system over the Bronze and Iron Ages.

These lectures all dealt with coastal and near-coast settlement areas.

In John Moreland's absence Henrik Thrane presented his paper "Exposing the Gaps in the Long-term History of the Peak District, Derbyshire, England" which illustrated the problems of an inland landscape seemingly devoid of archaeological remains from certain periods. By using simple morphological analyses of stone fences and applying test pits to a landscape where field walking has no value it became possible to close some gaps and explain others. It was a useful demonstration of how the eternal problem of the meaning of the apparent lacunae in the archaeological record may be explored.

Fig. 1. The participants on the steps of the main building at Moesgård. Front row, left to right: Václav Furmanek, Henrik Thrane, Jens-Henrik Bech and Slawomir Kadrow, next row: Niels Björhem, Jan Blazek, Peter Turk, Eike Gringmuth-Dallmer and Bernhard Hänsel. (Preben Dehlholm phot.)

Bernhard Hänsel's lecture: *"Bronzezeitlicher Landesausbau in der östlichen Adria"* took us to a quite different landscape in Krajna, Slovenia where a fortified and well-preserved town with Cyclopean walls of the 18th – 17th century BC gave cause for a discussion of the aspect of Aegean (Mycenaean) influence in this coastal region. This aspect includes the influx of people to explain the development of concentrations of population in well-structured towns with craftsmen and very early wine growing. The long term development up to the Roman occupation was outlined.

Eike Gringmuth-Dallmer had chosen a part of the recent "Oder project" for his lecture on *"Strukturveränderungen einer Siedlungskammer im westlichen Osteseegebiet – die "Neuenhagener Oderinsel".* This took us back north, to a marginal area in the Oder river valley where the Late Bronze and Early Iron Age settlement exploited the area, using *"Plaggendüngung".* He demonstrated how the continuous land use could be observed with different methods, not just normal archaeological ones but especially direct and indirect observations of the environment *(Bodenkunde).* The exploitation left the landscape de-settled till the Slavic *landnam* after 1000 AD. The effects of sand drift and soil-fertilising on the archaeological record were demonstrated.

Slawomir Kadrow had analysed a smaller part of Little Poland – 700 km^2 – dividing it into landscape types in his paper "Settlement development in Little Poland during the Bronze Age." The settlements were small and post-holes or other clear house indicators were absent – which is typical of several landscapes. Pits and graves combined with pottery typology and 14-C dates on bones were analysed to observe the structure and development of the settlements. The area was actually without metal during most of the Bronze Age, so the culture was a Bronze Age culture more nominally than in practice until the Late Bronze Age.

Jan Blazek from Most in the neighbouring Czech Republic presented another example of large scale archaeology: "Bronze Age Settlement Structures in Northern Bohemia". Here ½ km² is annually destroyed completely by the enormous open air brown coal mining operations. This has given a great deal of insight into the development of the individual settlements and the settlement structure (pattern) of the area west of the Elbe during the Bronze and Early Iron Ages. Here the nature of the settlement elements varied from period to period. Problems such as settlement mobility, short or long distance and the problem of single farms were tackled. The lack of dating material such as bronzes and graves, functional differences and population/settlement density as well as intensive/extensive field research strategies were also treated.

Václav Furmanek talked about *"Mittelbronze- und urnenfelderzeitliche Siedlungsstrukturen in der Slowakei".* He concentrated on settlement from another angle i.e. the settlement of the individual cultures in Slovakia, using the bronzes as indicators. He illustrated the importance of cultural geography in external relations during the Bronze Age. Mobility was, again, taken up and seen in the light of migrations and expansion of populations from the south, east and north. The role of the fortified settlements, which have become so important in this area, was taken up.

Peter Turk took us back to Krajna with his lecture on "Late Bronze Age Lowland Settlements in Central Slovenia – hamlets, villages or protourban centres ?" He had excavated a lowland settlement and looked at a nearby hillfort. Here the role of bronze hoards in relation to the settlement and their economic role in local and wider contexts were examined, including relations to Upper Italy. Once again the importance of local conditions for the possibility of identifying house structures was examined. Post-holes play a crucial role in this process as well as contexts with fences etc. – just as in several of the other papers presented at the workshop.

Conclusions

A variety of subjects and problems was discussed and several relevant and lucid cases presented. There is no doubt that highly qualified work is going on all over the area represented by the workshop. Much of it could undoubtedly serve as inspiration for other regions.

Let us just mention: specialised production, mobility/movements of individual settlements, whether they be farms or villages, macro or micro level mobility, territories, the application of the model of intensive research(excavation) combined with extensive research in the same region. The use of field surveys was discussed, how far can they take us, are they still necessary and to what extent should they be complemented by other methods? Other themes were the analysis of settlement structures without clearly identified houses and the analysis of settlements with houses, how to define what is contemporary and what was functionally conditioned.

The influx of new elements, groups, traditions and populations and their definition are ever present problems which of course cannot be solved in a workshop. The influence of environmental factors on the choice of settlement sites and on our ability to observe past behaviour in the landscape are perhaps more to the fore now when source criticism has become as important for archaeology as it has been for history.

The use of previous research as platforms for future research projects in order to improve standards and return to old questions is a comparatively recent phenomenon. Flexibility in planning and adaptability in long term projects and in the application of fresh and varied methods to the field of settlement research have become indispensable in modern administrative and research work. The workshop clearly demonstrated three traditions within diachronic settlement research in Europe – even if the practices of Western Europe could not be covered.

1. A Northern tradition where posthole archaeology has become the norm and all-dominating practice during the last 30 years, even if some areas and some periods still lag behind. There is normally a good burial record available. Here development is seen in a sequence of relative periods, i.e. as a unilineal development where changes and even gaps may be caused by environmental changes rather than migrations or culture movements.

2. A Central European tradition dominated by other elements than post-holes. The structures are analysed according to individual potential and initiatives and the theoretical framework is a complicated system of cultures defined, above all, by the metalwork and pottery styles. The Danube continues to play a crucial role in the understanding of innovation. The graves show a rather varying intensity and amplitude during prehistoric times.

3. A South European tradition where massive, still standing stone architecture dominates over more modest settlement indicators but where modern research will be able to change the picture. Here the reaction to the influences from the east Mediterranean must be a major element when cultural developments, including population and settlement, have to be explained. The burial record is highly variable and erratic.

It is no wonder that the methods applied in the North, Centre and South vary so much as they were seen to do. The degree of collaboration with other disciplines and with the sciences is also highly diversified, but this may be rooted in other traditions and conditions.

Here the traditions were identified and their compatibility noted. If we are to integrate the traditions into a new common one further discussions and a wider circle are needed.

The absence of so many of the invited speakers was most irritating and of course reduced the geographical coverage and restricted insight into and discussion of the regional traditions. This sad experience should be taken as an opportunity to improve the communication in similar future projects so that such calamities are not repeated. The investment of resources in the preparation is the same, no matter how many researchers participate.

We were, however, able to make use of the depletion of the number in a positive way. We had more time for the presentations and for discussion. This created a relaxed and pleasant atmosphere with frank and good exchange of ideas and constructive criticism. So we were satisfied with the outcome of the scientific part of the workshop and hope that this report will convey this to the readers.

We now need to expand the circle geographically so that the missing parts may be included.

We also need to focus upon interdisciplinary work, both with other humanistic disciplines and with a broad range of scientific disciplines. This could be the topic for our next meeting and should be discussed at the Liège congress in 2001 at the latest.

It was agreed that the present company should form the core of the *Commission for Settlement Archaeology* of the international union of archaeologists UISPP. The chairman will be Henrik Thrane, vice chairman Bernhard Hänsel and secretary Peter Turk. Thus we hope to be able to continue the communication initiated at the workshop and expand the circle to further countries in Europe so that the workshop will have been just the beginning of a new and fruitful tradition.

Finally we want to thank all the participants for their good company and contributions.

Bernhard Hänsel   Henrik Thrane

Northern Europe

Diachronic Settlement Studies in the South Scandinavian Lowland Zone
– the Danish Experience

Henrik Thrane

Denmark has a long but rather discontinuous tradition of diachronic settlement research with very different emphases applied at different times during the period of the last 100 years.

At this point I should like to emphasize that my definition of diachronic settlement research focuses upon the long term development of settlement structures, not on individual settlements. My approach is more what the Germans call *"Genetische Siedlungsforschung"*, indicating that it is the genesis of settlement patterns (to use the Anglo-Saxon term) and their development through time which is important.

I define settlement archaeology as the study of human settlement in relation to the natural and cultural environment applying settlement historical methods and perspectives, thus including the internal and external relations between settlements, communication, exchange etc.

Apart from a single, warm-hearted attempt by the enthusiastic amateur Frederik Sehested, who was the first to look at the finds of a single region – his own estate – as a whole rather than just at individual sites (Sehested 1878), it took 100 years of incipient archaeological research before settlement archaeology was launched in Denmark.

The pioneer in this field, as in so many others, was Sophus Müller who in the years 1904-15 published a series of papers on the distribution of the prehistoric settlement in relation to the different Danish types of landscape as they had been formed by the Ice Ages.

Actually his first attempt dates from 1898 when he published the first maps of groups of Stone Age barrows (of the Single Grave Culture). Müller was the first to use the new "database", as we would call it now and as it has now become, the so-called "Parish Register" (*sognebeskrivelse* in Danish); gathered from 1873 onwards this register contains registrations of finds and monuments, i.e. dolmens and barrows, cemeteries, hoards and stray finds and other sites county by county. Müller was also the first to regard the landscape as an inalienable part of prehistoric society. Müller's thesis was that "a complete map of the tumuli is at the same time a complete map of the settlement" (1904). The burial mounds had been placed next to the actual settlement sites, he thought, but this remained a hypothesis that could not be tested until 50 years later.

Müller's thesis determined the discussion and research for the next two generations. The historian Vilhelm la Cour wrote the first dissertation concerned with settlement patterns (1927). He demonstrated the usefulness of the Parish Register in his study of the Neolithic and Bronze Age settlement of the island of Zealand. He reconstructed the settled areas, *"bygder"*, and land routes for the Neolithic and the Bronze Age. For the Iron Age the only source was the cemeteries without markings above ground and there was not much that la Cour could do with them.

Another approach for this period was attempted by another historian, H.V. Clausen (1916). His interest

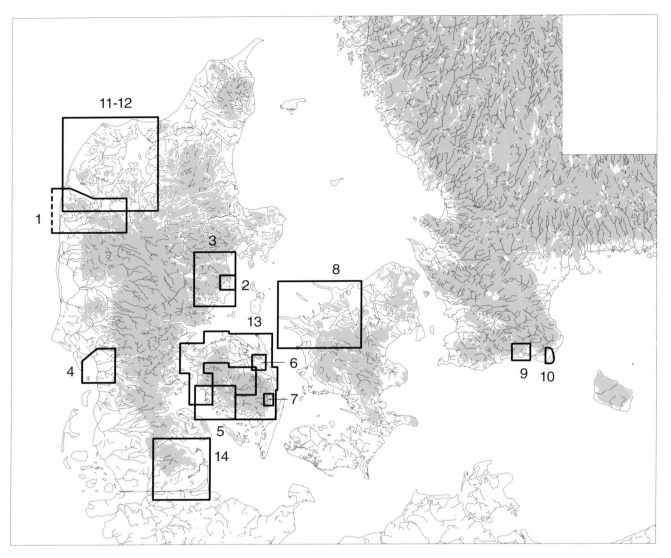

Fig. 1. Major diachronic settlement projects in the West Baltic Region, 1. Northwest Jutland, 2. Norsminde Fjord, 3. East Jutland, 4. Ribe Marshes, 5. Southwest Fyn, 6. Northeast Fyn, 7. Gudme, 8. Northwest Zealand, 9. Ystad, 10. Hagestad, 11.Thy, 12. Limfjord, 13. Atlas Fyn, 14. Kosel – Angeln – Schwansen.

was place names. He based his study upon the philological dating of groups of place names in a relative sequence. He reconstructed maps of the settled areas of the Pre-Viking period as seen against wooded land. He also used place names as indications of which areas had been forested until they were cleared in the Middle Ages.

An unexpected aftermath to this first phase was a strong reaction from an amateur. The agricultural consultant N. Overgaard turned Müller's thesis

round, viewing the situation from an agrarian's point of view (1932). His thesis was that the Bronze Age people of course had used the best arable areas for their subsistence and accordingly placed the burial mounds on the marginal lands. The distribution of the tumuli (cf. Baudou 1985), in his opinion, showed that the non-settled areas and the settlements had to be looked for where there were no barrows.

With this paper the discussion had reached a dead end. The same data could apparently be interpreted in directly contradictory ways and the situation had become slightly absurd. Theses about the distribution and land use of settlement were ardently discussed while the crucial archaeological sources remained absent. Although Bronze Age settlement sites were known, for many years the total number of sites known was less than 30. Before 1955 only rubbish pits were available as indicators of activity and there were no reliable house plans. This led to fruitless speculations about nomadism, in attempts to explain the absence of house remains from this period, in strong contrast to the Iron Age, the houses of which had by 1940 become fairly well known. Round post-hole settings were taken for houses, which they certainly were not (la Cour 1927).

Each of the attempts mentioned had a common source material: the Parish Register. No new field-work was involved. It was only during the 1930s that the situation changed. Therkel Mathiassen, fresh from the Arctic, took up the amateur approach of field-walking, directing his attention to the inland river system of Jutland in order to establish the existence of a Jutland equivalent of the Maglemosean of Zealand (1937). This project was successful in so far as a vast number of sites was found and a method established. Settlement sites could be found by field-walking and they existed in abundance, albeit only represented by flint tools and debitage. In Jutland the settlements from the Metal Ages produced only

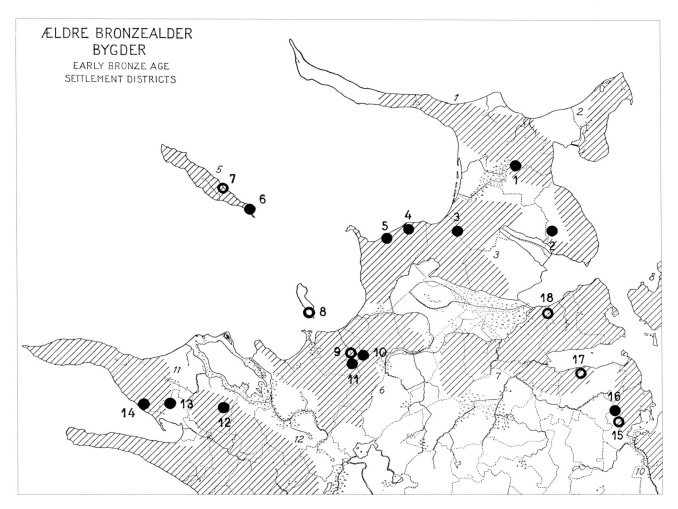

Fig. 2. Northwest Zealand, Mathiassen's map of the Bronze Age settlement areas (periods I – III) – hatched, with pottery dated settlements of periods IV – VI found between 1959 and 1971 – dots (Thrane 1971).

potsherds and other refuse from the rubbish pits, and the Neolithic and Bronze Age were still sadly under-represented. On the Danish Isles the situation was no better, apart from a cluster of pottery-rich pits in the Roskilde region.

During the war Mathiassen decided that the time had come for a comprehensive diachronic study of a whole region, inspired by the German *"Landesauf-nahme"* initiated by Alfred Tode and others after the bitter experience of the First World War. He chose an area of 1260 square kilometres in Northwest Jutland and had it field-walked, analysed and published rapidly (1948). The attempt was repeated equally rapidly and with the same methods in Northwest Zealand (1959). His aim was modestly stated as "an attempt to study the prehistoric settlement of a Danish region on a more solid basis than the existing".

Now nobody could complain of a lack of finds. Rather the opposite was the case. With 20 000 artefacts from Northwest Jutland and 50 000 from Northwest Zealand it was only possible in pre-computer times to present the material in a brief tabular form which did not exactly make the publications attractive. Even statistics were not highly developed or applied in the Humanities so perhaps we may say that the material was never exhaustively analysed.

As regards the Müller-Overgaard debate there was, strangely enough, little help. The settlement sites found on the surface by field-walking were characterized above all by flint and even the Iron Age sites had astonishingly little pottery to show. This meant that dating had to rely, above all, on flint typology, which presents problems for the Bronze and Iron Ages. Mathiassen had to conclude that he could not solve the issue. He had to rely on the burial mounds for the distribution of the settled areas – just as Sophus Müller had done. For the Stone Age his projects were important, however.

After Mathiassen's two great projects came an interval. At the National Museum it was felt that the usefulness of the approach had been exhausted and nobody wanted to continue or resume work in this way. There was a somewhat depressed attitude, and other concerns, such as rescue archaeology, also soon

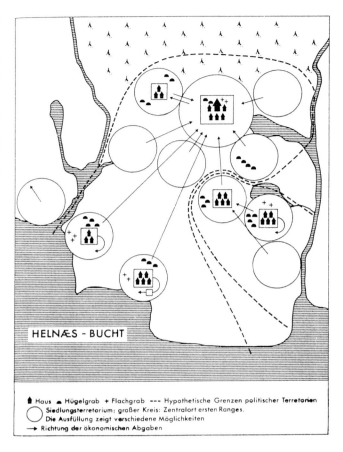

Fig. 3. Southwest Fyn, model of Late Bronze Age settlement system 1980 (after Thrane 1995).

came to the fore, fully occupying both thoughts and resources.

I happened to become involved in fieldwork in the 1960s in the area examined by Mathiassen on Zealand and was able to demonstrate that there was a perfectly good and simple reason for the failure of Mathiassen's work and that of the pre-Mathiassen era. When tractor ploughing reached its breakthrough in Denmark in the 1950s pottery all of a sudden began appearing on the ploughed fields. The reason was that the plough now went just a few centimetres deeper and thus turned up hitherto untouched levels. Now not only the technically better and therefore more climate-resistant Iron Age pottery but also Bronze Age and Neolithic pottery could be observed. Accordingly settlements from the pottery-producing periods could finally be located and dated with far greater precision (Thrane 1985). Needless to say, this opened new vistas for the study of land use and settlement patterns of the post-Mesolithic periods.

Another, less happy effect of the mechanised ploughing was the apparently inherent steady increase of ploughing depth as a result of increasingly more powerful tractors and bigger ploughs. With the early tractor generations the problem was not so great but with the tractors of the last 20 years this trend has come to mean much more. The ever increased ploughing depth has become the main cause of erosion – not only of the kind visible on the fields after heavy rains, but also, much more seriously for archae-

ology, erosion of the primary source material, which has now reached a depressing rate. This culturally caused erosion is the prime factor now destroying the hidden archaeological remains (or cultural heritage in modern terms) of this and other countries with a similar intensive agriculture. However, if we try to look beyond this sad, but irreversible development, we can point out that the tractors brought settlement archaeology to a point where proper analyses of the relationship of settlement sites to burials and the whole environmental sphere have, at last, become feasible. While the benefit may be estimated to have lasted perhaps 30-40 years the loss will be irreparable and will prove terminal within the next 20-30 years, at the most.

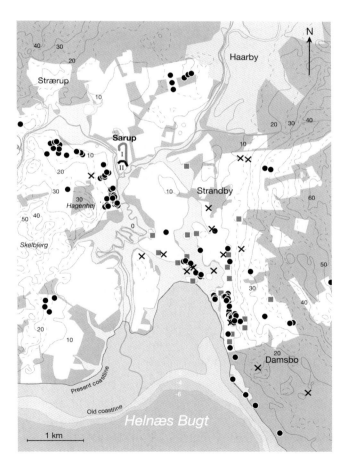

Fig. 4. The Early Neolithic settlement around Sarup light areas have been field walked. Sites contemporary to Sarup I and II are shown, square – settlement, circle – megalithic tomb, x – single find (after Andersen 1999).

When the opportunity arose, I tried to apply Mathiassen's method to a new area within my new working field, the island of Funen, which was a well studied region thanks to the very conscientious work by the single local archaeologist, Erling Albrectsen. The southwest Funen project from 1973-86 showed all the problems of this period (Thrane 1989). My goal was dual: 1. To form an overall idea of the antiquarian situation against the background just sketched, i.e. to observe how far the destruction had gone and what still remained to be found in the landscape. 2. To study the development of settlement and the changing settlement patterns in a typical East Danish landscape which was known to contain a rich archaeological record – above all, I admit, from my own period of interest – the Bronze Age. A preliminary report has been published and a comprehensive catalogue of the Late Bronze Age material is approaching printing. I have tried to expand the survey by concentrating on excavations of burial mounds etc. for several years, including the rescue excavations at the locus classicus of Danish Bronze Age settlements – Kirkebjerg at Voldtofte (Berglund 1981). Currently I am working on the publication of this important material. The animal bones and the carbonized grain have been analysed but the pottery and the other finds, including the painted wall plaster, remain to be studied. A model for the settlement structure of the region with a hierarchical system of the settlements was proposed (fig. 3), placing the settlement on Kirkebjerg at the top of the pyramid as the residence of the ruler of the area north of the bay of Helnæs. At a more modest level a model for a "normal" settlement was put forward (Thrane 1999).

The Neolithic has become one of the best investigated periods and is very much an ongoing project. The completely excavated causewayed camp of the Early Neolithic (3200 BC)) has been the core of Niels Andersen's research which is now accessible in three imposing volumes (Andersen 1997 & 1999). The surrounding landscape has been field-walked with astonishing results and a long term project of rescue excavations of megalithic tombs – and recently a new causewayed camp – is still continuing annually. The territorial pattern of the Neolithic phases has been reconstructed according to two different methods (Thrane 1989 figs. 22-23).

As had happened with Mathiassen's two projects, it turned out that the Southwest Funen project was also too early in some respects; computers, GIS, GPS and metal detectors were unknown, unavailable or useless when we did our fieldwork. It is rather irritating to see how easily and how much more precisely the plotting of finds can be made with GPS compared to the old fashioned methods that we had to use. We realized that for special problems we had to look elsewhere, so the origin of the medieval villages and the Late Iron Age settlement history (Migration-Viking period) had to be examined in separate projects elsewhere on Funen, contrary to my original intention. We did not succeed in closing the gap in the prehistoric record after the Roman period – because we did not then know that settlements of this period behave archaeologically differently from the earlier Iron Age settlements. I called this the Gudme problem because it was best illustrated by the extraordinary concentration of Migration Period gold around Gudme in East Funen where settlements and burials were absent – just like everywhere else in Denmark (Thrane 1987). It turned out that there was no gap in the settlement history caused by emigration but rather a change in how the archaeological sources behave. Metaldetecting yielded a vast amount of bronze and precious metal objects near the present village of Gudme. Excavations proved that these hundreds of metal objects had been ploughed up from an extensive settlement which we now regard as the central site during the 3rd- 6th centuries AD with its own landing site on the nearby coast of Storebælt – but that is another story (Nielsen & al. 1993).

In Southwest Funen we did not manage what I had intended in terms of area and intensity, but that was mostly an effect of our limited resources.

My inspiration came from Mathiassen and the Landesaufnahme in Schleswig-Holstein but also from Sweden, where Märta Strömberg had launched her Hagestad project in 1961. She applied a new model which is highly recommendable, I think. While her "core area" was rather small, just the parish of Hagestad, she made comparative excavations at sites outside Hagestad but within the "reference area" of south-east Scania (1980). Her publications of some of the issues that interested her most have shown how fruitful this approach can be when this combination of intensive area research with extensive excavations of specific problems is applied over a sufficiently long period of at least 30 years. This prolonged time horizon is important.

When it was discovered how frightening the effects of the new agricultural mechanization had become, Carl Johan Becker persuaded the Danish Research Council to finance a five year project from 1969 with the purpose of saving at least a selection of cemeteries and settlements of the Bronze and Iron Ages (Becker 1982). Becker himself had excavated the important group of sites centered round Grøntoft in western central Jutland and managed to apply the new mechanics to the excavation process, thus uncovering the first whole villages and house agglomerations of the Late Bronze Age and Early Iron Age (ibid.). This innovation set off the trend which has since been ruling settlement excavations in Denmark: large-scale area excavations, stripping the top soil mechanically and concentrating on the post holes.

South of the border the most ambitious diachronic project was carried out in the landscapes of Angeln (of a certain interest for the English) and Schwansen in order to examine the famous settlement gap of the Late Iron Age, but of importance to Bronze and Iron Age settlement as well. This project is well published – in contrast to most of the other projects (Willroth 1992).

We have been through three stages of Danish settlement archaeology: 1. the tumulus stage where no further sources were available, 2. the pit and surface find stage with excavations limited to the odd pit or trench or to field-walking and 3. the post-hole (large area excavation) stage characterized by the removal of the topsoil and concentration on the features dug into the subsoil.

So instead of the old midden *("Kulturschicht")* archaeology from the *"Kjøkkenmøddinger"* – kitchen middens of c. 1850 onwards – we now live with post-hole archaeology, practically excluding any other methodology (Näsman 1989). Maybe we should discuss the effects of this change.

The excavations by the settlement council created by Becker remained unpublished till a new Research Council financed project "Farm and Village" from 1993-98 was set up to analyse and publish this important material (Fabech & al. 1999). We still await these publications, however.

Several settlement projects have been initiated over the last 20 years but few have been finished or published. I should mention the East Jutland project centered on the Moesgård institute. It continues, but at a very low level of intensity. Originally the area selected was a limited one in the east, along the coast, not far from Norsminde Fjord where the institute had its excavation training and a study of the settlement system with focus above all on the Ertebølle culture, but later diachronically, was made during several years (Andersen 1991). The Neolithic period was the original focus of the East Jutland project (Madsen 1984) but the idea is diachronic and fresh blood has been added by new, landscape-oriented work around Lake Tåstrup where we currently teach our students field-walking (Näsman 1997). Still, the project is very much determined by the interests of the individual teachers.

One rather different project was the Ribe Marsh project conceived by Stig Jensen in 1980 and published in 1998. Here no fieldwork was undertaken, apart from minor excavations on special problems. The idea was to use the Parish Register supplemented by registration of what the farmers had found and observed. A central aspect was source criticism which had been taken up in Denmark during the 1970s and which is, of course, crucial to an understanding of what the archaeological sources are able to show, how representative they may be and how different periods show themselves in the archaeological record.

Another new approach was initiated by Ole Crumlin-Pedersen with his background in the maritime research centre at Roskilde. The idea was to explore the coastal zone and investigate the relationship between conventional terrestrial settlement archaeology and the maritime zone which is so important to a landscape like the Danish one. The island of Funen was chosen because it had an easily accessible source material, and by 1986 this material had been registered in the national database at the DKC *("det kulturhistoriske centralregister")* at the National Museum in Copenhagen. The work by Erling Albrectsen in the period 1940-1971 had provided a solid corpus of material, above all for the Iron Age (1971).

The Atlas of the Coast of Funen was devoted to the period 500 BC to 1500 AD and conceived as an interdisciplinary work (Crumlin-Pedersen & al. ed. 1996). Fieldwork by geographers was done at the coast to investigate the geographic conditions, how the coasts were formed by abrasion or sedimentation and where landing sites of the later Iron Age could be located or expected. The role of the medieval towns in the exploitation of the coastal zone was also explored. This attention to the marine cultural resources and to the contact zone where the traditional settlement zone meets with the maritime zone may well be one of our major contributions in a wider methodological context.

The international Thy project is presented by the local expert Jens-Henrik Bech so I shall not intrude upon his paper.

Recently we have seen settlement aspects in the interdisciplinary projects initiated by the Research

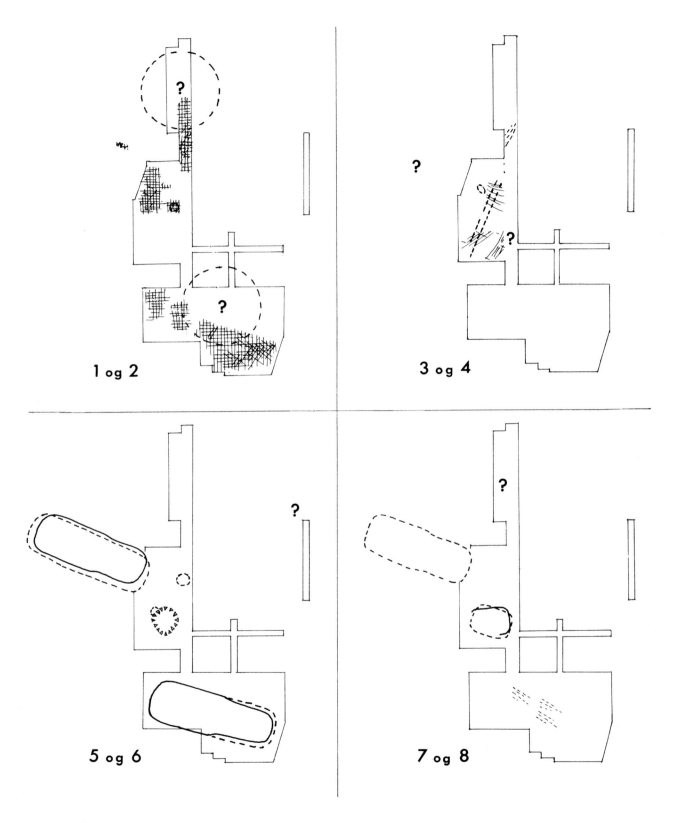

Fig. 5. Fragtrup, the sequence of the Late Bronze Age settlement (after Draiby 1985).

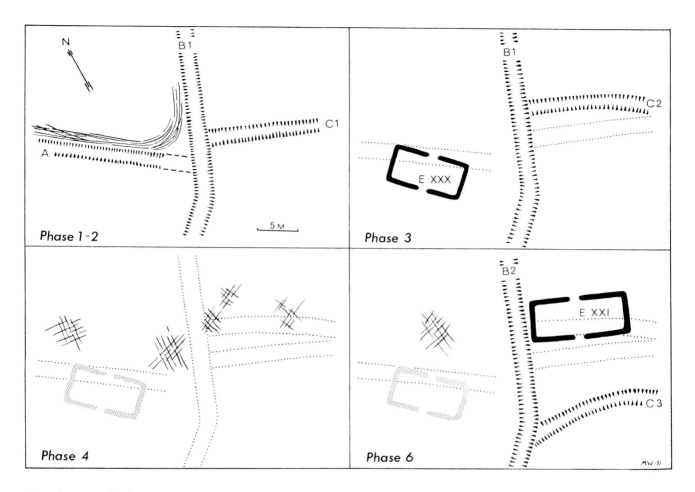

Fig. 6. Grøntoft, the sequence of the Pre-Roman Iron Age settlement (after Becker 1973).

Councils. Once again we see that archaeology is not the leading discipline. The areas selected for the Agrar 2000 project (Näsman 1997; http://www.natmus.dk/ agrar 2000) depend upon the availability of suitable lakes for diachronic pollen analysis – which is how it used to be. Only rarely have diachronic pollen diagrams been worked out with the relation to the settlement as the prime objective – as at Gudme fig. 7 (Odgaard & Rasmussen 2000). This touches upon a major problem in Danish settlement research and one that puts us in a negative light compared with our neighbours. We have had to focus upon the problems using an exclusively archaeological approach, sometimes tempered with a sprinkling of toponymic or historical analysis. We look with envy at recent Swedish projects like the Ystad project in Scania (Berglund

1991; Larsson & al. 1991) and hope that a new era will begin before it is too late. There are openings which make me optimistic, but there is a long way to go before we reach a satisfactory level of scientific participation in our settlement projects. Denmark is still not covered by a net of pollen diagrams enabling us to study the vegetation development and the impact of Man for all Danish regions. What we have achieved, however, is an integration of historical sources such as the first detailed maps from the decades around 1800, taxation statistics and place names down to field and site levels.

Now the application of GIS to the mapping of landscape and archaeological remains is being developed and holds great promise for the analysis level. We are to some extent involved in this development at our institute, but for projects like Southwest Funen or for Mathiassen's it is unfortunately too late (or too expensive).

Although there have been several diachronic projects that aim at a time-span from the arrival of Man to the medieval (or even later) period there has been a clear tendency to concentrate on shorter lengths of time. This has advantages for the in-depth understanding and analysing of the settlement patterns and their development but at the cost of the long term perspective, which we archaeologists always boast of as our main advantage over history. This is one of the reasons why we have given this workshop a special focus on an in-between period, simply in order not to confuse the issue by mixing Neolithic, Mesolithic and Late Iron Age, each of which has its own specific settlement types and problems. From the Neolithic onwards the cultures share the basic agricultural economy and are therefore more mutually compatible.

Gaps in the record – even in spite of serious specific efforts to find material for the critical periods – have been observed in most parts of Europe. They need explaining if we are to understand the development and John Moreland's lecture takes up this point. In Denmark we have gaps in the earliest Neolithic, in the earliest Iron Age – 500-300 BC – and in the Migration and Merovingian periods (Thrane 1987) – cf. the classic case of the landscape Angeln connected to the emigration of the Angles.(Willroth 1992).

Now that individual settlements are no longer the great problem that they (or rather their absence) used to be in Müller's time it is time to focus upon the settlement systems or patterns. In Denmark we now have a well documented series of long houses from the Late Neolithic (c. 2400 BC) far up into the Medieval period (13th century at least). We know hundreds of settlements with longhouses from the Bronze Age and from the Iron Age periods, while the Early and Middle Neolithic periods are slowly joining the party. The major problem remains however: when were the first villages built – and why? We know of agglomerations of long houses but we have no undisputed villages before c. 300 BC when the first fenced-in house/farm concentration is attested at Grøntoft B (Becker 1982). This does not mean that villages did not exist earlier. It only means that we are unable to prove their existence in the absence of delimiting fences or palisades or floors and other deposits interlinking the individual houses. The Late Neolithic, the Bronze Age and the earliest Iron Age (period I) are filled with longhouses, sometimes with stable ends (byres), sometimes accompanied by small houses, but we dare not propose that more than two or three farms co-existed at any time.

Another important issue is the fate of the individual farms and villages. How long did they last and how stable were they? Becker's excavations at Grøntoft – fig 6 (1973; Rindel 2001), Lise Thorvildsen's excavations at Fragtrup – fig. 5 (Draiby 1985) and my own at Lusehøj (Thrane 1984) all point to a labile settlement system. We call it the mobile or wandering settlement. It seems that individual settlements moved after a certain time, but that the distance involved in the move was not very great. The intervals are difficult to assess with any accuracy. Indeed we think that each settlement of village population size would have occupied a specific territory. Within this they would move the settlement until this process stopped at a time in the Late Viking period (Jeppesen 1981). The villages have remained until the present day in the same position that they had reached c. 950/1050 AD. This problem has only been investigated successfully in the late 1970s after decades of speculations and is a good example of how archaeology can contribute to the solution of vital historical problems. The "wandering village" is a major innovation in Danish settlement archaeology which forces us to examine each case individually in order to ascertain whether this or that settlement is the product of repeated occupation or simply a single occupation. The problems of dating and separating the 29 houses from a period of 1000 years at Højgård, covering 29650 m^2, is a good example (Ethelberg 1993). The theory also leads to new speculations over the land-use patterns and other important issues in the economic and social spheres.

One of the most striking gains of recent Danish settlement research is the claim that central places – however relative the interpretation of this term may be in the context of different periods – existed in the

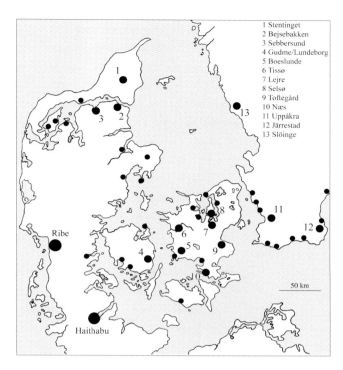

Fig. 7. Metalwork rich settlements of the later Iron Age – c. 200 – AD (Lars Jørgensen fec.)

Bronze Age, at Voldtofte and Boeslunde, and in the Iron Age (Madsen 2000) beginning with the cemeteries from the last century BC, such as Langå from East Funen and Hedegård in East Jutland and continuing in the Roman Iron Age with the Stevns concentration e.g. Himlingøje on East Zealand and Migration period Gudme near Langå and so forth – not forgetting the truly royal site of Jelling. The ways in which these centres express themselves differ and only rarely are we able to combine the rich burials with other sources like settlements or clusters of rich treasures – as is the case at Voldtofte, Hedegård and Gudme.

So, where are we now?

We are continuing to accumulate an enormous mass of information in our archives and databases because of the ever increasing volume of rescue excavations. Large numbers of relevant settlement sites are exca-

vated, albeit not all at a satisfactory level (Mikkelsen 1998). The local museums make their own small scale settlement projects covering specific periods such as the battle-axe culture, or on a diachronic basis, covering a longer period or periods, which is good. They plan them solely for their own benefit without any coordination or even regional planning, which is bad. What remains a problem is the lack of integration of relevant disciplines due to the absence of funding or relevant researchers. Another problem is the delay or even absence of publications. Without publications we have no means of asserting what has been achieved and what could be learned from these projects or how similar research may be improved. This aspect is one of the basic ideas behind this workshop. We should all learn from each other's mistakes – and successes.

One of the heaviest drawbacks in Danish settlement research has been the scale of scientific co-operation. We have had a crisis in scientific collaboration for decades. When the Southwest Funen work was in process we had to go to Sweden to have pollen diagrams made. Samples may have been taken from excavations but the chances of having them analysed before too many years elapsed were nil. Now we have very good botanists and other scientists at work, but there are far too few of them to play the role that I would like to see them play in settlement research.

I will make a short digression in order to stress an important point about a traditionally indispensable element of any regional settlement analysis – pollen diagrams. Before c. 1980 they were all very conscientiously made, – indeed Danes like Axel Jessen, Johannes Iversen and Jørgen Troels-Smith were pioneers in this field. One element was by necessity absent, i.e. absolute datings. Each pollen diagram had its own "floating chronology". With new separation techniques it is now possible to date not only peat samples but also for instance soil samples from drillings or sections in barrows by AMS 14 C-dates. New sophisticated techniques inform us about dust sedimentation (from fields) and about nitrogen and phosphate contents as indicators of agricultural practices in the catchment area. The new diagrams provide so much new informa-

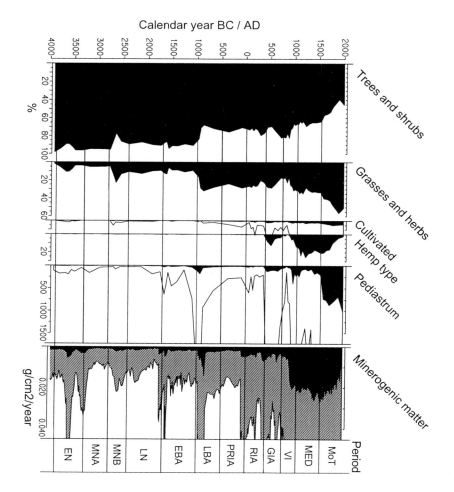

Calendar year BC / AD

Fig. 8. Pollendiagramme from Lake Gudme, Funen, Denmark with summary pollen curves for trees & shrubs, grasses & herbs, cultivated plants and hemp type pollen (a proxy for hemp retting in the lake) plus a summary curve for the green alga Pediastrum (a proxy for nutrient concentrations in the lake) and a curve for accumulation rate of minerogenic matter (a proxy for lake catchment erosion) (curves with 10x exaggeration). The diagram, which covers the period of agricultural impact on the Danish landscape, i.e. the last 6000 years from the Early Neolithic (EN) to Modern time (MoT), shows correlations between increasing anthropogenic impact on the vegetation (forest clearance, expanding agricultural land, intensified arable cultivation) and increasing soil erosion and nutrient concentrations in the lake. (Analyst: Peter Rasmussen, Geological Survey of Denmark and Greenland, GEUS).

tion that they are no longer comparable to the old ones when it comes to their relevance for archaeology, mainly settlement archaeology. In order to exploit the new approaches ideally a series of new diagrams should be made on fresh sites – and on some of the old ones.

The diagrams already available show extensive clearing from the Late Neolithic c. 2400 BC through the Bronze Age, with much more pronounced local variations in the Iron Age.

The Danish tradition is an example of the interplay between mainly humanistic disciplines rather than between archaeology and science. The place names were ordered chronologically at the end of the 19th century and this relative chronology formed the basis for the first attempts at a settlement history for the Medieval, Viking and Iron Age periods such

as H.V. Clausen's. The archaeological material had similarly been ordered in nearly all details by the time of the First World War and a discussion of the use of the place names and their relevance for the settlement history of the Pre-Viking period was resumed in the 1970s, forcing the toponymists to return to their chronology and refine it and reconsider the source critical position. Lately it has been the sacral place names which are in focus because of the surge of interest in the Migration period centres of wealth (Brink 1999).

Another game of ping-pong was played across the borders. I mentioned the Landesaufnahme as inspiration for Mathiassen's work. He in turn inspired Märta Strömberg's Hagestad project which was one of my ideals. The Southwest Funen and the village projects in their turn served as inspiration for the Ystad Project and an exchange of ideas also took place between Kiel and Odense in the 1970s. I am sorry to say that our horizon has been rather limited to our immediate neighbours. Although I did check for similar work in Norway, Britain, Poland, the Netherlands and Germany, I found either the conditions or the organisation too different.

Another important experience is that no matter how up to date we think we are, or try to be, we are limited by some restrictions caused by our position in time and space. I mentioned how Mathiassen's timing was unfortunate in so far as it was just too early to catch the impact of the mechanization of our agriculture – which on the other hand meant that we now have detailed knowledge of how the archaeological sources presented themselves in the period between the mid 19th century and the mid 20th century. In a research-historical perspective this is not unimportant. Again, we were too early on Southwest Funen to apply metal detectors and other modern techniques. They were not available then in editions that were useful in field-walking – and nobody suspected that they would be much use, anyhow, because so little metalwork was known by then. We missed the Late Iron Age settlements that must have been there at our feet. That was not only because we had no metal detectors but also because we did not imagine that there could be such a difference between the Early Iron Age (Pre-Roman and Roman Iron Age) and the Late Iron Age (Migration period – Viking Age) in the settlement indicators. It was by pure accident that we discovered this during rescue excavations in advance of the laying of gas pipe lines in the 1980s (Anon. 1989). Now that we know what to look for we ought to go back to Southwest Funen and check.

That leads to a favourite idea of mine. Diachronic settlement projects should per se be eternal. It is impossible to know all the critical factors and act accordingly at any given point of time. Not only do the scientific techniques change, agricultural practices change – and sometimes this changes our opportunities drastically. Let me just mention the EU agricultural agreements intended to reduce the leaching of phosphate and nitrogen in order to improve condi-

tions for the environment. This laudable initiative has led farmers to shorten the period when land is left fallow so much that the conditions for decent field-walking may be there just for a fortnight – if at all – during a year cycle.

New aids like GPS, which would have been considered pure magic when we walked the fields in the 70s, not to mention what Mathiassen's crews would have thought of them, revolutionize the precision and speed of the process of location of material.

Needless to say, we hope that progress will be made in the field of archaeological theory and method so that new considerations and strategies may be applied over the years. Any short term project like Mathiassen's is therefore bound to remain incomplete if it is not followed by control projects of selected areas or periods or types of monuments in the following generations. A permanent or at least semi-permanent presence in the area is vital, not least in order to keep tabs on, what is happening locally.

A diachronic settlement project should continue long enough to be able to incorporate changes in the methodological approach and to apply new techniques. The world of invention has not come to a stop with GIS and GPS. Field-walking should be carried out at least twice with an interval of some years.

References

Abbreviations:

Aarbøger	Aarbøger for nordisk Oldkyndighed og Historie, København
AUD	Arkæologiske Udgravninger i Danmark, København
FMS	Frühmittelalterliche Studien, Berlin
JDA	Journal of Danish Archaeology, Odense
PZ	Prähistorische Zeitschrift, Berlin
PPS	Proceedings of the Prehistoric Society, London

Albrectsen, E. 1971: Den ældre jernalders bebyggelse på Fyn, *Kuml 1970*, 123-44.

Andersen, N. H. 1997: *The Sarup Enclosures, Sarup 1*, Jysk Arkæologisk Selskabs skrifter, Højbjerg.

Andersen, N. H. 1999: *Saruppladsen, Sarup 2-3*, Jysk Arkæologisk Selskabs skrifter, Højbjerg.

Andersen, S. H. 1991: Norsminde. A køkkenmødding with Late Mesolithic and Early Neolithic occupation, *JDA* 8, 13-40.

Andersen, S. H. 2000: "Køkkenmøddinger" (Shell Middens) in Denmark: a Survey, *PPS 66*, 361-84.

Anon. ed. 1989: *Danmarks længste udgravning* (with Engl. summaries), Herning.

Baudou, E. 1985: Archaeological Source Criticism and the History of Modern Cultivation, K. Kristiansen ed: *Archaeological Formation Processes*, 63-80, Copenhagen.

Becker, C.J. 1973: Früheisenzeitliche Dörfer bei Grøntoft, Westjütland, 3. Vorbericht *Acta Archaeologica* XLII, 79-110.

Becker, C.J. 1982: Siedlungen der Bronzezeit und der vorrömischen Eisenzeit in Danemark, *Offa* 39, 53-71.

Berglund, B.E. ed. 1991: The cultural landscape during 6000 years in southern Sweden – the Ystad Project, *Ecological Bulletins 41*, Copenhagen.

Berglund, J. 1981: Kirkebjerget – a Late Bronze Age Settlement at Voldtofte, Southwest Funen, *JDA 1*, 51-64.

Brink, S. 1999: Social Order in the Early Scandinavian Landscape, Fabech & Ringtved eds: Settlement and landscape, 423-39.

Clausen, H.V. 1916: Studier over Danmarks Oldtidsbebyggelse, *Aarbøger 1916*, 1-226.

la Cour, V. 1927: *Sjællands ældste Bygder*, Kjøbenhavn

Crumlin-Pedersen, O., E. Porsmose & H. Thrane eds. 1996: *Atlas over Fyns kyst*, (Engl. summaries), Odense.

Draiby, B. 1985: Fragtrup, en boplads fra yngre bronzealder, *Aarbøger 1985*, 127-216 (Engl. summary).

Ethelberg, P. 1993: Two more house groups with three-aisled long-houses from the Early Bronze Age at Højgård, South Jutland, *JDA 10*, 136-155.

Fabech, C., S. Hvass, U. Näsman & J.Ringtved 1999: "Settlement and Landscape" – a presentation of a research programme and a conference, C. Fabech & J. Ringtved eds.: *Settlement and Landscape*, Aarhus.

Jensen, S. ed. 1998: *Marsk, land og bebyggelse. Ribeegnen gennem 10.000 år*, Jysk Arkæologisk Selskabs skrifter, Højbjerg

Jeppesen, T. Grøngaard 1981: *Middelalderlandsbyens Opståen*, Fynske Studier 11, Odense.

Larsson, L., J. Callmer & B. Stjernquist eds. 1991: *The Archaeology of the cultural Landscape. Fieldwork and research in a south Swedish rural region*, Acta Archaeologica Lundiensia ser. in 4° no. 19, Stockholm/Lund

Madsen, T. 1982: Settlement Systems of early agricultural societies in East Jutland, Denmark: a regional study of change, *Journal of anthropological archaeology 1*, 197-236,

Mathiassen, T. 1937: Gudenaakulturen, en mesolithisk Indlandsbebyggelse i Jylland, *Aarbøger 1937*, 1-186.

Mathiassen, T. 1948: *Studier over Nordvestjyllands Oldtidsbebyggelse*, Nationalmuseets Skrifter Arkæologisk-historisk Række II, København

Mathiassen, T. 1959: *Nordvestsjællands Oldtidsbebyggelse*, Nationalmuseets Skrifter Arkæologisk-historisk Række VII, København.

Mikkelsen, D. Kaldal 1998: Bopladsudgravninger: en forskningsmæssig status, *AUD 1997*, 7-20, (Engl. summary).

Müller, S. 1904: Vei og Bygd i Sten- og Bronzealderen, *Aarbøger 1904*, 1-64

Müller, S. 1914: Sønderjyllands Bronzealder, *Aarbøger 1914*, 169-322.

Nielsen, P. O., K. Randsborg & H. Thrane eds., 1993: *The archaeology of Gudme and Lundeborg*, Copenhagen.

Näsman, U. 1989: Hus, landsby og bebyggelse, Anon. ed.: *Danmarks længste udgravning*, 69-86, (Engl. summary) Herning

Näsman, U. 1997: Landskabsudvikling i 6000 år, S. Andersen ed:, *Det agrare landskab i Danmark*, 52-61, København.

Odgaard, B. V. & P. Rasmussen 2000: Origin and temporal development of macro-scale vegetation patterns in the cultural landscape of Denmark, *Journal of Ecology 88*, 733-48.

Overgaard, N. 1932: Vestjyllands Oldtidsbebyggelse, *Jyske Samlinger 5*, 1-99, Aarhus

Rindel, P.O. 2001: Building typology as a means of describing the development of early village communities in the 5th-3rd centuries BC at Grøntoft, J.R. Brauet & L. Karlsson eds: *From Huts to Houses*, 73-87, Stockholm

Sehested, N.F.B. 1878: *Fortidsminder og Oldsager fra Egnen om Broholm*, København, (French summary).

Strömberg, M. 1980: The Hagestad Investigation – a Project Analysis, *Meddelanden från Lunds Univeristets historiska Museum 1979-80*, 47-60, Lund.

Thrane, H. 1984: *Lusehøj ved Voldtofte – en sydvestfynsk storhøj fra yngre broncealder*, Fynske Studier 13, Odense.

Thrane, H. 1985: Bronze Age Settlements, K. Kristiansen eds: *Archaeological Formation Processes*, 142-151, Viborg.

Thrane, H. 1987: Gudme und das Gudme Problem, *FMS 21*, 1-48.

Thrane, H. 1989: Siedlungsarchäologische Untersuchungen in Dänemark mit besonderer Berücksichtigung von Fünen, *PZ 64*, 5-47.

Thrane, H. 1995: Stand und Aufgaben der Bronzezeitforschung im westliche Ostseegebiet während der Per. III-V, P. Schauer ed: *Beiträge zur Urnenfelderzeit nördlich und südlich der Alpen*, 429-452, Mainz

Thrane, H. 1999: Bronze Age settlement in South Scandinavia – territorality and organisation, A.F. Harding ed: *Experiment and Design. Archaeological Studies in honour of John Coles*, 123-132, Oxford.

Willroth, K.H. 1992: *Untersuchungen zur Besiedlungsgeschichte der Landschaften Angeln und Schwansen von der älteren Bronzezeit bis zum frühen Mittelalter*, Neumünster.

Settlement structure in south-western Scania
– a local perspective

Nils Björhem

This article deals with two large-scale archaeological projects carried out in Malmö during the last two decades. In Sweden, laws protecting ancient monuments are strong. The Ancient Monuments Act (*Kulturminneslagen*) of 1988 is the latest version of a tradition stretching back to the 1600s (SFS 1988:950). The law states that when construction takes place the landowner must in general pay for an archaeological investigation if no possibility of preserving the ancient remains exists, which is the course the law prefers. This law also covers ancient remains hidden beneath the surface of the ground, meaning in practice that all traces of human activity are legally protected.

Contract archaeology in the Malmö region

In Sweden, there exists a comprehensive system of excavations based upon contracts in conjunction with the development of land. Excavations take place mainly under the authority of the government, but county and city museums also conduct excavations. Malmö Cultural Resource Management (*Malmö Kulturmiljö*), of the City of Malmö, formerly known as the Department of Antiquities (*Stadsantikvariska avdelning*), sets the agenda concerning ancient monuments and historic buildings within the City of Malmö and also, more recently, in the near vicinity.

Malmö lies in Scania, in the very southernmost part of the country. The city is Sweden's third largest in size, and is built upon extremely fertile soils. South-western Scania belongs to one of the most densely and continuously occupied parts of the country (fig. 1). The physical geography of the area is reminiscent of Denmark, and the province was a part of Denmark until the second half of the 1600s, which, among other things, is evident in architectural styles, and to a lesser extent in the language. The area consists of moraine land with clay and sand, but with none of the large rocks which are so common in other parts of Sweden, while the coastline is smooth and lacks islands or skerries. Forests of spruce are a very typical feature dominating great parts of the Swedish landscape; however, the spruces found in Scania have been planted during the last hundred years. The south-west is, and has long been, a flat, cultivated landscape.

Archaeological excavations in Malmö have been carried out by the Museum. These increased in number and scope as they did in many other parts of the country during the 1960s and 1970s. More distinct archaeological projects did not occur in Malmö until later, with precisely defined project programmes and pre-excavation research aims being a phenomenon of the last decade.

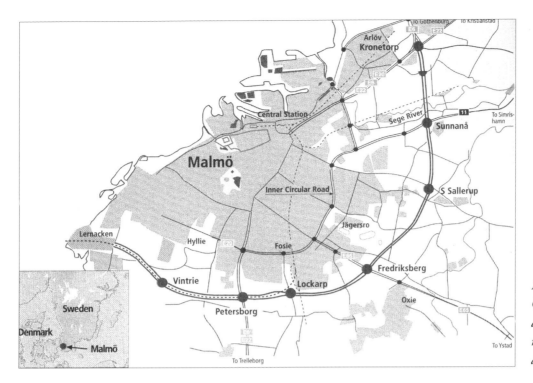

Fig. 1. Map of the Outer Circular Road around Malmö connected with the Bridge and the Continent.

Fosie IV

In 1979, a continuous expansion of the Fosie Industrial Estate in the southern part of Malmö was initiated. This project was named Fosie IV, and was distinguished from previous developments in that an area was prepared for a whole industrial estate at once rather than separate plots at a time (Björhem & Säfvestad 1989; 1993). The area was 2000 x 300 m in size, and topsoil was to be removed over an area of 400 000 m^2. The normal procedure at this time was for archaeologists to follow the excavating machines as the topsoil was stripped. Working procedures were decided by the builder, which usually meant the local authority and its entrepreneurs. The ravages of the excavating machines resulted in an indistinct surface covered in caterpillar tracks or in a surface compromised by large rubber tyre marks. The archaeologists marked those darker patches they could distinguish with sticks, these usually being obvious remains such as groups of stones, hearths and pits or occupation deposits with sooty fills. Post-holes, and other small or diffuse remains were not discovered except when

they lay in close vicinity to those pits and occupation deposits which were cleaned by hand. After topsoil stripping, the settlements consequently consisted of scattered features which were treated as wholly separate objects of investigation. Conversely, the areas between them were regarded as lost and even devoid of information. The entrepreneurs who removed the topsoil left a layer of silt between the topsoil and the lighter moraine. We archaeologists therefore had to demand help from the excavation machine to carry out another removal. As a result, we decided to do more than merely take care of what 'happened' to turn up. As an example, the excavation involved among other things a hill upon the slopes of which extensive Bronze Age settlement remains had been found. Attention was subsequently focused upon the summit of the hill in particular. Because of the workload, the Museum had engaged several Danish archaeologists that season. Some of those archaeologists made us aware of the possibility of finding house remains similar to those that had earlier been found in Denmark. When the settlement plateau was stripped, rows of post-hole discolourations which could quite quickly be grouped together into house remains from both the Bronze and Iron Ages were discovered. After this, the excavation strategy was changed, with more careful machine stripping henceforth being carried out with the excavator's scoop. The result was about a hundred house remains from a variety of periods.

As a consequence, our picture of the presence of prehistoric houses has changed completely since the first clear longhouses were discovered in Scania's arable fields. Today, the remains of post-built longhouses are commonly found in arable land throughout the whole of Scandinavia, from the south to the north, with a concentration still to be found in Denmark and the old Danish provinces of Sweden. However, the existence of areas completely without such finds can best be explained by a lack of land development.

The discovery of all these house remains was in itself a great step forward, but it was above all the realisation of the extent of a settlement in all its different parts, with its buildings, waste pits, clay pits and wells, which most influenced the investigations of the last decades. The investigation area at Fosie IV with its very gently rolling terrain adjacent to wetlands and a small river provided very good conditions for the delimitation of constructions and activity areas in relation to one another. The delimitation of these spatial elements also facilitated a clarification of chronological elements within the settlements and between them. Few unknown areas were discovered between the settlements, and these were, due to the large working area, if not completely, at least relatively well defined. In this respect it became possible to talk of a total investigation.

The investigation, which continued for four and a half years, resulted in remains from the end of the Early Stone Age up to the Viking Age, divided into six more or less well-defined settlements. Remains of post-constructed houses from the Late Neolithic until the Viking Age were present, with a preponderance of material from the Late Bronze Age, Roman Iron Age and Late Iron Age (fig. 2).

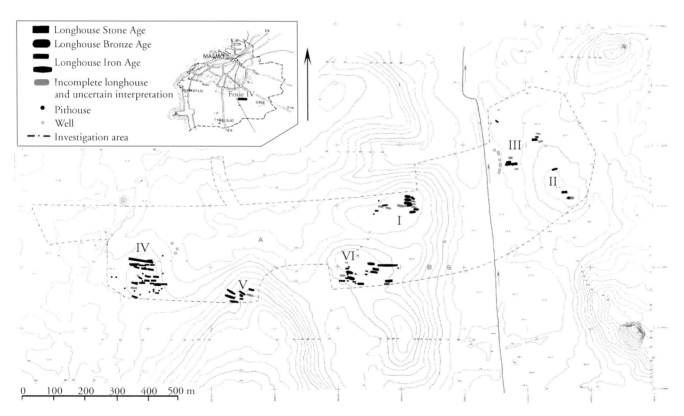

Fig. 2. The Fosie IV area.

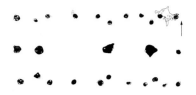

Fig. 3. Late Neolithic house from Fosie IV (house 13). Scale 1:200.

The Late Neolithic longhouses were unique when first discovered, but the type has now shown itself to be generally valid for large parts of primarily southern Scandinavia (fig. 3). Today we know that longhouses from the Later Stone Age can be identified by a row of posts placed under the central axis of the roof. This construction type was replaced during the Early Bronze Age by houses with two rows of roof-bearing posts placed in pairs. Certain local features can be noticed, however, in the material from Scania and the Malmö area.

The find material was dominated by pottery and flint from the Late Bronze Age. The reason for this was that the settlements here, as at other sites, included many large pits. These were investigated with appropriate attention, resulting in extensive find material. An important result was that it was possible to divide the settlement ceramics from the Late Bronze Age into two separate chronological periods, the A-phase from around the 1300s to the 800s BC, and the B-phase from the mid-800s until around 400 BC.

It became possible to sketch out building patterns in the area over a long time perspective for the whole period Late Neolithic – Viking Age. The limited size of the area meant that the results were uncertain when applied outside the local horizon. The lack of find material and accelerator dates resulted in much of the reasoning concerning above all the Iron Age constructions becoming very hypothetical. However, it was still possible to make descriptions and even certain interpretations of causes of change. These can be summarised by a simple sketch of the investigation area divided into different construction phases (fig.

4). A certain concentration of construction is hypothesised to have taken place during the transition between the Late Neolithic and the Early Bronze Age. During the Late Bronze Age, an expansion in construction began which can be discerned both as division and new establishment of constructions. At the same time, changes in the find material took place, as they did in bone, macrofossil and pollen material (fig. 5). The occurrence of different types of features in the settlements also indicated an intensification of both agriculture and animal husbandry (Berglund et al. 1991, Fig. 5.13:5; Björhem & Säfvestad 1993, 356 f.; Gustafsson 1995). A change in the appearance of pottery and the proportions of the houses indicated a more pervasive cultural change in Bronze Age society than just an increased exploitation of the landscape. This expansion continued during the Pre-Roman Iron Age. One purely hypothetical consequence of this intensification could have been that certain settlement areas came to consist of a large number of dis-

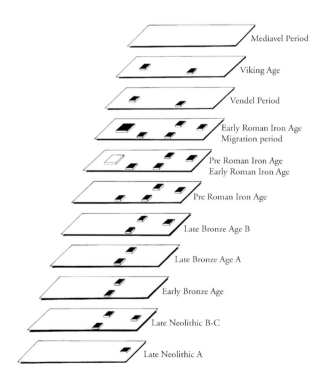

Fig. 4. Habitation development on the settlements within Fosie IV.

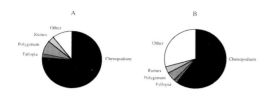

Fig. 5. The percentage distribution of arable weed seeds from: A: 1000 BC – 800 B.C; and B: 800 BC – 500 BC (from Gustafsson 1998).

Fig. 6. Use of resources during the later part of the Late Bronze Age. 1. Field systems. 2. Wetlands. 3. Settlements.

persed farms surrounded by cultivation areas bordering each other (fig. 6). Even if the local constructions as a whole could be defined as lone farm buildings, co-ordination would probably have been necessary when it came to animal husbandry – however, socially seen, the distance between the farms would not have been any problem as they lay within view of each other. One can presume that the landscape gradually became fully colonised. During the course of the Early Iron Age, a change in building structure took place, resulting in a reorganisation of the constructions into villages or village-like concentrations. A reorganisation to a system of in- and out-field based agriculture also probably took place. This may even possibly have involved several different adjustments. In the archaeological source material in Malmö at the beginning of the 1990s, there still persisted an uncertainty about how large this expansion was and

whether it had caused a restructuring of buildings and cultivation geography.

An important by-product of the Fosie IV excavations has been to illustrate the possibilities that contract archaeology can have if one attempts to view it as a whole and construct syntheses instead of only producing as administratively neutral a report as possible in the hopes that somebody else will be able to link the results together afterwards.

The *Öresundsförbindelsen* ('Öresund Fixed Link')

In the summer of 2000, Denmark and Sweden were joined together via a bridge over the Sound, with the Scandinavian Peninsula and the Continent becoming permanently linked. The archaeological work for the land approach to the bridge on the Swedish side began in 1993. The County Administrative Board charged the then Department of City Archaeology with the commission of carrying out an inventory and formulating what would be of importance before construction of the 25 km long motorway around Malmö, with approach roads, roundabouts and connecting rail links (fig 1). The railway over the bridge meant that 10 km of lines needed to be widened to close to 200 m. One difference from earlier contract-based excavations in the area was that we were now actively forced to choose what would be excavated. The point of departure was that this selection would be made on the basis of research aims rather than solely the occurrence of ancient remains hidden below the surface. The reason for this was partly the extent of the commission, but also the changing perception of how contract archaeology should be carried out (Proposition 1993/94: 177).

An overall goal for the project was to work with a large-scale perspective, to consider the cultural and natural landscape as a unity which in addition to remains of settlements and graves also includes cultivation areas, sacrificial locations and resource

Fig. 7. Archaeologically investigated areas in Malmö. The outer circular road and later investigations marked as trial trenches. Dots = Early Iron Age settlements known before 1994. Dotted line = sea level ca. 4000 BC.

areas. It was also decided that the proportional input should be quantitative, and that no areas should be downgraded in priority as being of lesser value without a survey excavation having first been carried out according to the rules and possibilities presented by the Ancient Monuments Act in the form of various phases of investigation such as site assessments and survey excavations (Björhem 1994). Bearing in mind earlier experience of how much lay hidden beneath the topsoil, it was therefore accepted that this inductive phase would involve a thorough examination taking the form of the opening of exploratory trenches. This was carried out over the whole of the planned road areas, including the area planned for landscaping, an area of c. 5 000 000 m^2 (fig. 7). The prioritisation which was demanded resulted in a planned varied level of documentation regarding the delimitation and excavation of individual settlements rather than

completely excluding or refraining from investigating certain locations. About fifty sites were therefore investigated to varying extents.

To be able to study the areas of greatest importance and avoid merely collecting fragmentary knowledge, several sub-projects were created. Through these sub-projects, the material could be both elucidated in a long chronological perspective and described in more synchronous conditions. This involved quantitative comparisons between sites, but also analyses of individual locations. Interdisciplinary knowledge and methodical approaches were emphasised. The sub-projects were named: the Hunter-Farmer Landscape (*Jägar-bondelandeskapet*), which was to deal with issues of the coastal and inland complex of problems during the Mesolithic and Neolithic; the Longhouse Landscape (*Långhuslandskapet*), which was to deal with construction patterns over a long time perspective; the Organised Landscape (*Det organiserade landskapet*), looking at the problems of the dynamic in construction and the cultivation landscape during the Middle Ages, among other things; the Ritual Landscape (*Det rituella landskapet*), which was to analyse sacrificial, funerary and settlement finds; the Functional Landscape (*Det funktionella landskapet*), which was to elucidate problems centring around the functions of individual settlements, among other things; the Fully-Cultivated Landscape (*Fullåkerslandskapet*), within which conditions of preservation and methodical issues were to be studied; and Environmental Archaeology (*Miljöarkeologi*), dealing with the landscape and land use from quaternary geological and cultural geographical aspects. With the help of these sub-projects, the intention was, at a general level, to provide an account of the extent of construction and different aspects of the use of the landscape from the Stone Age until the Middle Ages. Laboratories and institutions in several of the country's universities are represented in the project, collaborating in dating, problems concerning assemblages of species, cultivation environments and other specific activities.

The Longhouse Landscape

The Öresund Fixed Link provided an excellent opportunity to test the results of the Fosie IV investigation over a significantly larger area. One of the results from Fosie IV was that the existing view of prehistoric construction as a "wandering village", which was so effectively popularised for the Bronze and Iron Age constructions of Jutland, could not be properly verified here (Becker 1973, 108; Hvass 1982, 194f). Over the long perspective, a picture of sporadic spreading, expansion and concentration of constructions presented itself. An important fact was that the investigation area was sufficiently large to allow the changes to be perceived both in the individual settlement surfaces and also between the settlements.

These concentrations and expansions in construction were presumed to be easier to perceive in

a larger perspective. The landscape around Malmö was therefore divided into four zones on the basis of topographical characteristics. From the Sound in the west, these were named (I) the coast, (II) the coastal inland, (III) the outer hummocky landscape, and (IV) the Sege River area (fig. 8). These areas are not distinctly differentiable; if one does not travel in the right direction or does not pay attention to the proportions of the landscape, no obvious zones will be perceived. No part of the road lies further than 7 kilometres from the original coastline. The coastline lay about 5m above its current level at its highest point during the transition between the Mesolithic and Neolithic. During the Bronze and Iron Ages it was not significantly different from today, if one excepts all later land reclamation connected with the growth of the city (fig. 7).

The hypothetical development of buildings can be considered as a model illustrated with a graph in which the X and Y axes represent topographical zones versus chronological periods relevant to the better perception of changes. Stated in general terms, our knowledge regarding longhouse construction was limited when the Öresund Fixed Link project was launched, except with regard to Zone II, where Fosie IV was situated (fig. 9). It proved to be suitable to work with three levels: within the settlement, between settlements and within the territory. Synonymous appellations are settlement surface, settlement area and resource area. Similar concepts with slight differences in significance have also been used within, for example, the project "The Cultural Landscape during 6000 years in southern Sweden – the Ystad Project" (Berglund 1991; Tesch 1993, 18).

It was possible, in the first place, to define settlement surfaces on the basis of traces of activity (i.e. features) in relation to specific topographical conditions. The evaluation of a settlement demands simultaneous detailed analysis of the source material as most settlement surfaces consisted of several settlement phases of differing size and extent. This also applies to the relationship between the settlements. The latest level had already been defined at the assessment stage as the four landscape zones referred to above. In this

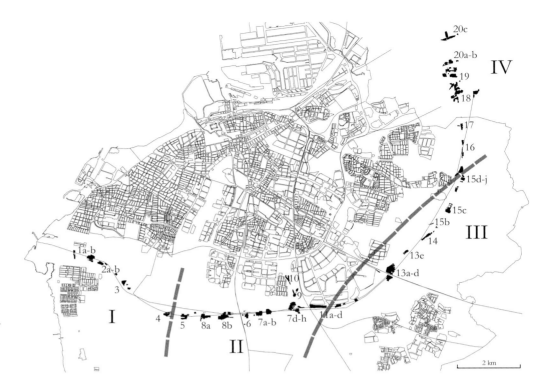

Fig. 8. The Öresund
Fixed Link Project.
Investigated areas (1-
20) and topographi-
cal zones (I-IV).

chronologically vertical study with spatial variation, changes could be perceived in the distribution of activities. This quantitative state of relations demanded an investigation area with a representative division of settlements. The intensive but uneven distribution of archaeological investigations in the Malmö area generally hindered such studies and despite the extensive development areas within the project, the spatial perspective was on the whole limited to a local level. The changes in the local placement of a building which occurred due to the relocation, division or expansion of the construction meant that it could not be followed in its entirety nor as an addition to the area under development (Callmer 1986, 173ff.). Conversely, the large and continuous investigation surfaces made it possible to study building structures within and between individual settlements.

The consequences of the above reasoning were that the documentation of settlements and construction was carried out over the whole area of investigation, and that large investigation areas were striven for. Analysis of the inner structure of the settlements and the relation between different construction units re-

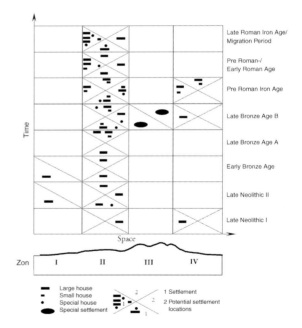

Fig. 9. Model of "The Longhouse Landscape". Settlements
with remains of houses grouped in suitable periods and
topographically defined environments. The levels of space:
region, resource area = zones; settlement area = rectangle; settlement and potential location for a settlement are
marked with one or more diagonal.

quired that the topsoil should be removed over large surfaces and that careful documentation was carried out. Studies of the relationship between settlements demanded a good knowledge of where one construction stopped and another began. In order to establish clear control over the division of settlements within the zones during the different periods of time, as many settlements were investigated as possible. The investigation surfaces were therefore divided into intensive and extensive areas. Total investigation was intended through the intensive investigation of surfaces. This meant that all of the free-lying surface was documented in plan and that a large proportion of the revealed features were excavated to at least 50%. These extensive investigation surfaces were managed so that within a larger accessible surface only certain parts were opened up, these being selected as the stripping proceeded and knowledge of the area increased. Prioritisation took place at first hand on the basis of these criteria, and to a lesser degree through the exclusion of complete settlements or areas from investigation.

Some of the research aims which were formulated have now, after the conclusion of the field-based part of the project, been evaluated. These include the following.

The Late Neolithic – Early Bronze Age

In order to elucidate construction patterns and relations between zones and settlements during this period, we must turn our attention to the coast. Only 900 m from the contemporary coastline at Elinelund (2A), remains of both two and three-aisled houses plus small constructions with three pairs of posts occurred (fig. 10). Judging from appearances, it seemed clear at an early stage that the three-aisled houses were from the Bronze Age. This also fitted into the pattern of settlements undergoing expansion at the end of the Bronze Age, which was one of the theories under consideration. The large and numerous pits so typical for

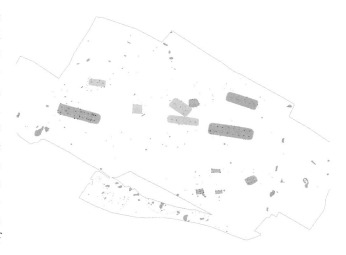

Fig. 10. Late Neolithic and Early Bronze Age settlement Elinelund 2 A. Light shading marks Stone Age, dark shading marks Bronze Age. Scale 1: 1000.

this period were missing, something which needed to be explained. One theory proposed was that the settlement lay in a newly established and more densely wooded area, and that the houses therefore did not need clay-daubed walls. Another interpretation came from environmental archaeology, as the assemblage of macrofossils indicated that the material came from the Early Bronze Age. This was soon confirmed by carbon 14 dating of the samples from the post-holes. These dates indicated that the settlement was occupied during the Late Neolithic and Early Bronze Age and came to an end during the transition to the Late Bronze Age. Judging from these widely-spaced carbon 14 datings, the settlement could have been abandoned for a period. The known transition between two- and three-aisled longhouses at the beginning of the Bronze Age, as earlier established, had been confirmed once more (Boas 1993, 133f; Ethelberg 1993, 154; Sarnäs & Nord-Paulsson 2001).

Six hundred metres east of this settlement, a settlement (2B) with three more two-aisled houses, each with only three central posts, was investigated. The buildings had not existed simultaneously, but appeared, interestingly enough, to have been enclosed by a fence or post construction. It was discovered that this house group included another Late Neolithic site with a group of three houses which had replaced one another, following which the settlement had been abandoned (Björhem & Säfvestad 1989, 125). This indicated that the settlements had a certain permanence and stability, but that, seen over the perspective of about a hundred years, they moved. Without being certain that only these two settlements were in successive use, it seems however possible that at least four building horizons can be counted within this limited area during the Late Neolithic and Early Bronze Age. It is also possible to follow a progression among the houses from very small two-aisled houses with three heavy central posts to longer, but possibly somewhat narrower constructions, which in turn were replaced by large three-aisled buildings.

Early and Late Bronze Age

Judging from both earlier investigations and the basic data beginning to take form, a concentration (and increase) of settlements occurred during the transition between the Early and Late Bronze Age. The settlements by the coast also fitted into this pattern as they came to an end at the same point in time. However, hearth pits connected with Litorinavallen (1A) have been dated to this period of time and surprisingly do not indicate that there were any people who actually lived seasonally or transiently on the shore.

One issue raised by the results of the Fosie investigation was whether construction became "monumentalised" during the course of the Early Bronze Age, something which was first expressed by the placement of burial mounds in topographically eminent positions. This question is closely linked with the concentration of buildings discussed above. The rich occurrence of settlement remains from Zones II and III during the later part of the Early Bronze Age and the first half of the Late Bronze Age does not completely answer this question. One problem was that clear settlement traces from the Late Neolithic and above all the Early Bronze

Age were difficult to find. However, the preliminary results from the settlement at Svågertorp (8B) corresponded well with the questions posed. The settlement was situated at the highest point in its immediate environs in the middle of Zone II, in a part of the landscape where the rise from the coast levels out and transforms into a rolling landscape. The Sound and the coastline were easily visible from the elevated ridge known as "Mallhög" (the great mound or height) in older cartographic material. The complex, with the exception of some remains, was dated to the Early Bronze Age and the first part of the Late Bronze Age, both on the basis of finds (from the A-phase), and carbon 14 results. The hill itself was not occupied during the later part of the Late Bronze Age. Minor remains were however present, situated near a wetland at the foot of the hill (8C) (von Rostoványi & Hydén 2002). Further afield, in a lower lying settlement slightly to the west (8A), remains from the Late Neolithic and Early Bronze Age as well as remains from the A- and B- phases of the Late Bronze Age were found (Rosberg & Lindhé 2001). The material consequently corresponded with the above hypothesis. Settlements have been found in the whole area, with the most topographically eminent positions being completely dominated by A-phase material. One more settlement (20C), with a monumental situation and a fine view over the valley of the Sege River lay in the area's north-easternmost part, at the transition to the Lund plain. Comprehensive settlement material from the A-phase was also collected here (Berggren & Celin in press).

Another problem surrounding the Bronze Age material from Fosie was to what degree changes occurred in aspects of culture, community and economy to correspond in time with the transition between what have been named the A- and B-phases. Among other things, did the splintering and increase of building units that took place during the later part of the Late Bronze Age, which the material from the Öresund Fixed Link project et al. was expected to indicate, result in the launching of new constructions in the coastal zone? This could also be confirmed. Even if we have not yet analysed all the excavation material from the outer hummock landscape (Zone III), a slight question mark can still be placed beside the concept of an expansion. There can be no doubt that settlement remains from the B-phase have been found in newly-settled locations on several sites. However, it is not a question of a one-sidedly clear picture of core buildings with an expansion to satellite settlements in the surrounding areas. Many settlements lasted over the entire Late Bronze Age, but examples also exist of settlements with A-phase material where a subsequent construction from the end of the Bronze Age and the first centuries of the Pre-Roman Iron Age could not be observed upon exactly the same surface. Instead, the settlement remains were found in nearby locations. The only traces from the B-phase on one of them (7A) (Sarnäs 2000; Rudin & Brink 2002, 76ff) was a hearth placed on top of an erosion layer on one of the hill's slopes. This layer was interpreted as being the remains of fields which formed faint terraces upon the slope and thereby escaped being completely obliterated by modern cultivation, which is remarkable in the intense cultivated landscape of Scania. In these cases, consequently, we are dealing with a transference and division of buildings rather than an obvious expansion and increase. Neither did the hummocky landscape constitute some kind of clear zone for fresh colonisation – this was not actually completely new knowledge. The buildings were already established and evidence was found of large erosion layers which stratigraphically separated radiometrically-dated material corresponding chronologically with the A- and B-phases (14). It would therefore be most reasonable to speak of a restructuring and change in construction patterns, which was a consequence and perhaps even also a cause of an expansion of settlements during the transition to the Iron Age.

Iron Age

One of the expected results was that buildings from the end of the Late Bronze Age and beginning of the Iron Age would be present in the coastal zone. This expectation was based upon the concept of division, increase and relocation of the buildings situated slightly inland

from the coast. This was also confirmed, with a settlement in Zone I near the coast (3A and B) consisting in the main of pits and wells, but also with a few house remains, which could be dated to the Pre-Roman Iron Age. Some carbon 14 dates from the 8th century BC, with the usual large outer values due to the calibration curve, were also obtained (fig. 11).

One question which was posed was whether the more village-like structures from around the birth of Christ that had been suspected of having a connection with the constructions within Fosie IV could be confirmed and clarified. There was also the question whether this involved a couple of greater phases of restructuring or changing of the buildings during the Iron Age. This proposition is a little vaguely formulated, but can be answered. Observation during analysis

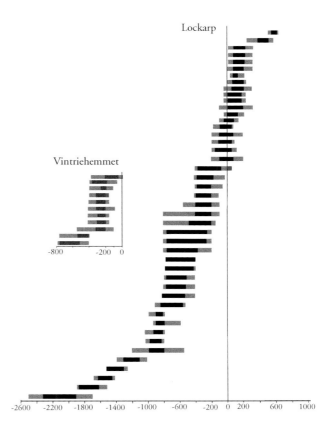

Fig. 11. Radiocarbon datings from a settlement in the coastal zone (Vintriehemmet 3 A) and a settlement in the coastal inland (Lockarp 7 B).

does not just consist of assessing the basic data of the settlements, but also involves really taking advantage of the opportunity to study many settlements, notably those nearby. A change in one place can always be assessed in relation to "where the neighbours live". We can see that the houses are changing, from the evidence of different dating elements, but these differences are also easier to detect since the houses are located on different sites. This situation of constructions on different sites at separate points in time has often been interpreted as a sign of so-called "itinerant construction", a form of regular relocation of units with construction first becoming stabilised during the transition between the Viking Age and the Middle Ages. If one moves one's settlement, and thereby also one's house, one also has the incentive to change the appearance of the building. In a fully exploited landscape, such as we continue to see during the Early Iron Age in the area, almost all major relocations of buildings would affect the "neighbours", which would provide a foundation for a simultaneous creation of new house types. The occurrence of a new type of house could consequently indicate a more uniform and co-ordinated shifting of territories.

Settlements from the first half of the Pre-Roman Iron Age consisted of relatively insubstantial house remains, with a few holes from wall-bearing posts. The longhouses assumed to be dwellings were up to 20m long, although many were only about 10m long. Large pits and pit systems were present at the settlements, as they were during the Late Bronze Age (fig. 12). These are assumed to be clay pits. This indicates that the walls were clay-lined, which in turn indicates a relatively open and deforested landscape. They lay dispersed in many different parts of the landscape and down to the coast, and can be considered traces of farm buildings. They were followed by constructions most often consisting of well-built houses, closer to 40m long with densely-positioned wall posts. These posts were occasionally placed in dug-out ditches, with in some cases presumably different types of walls in separate parts of the house. The construction of the gables often varied within the same building. The houses could have had some kind of gable door. Smaller houses, e.g. possible

workshops were also present. A very important connection was that the houses in a number of cases were surrounded by stakes or small palisades (fig. 12). On the basis of carbon 14 analysis, the houses have been dated to the later part of the Pre-Roman and Early Roman Iron Age. The settlements were now situated inland from the coast, but continued to cluster a short distance from the coast, and in some cases it becomes appropriate to talk of the formation of villages (7D-H). The third type consists of constructions featuring, among other things, houses situated one after the other in rows, making it very difficult to determine the length of each house. As a rule, these structures lack traces of walls. The inner roof-bearing construction is narrower than earlier, and the house-lengths vary, as does the placement of posts both within and between houses. It is difficult to define a typical house plan. However, exceptions existed in the form of houses with a seeming division into several different rooms. Sunken-floored huts also occurred in connection with this type of construction (fig. 12). Within the Öresund Fixed Link project, this type of construction could only be identified at Lockarp (Fosie 11A), directly connected with Fosie IV. The buildings consisted of a large number of longhouses and around thirty sunken-floored huts which were documented. Most of the constructions were dated to 300-600 AD (Hadevik & Gidlöf). Towards the end of the prehistoric period, constructions consisting of broad houses and separate buildings positioned in a north-south direction occur. These also had associated sunken-floored huts. These constructions were dated to c. 700-900 AD. They occur again dispersed in the landscape, but the coastal zone is never again rebuilt upon (Björhem 2000, 153).

The difference which exists between the two first settlements is best explicable, with our current knowledge, as a form of *rotation*, linked by inference with changes in cultivation and grazing lands. Old settlements were abandoned and new ones founded. The coastal zone was abandoned and the inland coastal areas more densely settled. Some form of major reorganisation consequently took place during the second century before the birth of Christ. The houses changed, and were enclosed with stakes heavy enough

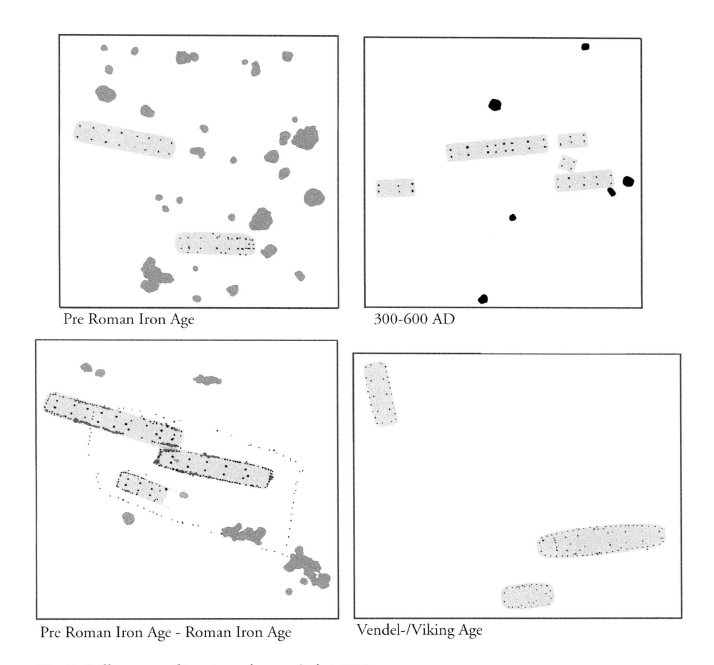

Pre Roman Iron Age

300-600 AD

Pre Roman Iron Age - Roman Iron Age

Vendel-/Viking Age

Fig. 12. Different types of Iron Age settlements. Scale 1:1000.

to have left preserved traces, in fact so heavy that it was necessary to dig post-holes.

The next clear change in construction during the Iron Age took place during the 4th century AD. The clear enclosed farmsteads disappeared at this time, with carbon 14 dates from this century suddenly becoming very scarce. However, this is not a case of a total abandonment of the area. Settlement remains dating from the 4th century occur to a very limited extent on other sites, but not however within the whole stretch south of the Fosie IV area (11a-d). The concentration and transplantation of the Iron Age buildings towards the west in this area is supposed to have its cause in a connection to the main thoroughfare linking the towns of Lund and Trelleborg, which passed nearby. It probably had a prehistoric forebear (Sköld 1963; Erikson 2001; Samuelsson 2001). The interesting thing is that the reorganisation and re-establishment that was perceived in that little area 10-15 years ago also turned out to be just as valid for this larger area. The concentration and consequent great reduction of construction which is perceptible in the larger material was the counterpart of the increase we saw in buildings from the Late Iron Age in the earlier investigation area (fig. 4). In the "little" Fosie IV perspective, a displacement and re-establishment of construction took place along the course of the road during the Iron Age. In the larger Öresund Fixed Link perspective, the same pattern could be observed. Corresponding dating evidence, although only in the form of remains of pits and wells, was retrieved from one more location (13A). It should be noted that this settlement lay immediately adjacent to a corresponding road, as was earlier reported, connecting together just before the passage of the Sege river. It is, of course, not realistic to imagine that all construction taking place in the Malmö area during the 4th century occurred at just these sites, but this does illustrate what was probably an all-embracing change and reorganisation of settlement in which communication also played a part. The reasons for the concentration of construction in this area are not clear, and can perhaps not be explained solely from the results of the Öresund Fixed Link project either. It is even less likely that they should only be connected with agricultural conditions and land use. The changes in construction and associated chronology correspond with the Danish material (Hedeager 1992, 202).

Summary

In a similar way to what happened in the Fosie IV area, a picture emerges of the whole investigation area, with buildings scattered over the landscape during the Late Bronze Age and, even more so, during the Early Iron Age. A few centuries before the birth of Christ, the settlements in Zone I nearest the coast came to a halt. It is interesting to note that the dates of the building-remains roughly range over the 4th century AD, with some few gaps in the material. The varying life-spans of the buildings imply that movements and relocations of the settlements have taken place, and this has also facilitated the identification of mutually separate house and construction types. From a situation where buildings are scattered in the landscape and house-remains are relatively fragmentary and indefinite during the first half of the Pre-Roman Iron Age, traces of them become more evident, with houses leaving clear traces of walls in the form of post-holes and ditches, in the last centuries BC. Several of the settlements now also show traces of enclosures around the houses. As a rule, they do not lie in the same place as they did during the preceding period of time, and some restructuring and shifting of the buildings can be supposed. After this, from the later Roman Iron Age and Late Iron Age on, the settlements become less common. The remains of houses again become more ill-defined, and traces of the walls, as a rule, are lacking. Sunken-floored huts are now also included in the settlements. From the end of the Merovingian (Vendel) Period and the Viking Age, examples of houses with traces of walls are again present, and these can also be found oriented in a north-south direction. Variation among house types is great. The number of locations also increases markedly compared with the previous period.

In a material of this extent, where a close spatial connection runs between investigation areas and a strong chronological continuity exists both in the actual history and in the analysis of the source material itself, the possibilities of processing and interpreting the material from many starting-points are good. In the Öresund Fixed Link project, for example, detailed analyses of the macrofossil content of the post-holes, magnetic and chemical soil tests and so on were carried out for individual houses. Here, a primarily long chronological perspective with every possibility of perceiving greater changes and shifts has been noted. One strength of the material is that, despite the poor conditions of preservation and badly plough-damaged remains, one can still write a general local history without needing to base all interpretations on previously known material and accounts. Comparisons become therefore more a way of understanding emerging patterns than a way of finding their reflections and thus attaining new knowledge.

Acknowledgements

Thanks to Bengt-Åke Samulesson for viewpoints included in the manuscript and also Mimmi Tegnér and Chatarina Ödman for help with illustrations. Thanks to Callum McDonald for the translation.

Bibliography

Becker, C.J. 1973: Früheisenzeitliche Dörfer bei Grøntoft, Westjütland. 3. Vorbericht: Die Ausgrabungen 1967-68. *Acta Archaeologica* vol. XLII, 79-110, Copenhagen.

Berglund, B.E. (ed.) 1991: *The cultural landscape during 6000 years in southern Sweden – the Ystad project* – Ecological Bullentins 41. Copenhagen.

Berggren, Å. & Celin, U. in press. *Öresundsförbindelsen. Burlöv 20 C.* Malmö Kulturmiljö. Report.

Billberg, I., Björhem, N. & Thörn, R. (eds.) 1996: *Öresundsförbindelsen och arkeologi. Projektprogram och undersökningsplaner för arkeologiska undersökningar.* Stadsantikvariska avdelningen. Malmö Museer. Malmö.

Billberg, I., Björhem, N., Magnusson Staaf, B. & Thörn, R. (eds.) 1998: *Öresundsförbindelsen och arkeologi II. Projektprogram och undersökningsplaner för arkeologiska undersökningar.* Stadsantikvariska avdelningen. Malmö Museer. Malmö.

Björhem, N. & Säfvestad, U. 1989: *Fosie IV. Byggnadstradition och bosättningsmönster under senneolitikum.* Malmöfynd 5, Malmö Museer. Malmö.

Björhem, N. & Säfvestad, U. 1993: *Fosie IV. Bebyggelsen under brons- och järnålder.* Malmöfynd 6, Malmö Museer. Malmö.

Björhem, N. 1994: *Problemformuleringar inför arkeologiska utgrävningar i samband med Öresundsförbindelsen.* Unpublished. Stadsantikvariska avdelningen. Malmö Museer, Malmö.

Björhem, N. 2000: Bebyggelseformer. Björhem, N. (ed.) *Föresundsförbindelsen. På väg mot det förflutna.* Stadsantikvariska avdelningen. Kultur Malmö. Malmö.

Boas, N. A. 1993: Late Neolithic and Bronze Age Settlements at Hemmed Church and Hemmed Plantation, East Jutland. *Journal of Danish Archaeology* 10, 119-135.

Callmer, J. 1986: To Stay or to Move. Some Aspects of the Settlement Dynamics in Southern Scandinavia in the Seventh to Twelfth Centuries A.D. with special Reference to the Province of Scania, Southern Sweden. *Meddelanden från Lunds universitets historiska museum* 1985-86, 136-155, Lund.

Erikson, M. 2001: En väg till Uppåkra. *Uppåkrastudier 4. Acta Archaeologica Lundensia 35,* Lund.

Ethelberg, P. 1993: Two more House Groups with Three-aisled Long-houses from the Early Bronze Age at Højgård, South Jutland. *Journal of Danish Archaelogy* 10, 136-355.

Gustafsson, S. 1995: *Fosie IV. Jordbrukets förändring och utveckling från senneolitikum till yngre järnålder.* Rapport nr. 5. Stadsantivariska avdelningen Malmö Museer. Malmö.

Gustafsson, S. 1998: The Farming Economy in South and Central Sweden during the Bronze Age. A Study Based on Carbonised Botanical Evidence. *Current Swedish Archaeology,* 6, 63-71.

Hadevik, C & Gidlöf, K. in press: *Öresundsförbindelsen. Fosie 11 A-D.* Malmö Kulturmiljö. Report, Malmö.

Hedeager, L. 1992: *Danmarks jernalder. Mellem stamme og stat.* Århus.

Hvass, S. 1982: Ländliche Siedlungen der Kaiser- und Völkerwanderungszeit in Dänemark. *Offa* 39, 189-195, Neumünster.

KML. Lagen om kulturminnen m.m. SFS 1988: 950.

Rosberg, A. & Lindhé, E. 2001: *Öresundsförbindelsen. Svågertorp 8A.* Malmö Kulturmiljö. Report 13, Malmö.

v. Rostoványi, A. & Hydén, S. 2002: *Öresundsförbindelsen. Svågertorp 8 B-C.* Malmö Kulturmiljö. Report 14, Malmö.

Rudin, G-B. & Brink, K. 2001: *Öresundsförbindelsen. Lockarp 7 A.* Malmö Kulturmiljö. Report 16, Mamö.

Samuelsson, B.-Å. 2001: Kan gravar spegla vägars ålder och betydelse? Ett exempel från Söderslätt i Skåne.

Uppåkrastudier 4. Acta Archaeologica Lundensia. 35, Lund.

Sarnäs, P. 2000: Åker i mer än två tusen år, N. Björhem (ed.) *Föresundsförbindelsen*, 117-118, Malmö.

Sarnäs, P. & Nord-Paulsson, J. 2001. *Öresundsförbindelsen. Skjutbanorna 1B – Elinelund 2B*. Malmö Kulturmiljö. Report 9, Malmö.

Sköld, P.E. 1963: En väg och en bygd i gammal tid. *Ale* 1963:2, 1-15.

Tesch, S. 1993: *Houses, Farmsteads, and Long-term Change. A Regional Study of Prehistoric Settlements in the Köpinge Area, in Scania, Southern Sweden.* Uppsala.

Tesch, S. 1993: *Utbildning och forskning. Kvalitet och konkurrenskraft.* Proposition 1993/94:177. Stockholm.

The Thy Archaeological Project
– Results and Reflections from a Multinational Archaeological Project

Jens-Henrik Bech

Thy, in northwestern Jutland, is bordered to the west by the North Sea and to the east and south by the Limfjord. In this part of Denmark thousands of barrows were constructed, in particular during the Early Bronze Age (from 1500/1400 to 1000 BC). Wherever one turns, the eye meets one or several barrows on the horizon.

With its rich burial finds, Thy was ideal for a diachronic settlement project to test interpretations of Bronze Age society with the evidence of settlement and environment. This was the starting point of the Thy Archaeological Project (henceforward TAP).

TAP was an international venture bringing together archaeologists from Denmark, the United States, Great Britain and Sweden for field work and surveys during the years 1990-1998. Main themes in the project were settlement studies, household archaeology, social organisation and the ecological background – all seen in a long term perspective. The project was originally planned to cover development throughout a very long time sequence from the start of the Neolithic Period 4000 BC to 1800 AD, but faced with reality the main focus was narrowed down to the periods Late Neolithic and Bronze Age (2400-500 BC).

This short presentation of the project will deal with some of the results mainly regarding data from surveys and excavations of Bronze Age sites (for a more comprehensive presentation of the project and some of the main results see Earle et al. 1998; see also Thorpe 1997; Kelertas 1997; Steinberg 1996, 1997; Kristiansen 1998; Bech 1998; Bech & Mikkelsen 1999).

Pollen analysis

In the planning of TAP as an interdisciplinary archaeological settlement project, heavy emphasis was laid on pollen-analytical and palaeo-botanical studies in order to understand the vegetational history of the region and the exploitation of the area through prehistoric agriculture. The pollen-analytical data came first of all from two regional pollen-diagrams: One from a bog named Hassing Huse Mose and the other from lake sediments at the bottom of Lake Ove, both in central Thy, fig. 1 (Andersen 1995a-b). The distance between the two places where the pollen cores were taken was only 2.5 km. The pollen-diagrams demonstrated a major *"landnam"* during the early 3rd millennium BC, corresponding to the Bottom Grave Period of the Single Grave Culture (fig. 2). This is one of the most massive forest clearances in northern Europe (Kristiansen 1998) and the pollen spectra clearly show that coppice vegetation had been removed and was replaced by open land for fields and pastures during the Middle and Late Neolithic. Treeless areas increasingly expanded in the Early Bronze Age (1700-1000 BC), where tree vegetation became mainly restricted to wetlands. As will be demonstrated below, the archaeological data also indicate that already during Early Bronze Age period II problems of procuring quality building timber were a matter of concern to the Bronze Age people of Thy. Supplementary pollen spectra from soils that were enclosed in or under Early Bronze Age mounds tell the same story of extensive land-use, perhaps mainly based on animal husbandry (Andersen 1999). In the Late Bronze Age (1000-500 BC) treeless areas remained widespread, although some recovery of secondary forest took place, probably due to an intensification of agriculture (Andersen 1995a-b). This development continued into the Early Iron Age, where the extensive use in north-western Jutland of houses with sod walls during the period 500 BC-200 AD no doubt reflects lack of timber and the openness of this wind-exposed landscape facing the North Sea.

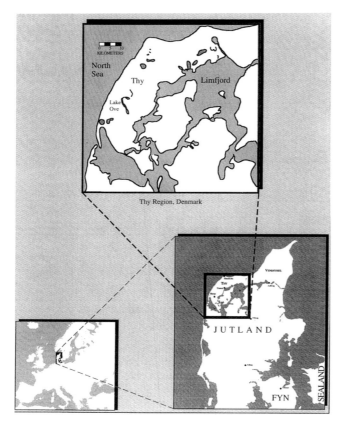

Fig. 1. The location of Thy, Denmark (after Earle 1997).

How are these pollen-analytical conclusions about land use reflected in the archaeological material? The deep regression of the woodland, especially during the Early Bronze Age, is no doubt indirectly reflected in the amount of burial mounds, which had to be seen in an open landscape – but what about settlements from the same period? Until about 10-15 years ago knowledge about Bronze Age sites in Thy was almost non-existent (Bertelsen et al. 1996), and there were also problems with the Neolithic period, although finds in museums and in private collections indicated a potential (Steinberg 1997). To shed light on these incongruities between the pollen-analytical evidence and the archaeological record, different methods can be used, ranging from recording of private collections of artefacts, field surveys, shovel tests, plough-zone screenings and ultimately to excavations – trial and real. Each of these methods has different limitations, but taken together they supplement each other. In the following, results from field surveys and excavations, mainly, will be used to show the archaeological evidence of man's impact on the environment during the Neolithic and Bronze Age periods, especially with regard to the "missing" Bronze Age settlements.

Field surveys

Today regional pollen-diagrams are believed to reflect the general vegetational history within an area up to 5 km from the sample site (Odgård & Rasmussen 2000). This is a reduction compared to earlier notions (Andersen et al. 1983), which is the reason why a 10 km circle was originally chosen by the Thy Project as the delimitation of the primary research area shown in fig. 3. (In Kristiansen 1998 fig. 1b the 10 km circle is indicated, but the scale is wrong). Two of the main areas for surveys were placed within the 10 km circle. One inland (Sønderhå/Snedsted/Hørsted – area 1) and the other along the Limfjord coast (Heltborg – area 2). In addition another Limfjord area to the north outside the circle was chosen (Sjørring/ Tilsted – area 3) to reflect the broad landscape variation

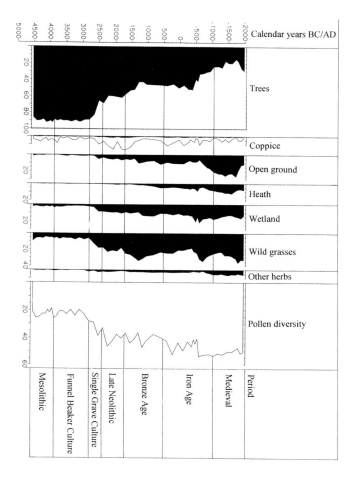

Calendar years BC/AD

Trees

Coppice

Open ground

Heath

Wetland

Wild grasses

Other herbs

Pollen diversity

Mesolithic · Funnel Beaker Culture · Single Grave Culture · Late Neolithic · Bronze Age · Iron Age · Medieval · Period

Fig. 2. Lake Ove. Pollen spectra for plant groups and curve for pollen diversity (after Andersen 1995b, fig. 10).

within the moraine soils of Thy, which inland primarily consist of sandy till and along the Limfjord mainly of clay till (DGU 1989, soil map of Denmark 1:200.000).

Survey finds

All in all 8.4 km² were surveyed using a standard procedure with line walking at 10 m intervals and detailed recording in 50 x 50 m blocks at sites.[1] Of the collected artefacts from the Late Bronze Age and the Iron Age more than 95% are ceramics while a very different situation is characteristic of material

from earlier periods, where flint flakes and flint tools make up the bulk of the survey finds. Although 3684 surface finds are recorded in the TAP-database, unfortunately only an extremely small proportion of them is datable to one main period. As illustrated in fig. 4, 16% of the datable stone artefacts belong to the Funnel Beaker Culture (AYT) while only 9% have a clear date to the Late Neolithic (AYS); the majority of the stone artefacts therefore can only be dated in more general terms. One large group of finds consists of small fragments of polished flint axes and other artefacts, which cannot be dated more precisely than to the Neolithic in general (AYX). 22% of the survey finds are dated to this group while almost 40% are only datable to either the Late Neolithic or the Early Bronze Age (AYS/BÆX). The last group consists of artefacts such as daggers, sickles and arrowheads made in pressure work technique, a technique which was in use in the Late Neolithic and the Early Bronze Age, and since survey finds normally consist of fragments, the dating can only in some cases be narrowed down to one of the two periods. To use those finds in the calculations below we therefore put forward the hypothesis that half of the total amount of the AYS/BÆX artefacts date from the Late Neolithic and the other half from the Early Bronze Age. In the same way it is presumed that half of the total artefacts dated to the Neolithic in general (AYX) belongs to the Funnel Beaker or the Single Grave Culture (AYT/AYE), while the other half is from the Late Neolithic (AYS). By doing this it becomes clear that the number of estimated Late Neolithic artefacts is much bigger than the number of artefacts from the earlier part of the Neolithic. This becomes even more evident when the length of the time periods in question is taken into account. Together the Funnel Beaker Culture and the Single Grave Culture lasted about 1500 years, while the Late Neolithic only covered about half the length of this time-sequence. The number of estimated artefacts per year in the Late Neolithic is therefore about three times as high as the level of estimated artefacts per year from the earlier periods. This picture does not change significantly if the Neolithic artefacts in the AYX-group are split up according to the length

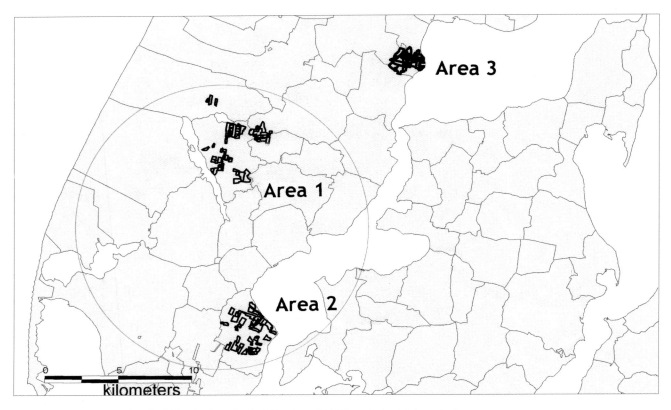

Fig. 3. Survey areas for the Thy Archaeological Project (TAP) and the 10 km circle.

	AYT	AYE	AYS	BÆX	BYX	TOTAL
Years	**1100**	**400**	**700**	**700**	**500**	
Artefacts	33 (16%)	4 (2%)	19 (9%)	9 (4%)	11 (5%)	76
AYX		47 (22%)				47
AYE-AYS			2 (1%)			2
AYS-BÆX				83 (39%)		83
BXX					4 (2%)	4
ESTIMATED ARTEFACTS	*61.5 (29%)*		*85 (40%)*	*65.5 (31%)*		212
ESTIMATED ARTEFACTS PER YEAR	*0,041*		*0,121*	*0,055*		

Fig. 4. Datable stone artefacts from TAP surveys. AYT: Funnel Beaker Culture (3900-2800 BC), AYE: Single Grave Culture (2800-2400 BC), AYS: Late Neolithic (2400-1700 BC), BÆX: Early Bronze Age (1700-1000 BC), BYX: Late Bronze Age (1000-500 BC).

of the time periods as well, so that 2/3 of the AYX finds go to the earlier time groups (instead of half the total amount to each of the time groups as described above).

This difference between the number of survey finds from the early and late part of the Neolithic is important and corresponds very well with the number of sites from the two periods. That survey finds from the Bronze Age are almost as unusual as finds from the Funnel Beaker and Single Grave Culture in the same calculation is first of all because ceramics are excluded from the calculations. As will appear below, sites from the Late Bronze Age and Early Iron Age with ploughed-up potsherds are frequently found (see fig. 5A-B).

Sites

Using results from plough-zone screenings as site signatures, Steinberg (1996; 1997) has clearly demonstrated great differences in flint production between sites. As a consequence some sites are easy to locate during surveying, while others are difficult or impossible to locate in this way. In spite of these obstacles the number and dates of the survey sites nevertheless add to the discussion above.

During the TAP surveys the term "site" was used as a rather broad category, not defined by e.g. a certain quantity of tools or artefacts per square metre. So whenever the survey crew found a concentration of flakes, stone tools, ceramics, fire cracked stones or dark charcoal coloured patches on the ploughed field surface the term was used. With reference to formal discussions about how to use the term "site", or if "sites" exist at all, we have been able to demonstrate by plough-zone screenings and shovel tests that our survey sites from the Neolithic and the Bronze Age really do exist as more or less clear concentrations of flakes in the plough-soil (Steinberg 1996; 1997).

As a consequence of the problems in assigning specific dates to the survey finds, many sites of course cannot be dated precisely either. From TAP surveys we therefore have 38 sites with such broad datings that they are useless in this context. From the listing in fig. 5A-B it becomes evident that, with regard to the datable survey sites, almost the same picture emerges as with the survey finds as a whole. This of course has its background in the fact that about 65% of all the survey artefacts are found on sites. The only difference to the calculations in fig. 4 is that ceramics are included as dating evidence for the sites as well.

To get as clear a picture as possible for this presentation, all sites with less than two datable objects from at least one of the time groups are left out. In other words a site is only dated to a specific period if two or more datable objects from the period have been found at the site. Using this definition a single object from another period is regarded as a "stray-find" and does

	AYT	AYE	AYS	BÆX	BYX	CÆX	TOTAL
Years	1100	400	700	700	500	900	
Sites	2	0	6	1	7	15	31
AYX		2					2
AYS-BÆX			11				11
BXX-CXX				1			1
BYX-CXX					3		3
ESTIMATED SITES	3	12,5	6,5	9	17		48

Fig. 5A. Datable sites from TAP surveys. AYT: Funnel Beaker Culture (3900-2800 BC), AYE: Single Grave Culture (2800-2400 BC), AYS: Late Neolithic (2400-1700 BC), BÆX: Early Bronze Age (1700-1000 BC), BYX: Late Bronze Age (1000-500 BC), CÆX: Pre-Roman and Roman Iron Age (500 BC-400 AD).

Time	AYT		AYE		AYS		BÆX		BYX		CÆX	
	TAP	SB	TAP	SB	TAP	SB	TAP	SB	TAP	SB	TAP	SB
NUMBER (%)	3 (3%)	3 (3%)	0	2 (2%)	12,5	11 (10%)	6.5 (6%)	2 (2%)	9 (8%)	8 (7%)	17 (15%)	38 (34%)
TOTAL	6 (5%)		2 (2%)		23.5 (21%)		8.5 (8%)		17 (15%)		55 (49%)	
YEARS	1100		400		700		700		500		900	
SITES PER YEAR	0,005		0,005		0,034		0,012		0,034		0,061	

Fig. 5B. Estimated number of datable sites from TAP surveys supplemented with other datable sites recorded at the National Museum in Copenhagen (SB) within the 10 km circle (sites along the North Sea Coast included). Abbreviations for time periods: see fig. 5A.

	Inland (3.216km^2)	Limfjord coast (5.182km^2)	Total
AYT + AYE	8 (0.0025 pr. km^2)	29 (0.0056 pr. km^2)	37
AYX	15 (0.0047 pr. km^2)	32 (0.0061 pr. km^2)	47
AYS + BÆX + AYS-BÆX	67 (0.0208 pr. km^2)	44 (0.0085 pr. km^2)	111

Fig. 6. Datable stone artefacts from TAP surveys. Distribution between inland (fig. 3, area 1) and Limfjord coast (fig. 3, area 2-3). Abbreviations for time periods: see fig. 5A.

not count. On this basis only two survey sites belong to the Funnel Beaker Culture, six to the Late Neolithic and eight to the Bronze Age, while 15 belong to the Early Iron Age (fig. 5A). The number of datable sites – few though they be – clearly shows for the Neolithic Period and the Bronze Age what we observed in dealing with the datable survey finds: the largest number of sites are those broadly dated to the Late Neolithic/ Early Bronze Age sequence. If these sites are divided equally between the two periods, some of the missing sites from the Early Bronze Age are no doubt accounted for, but still they only make up half the number of the possible Late Neolithic sites (fig. 5B).

To enlarge the database it is reasonable to add to the number of survey sites (TAP in fig. 5B) the datable sites within the 10 km circle, which are recorded in the national database at the National Museum in Copenhagen (SB in fig. 5B). From those data the rise in the settlement activity within the research area from the Late Neolithic onwards is still clearly visible. Using the number of sites per year this tendency is even more dramatic. As for the fall in the number of sites from the Late Neolithic to the Early Bronze Age in fig. 5B, this question will be dealt with in the section below about development in population density.

On the basis of this evidence we may conclude that the big jump in the exploitation of the Thy region took place in the Late Neolithic between 2400 and 1700 BC. Judged by the pollen data, however, the major impact already began in the Single Grave Culture a couple of hundred years earlier. The problem is that until now it has been impossible in the TAP material to date one single site with certainty to this time period (the site THY 3458 in the Sjørring/Tilsted area might have this date). But as grave finds from the

Single Grave Period demonstrate the presence of this culture group in the area (Glob 1944; Bech & Haack Olsen 1985), the settlement sites must be much more difficult to locate during surveying than those from earlier and later periods. Probably they are small ones like the Mortens Sande site in the Lodbjerg Area (Liversage 1988, see also Mathiassen 1948; Rostholm 1986; Hvass 1986). In the Heltborg and Sønderhå/ Hørsted area a number of flint axes in private collections are important for the discussion of the presence of the Single Grave Culture in the area. 2/3 of the 120 axes recorded belong to the thick butted type, and of these the majority are typical of the way axes were made in the Single Grave Culture. Therefore we may say with high probability that those axes were used in the first extensive clearings in the woodlands of Thy.

In conclusion it can be stated that the combined archaeological data from Thy confirm the picture derived from the pollen-analytical results.

Development in population density

When dealing with numbers of sites it must be taken into account that the sizes of the sites from the different periods are clearly not the same. In our count large Iron Age sites with space for many people have the same weight as small sites from e.g. the Funnel Beaker Culture. That the rising number of sites from the Neolithic to the Iron Age nevertheless indicates a rise in the population density cannot be questioned – but still we have no evidence that permits us to go into details. The hypothesis that e.g. a stabilization or perhaps even a decline in the population size from the Late Neolithic to the Early Bronze Age took place in Thy, as indicated by Timothy Earle (Earle 1997), may find some support in the survey data, but I find it much more likely that we are dealing with a question of different visibility of sites between those of the Late Neolithic and those of the Early Bronze Age. That Bronze Age sites can be difficult to detect during survey is evident (Mikkelsen 1991). A decline from Stone to Bronze Age in the number of diagnostic tools could also have an effect. Furthermore it is also somewhat unlikely that a decline in population density took place, taking into consideration the number of burials from the two periods, where the Early Bronze Age burials vastly outnumber those from the previous centuries. The results from the investigations by Thisted Museum and by Martin Mikkelsen in the Aas area facing the Limfjord just south of the surveyed area in Tilsted/Sjørring parishes also clearly demonstrate that for this micro-region the Bronze Age sites and excavated houses do not testify to any fall in the volume of activity and population size from the Late Neolithic to the Early Bronze Age at all. As the Bronze Age impact is much more clear than the Late Neolithic the opposite is more likely (Mikkelsen forthcoming).

Site distribution

With the restricted number of dated sites, diachronic changes in the settlement pattern can only be demonstrated tentatively and in very broad outlines. The main difference between the three surveyed areas is to be found in the Neolithic period, as the Funnel Beaker Culture preferred the Limfjord coast to the inland region of Sønderhå[2], while the Late Neolithic (and Early Bronze Age) impact is much more clearly seen at Sønderhå (fig. 6). This change no doubt mirrors the major opening up of the inland areas and the development from woodland to grassland that was reflected in the pollen samples. Regarding the Late Bronze Age and Early Iron Age the situation more or less seems to be the same in the three areas. Mean-

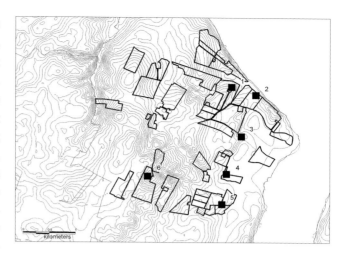

Fig. 7A. Datable sites from the Neolithic and the Early Bronze Age in Heltborg parish (fig. 3, area 2).Surveyed fields marked. 1-6: Sites (see note 3).

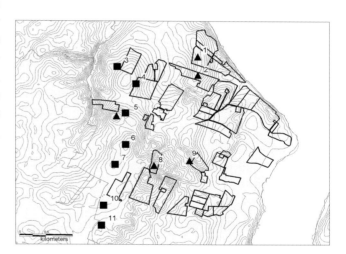

Fig. 7B. Datable sites from the Late Bronze Age (triangles) and the Early Iron Age (squares) in Heltborg parish (fig. 3, area 2). Surveyed fields marked. 1-11: Sites (see note 4).

while an interesting pattern can be observed along the Limfjord coast. Both at Heltborg (fig. 7A-B) and in the Silstrup area, to the north (fig. 8A-B), the sites from the Neolithic and the Early Bronze Age are much closer to the coast than those of the Late Bronze Age and the Early Iron Age. As the soils are the same, both near to the coast and further inland, the reason for this difference cannot be explained only in terms

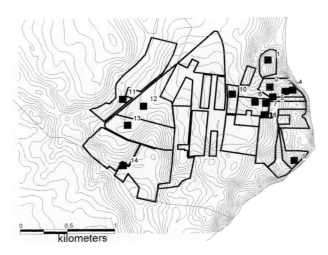

Fig. 8A. Datable sites from the Neolithic and the Early Bronze Age in Tilsted and Sjørring parishes (fig. 3, area 3). Surveyed fields marked. 1-14: Sites (see note 5).

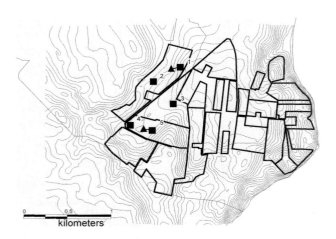

Fig. 8B. Datable sites from the Late Bronze Age (triangles) and the Early Iron Age in Tilsted and Sjørring parishes (fig. 3, area 3). Surveyed fields marked. 1-5: Sites (see note 6).

of a decrease in the importance of the resources from the Fjord, but has perhaps also some strategic implication. Evidence of raiding by boat in southern Jutland in the Pre Roman Iron Age is provided by the Hjortspring warrior ship (Rosenberg 1937), so if any external phenomenon threatened the village communities of the Early Iron Age in Thy it no doubt came from the Fjord. The observed change in the preferred posi-

tion of the sites can therefore tentatively be explained as the introduction of a kind of buffer zone to the coast for security or other reasons. In a study of the prehistoric settlement of Eastern Jutland, Bo Ejstrud is able to demonstrate a similar shift away from watercourses – even small ones with no obvious security aspect – in the Late Bronze Age and Early Iron Age (Bo Ejstrud personal communication). This indicates that other more general patterns of relocation of sites could also be a reason for the observed change in the Limfjord region.

Likewise the need for transport of goods and better communication between sites could have played a role in the location of Early Iron Age sites as well, favouring the higher lying areas away from the Fjord. Perhaps it is not a coincidence that the main road along the Limfjord in the Heltborg region is situated in the same area as the North-South row of Iron Age sites on fig. 7B.

Early Bronze Age sites at Sønderhå

While the Late Neolithic presence in the inland region of Thy is very clear, it is, on the other hand, impossible to see what happened in the Early Bronze Age using the TAP survey data alone. As demonstrated above, one of the disadvantages of the survey method is that it does not produce many clearly datable objects. To overcome this problem, recordings of private collections were used, as has been done by many others before in studies of settlement patterns (Mathiassen 1948; Vedsted 1986). By doing this we more than doubled the amount of datable finds. But what was gained in the quantity of finds was to some degree lost in precision, as the actual find-place sometimes could not be remembered exactly by the collectors. Nevertheless, looking through three private collections in Sønderhå, with 359 artefacts, we actually found evidence that the distribution of Late Neolithic daggers (or fragments from daggers) in the northeastern part of Sønderhå clearly overlaps the distribution of a special type of Early Bronze Age pressure-worked flint sickle (Bech 1997). The conclusion is easy to reach: the Bronze Age sites are not missing, but are to be found within the same general topography as the Late Neolithic sites (see also Kristiansen 1998). Based on the survey data we may add that with only one field-walking exercise the Late Neolithic sites are perhaps easier to locate than the sites from the Early Bronze Age. This could very well be caused by the rising specialisation from the Late Neolithic to the Bronze Age, where the sites from the latter period seem to have had a more varied degree of flint production than in the previous period (Steinberg 1996; 1997). The Legård site at Sønderhå illustrates this point. Despite its size and the number of houses the site did not have much worked flint on the surface (Earle et al. 1998). On the other hand, a nearby Bronze Age site (THY 2788) was very easy to track both in shovel and plough-zone tests (Steinberg 1996; 1997). From this site there were also a number of Early Bronze Age flint sickles which came to light in a private collection, but in contrast to Legård there were only a few structures from one phase of a single farmstead that were revealed by excavation (Earle et al. 1998).

Early Bronze Age households

Legård

Excavations at the Legård site uncovered structures from at least 15 Bronze Age longhouses, of which 12 were excavated in their full length (Mikkelsen & Kristiansen 1996; 1997; Earle et al. 1998). The houses represent different stages in the development of a single farmstead during the Early and Late Bronze Age. Houses III and IX are the best dated longhouses, which, according to 14C-dates, belong to the Early Bronze Age period II (AAR-6552, 6553, 6564, 6565).Two 14C- dates from the same structure in house III gave results that were too old, as the dated material (charcoal) came from the Mesolithic Late Ertebølle Culture and the Late Neolithic respectively?

(K-6906 +6907). The charcoal was taken from a fire pit in the centre of the "living room", which, without any doubt, was contemporary with the house, and the only reasonable solution to this puzzle is therefore that the inhabitants of the house used peat containing old wooden branches. That peat was actually used for fuel in the Early Bronze Age of Thy is documented from another excavation in Sønderhå, where the remnants of a funeral pyre from the Early Bronze Age period III contained burnt peat from shallow wetland deposits (Olsen & Bech 1996).

Of the two Legård houses, house III is the best preserved, with dimensions of 33 x 8 m, while house IX was somewhat smaller, about 30 m long and 7.5 m wide (fig. 9). They lay parallel to each other with a distance of only about 8 m between them. As they were of the same general outline, and apparently had identical inner layouts, it is reasonable to argue that they did not exist at the same time but succeeded each other. With a roofed area of between 225 m² and 264 m² these are big houses – not so far surpassed in Thy by other Bronze Age houses – and they belong to a group of houses of seemingly "chieftain" status built at the same time over most of Jutland (Rasmussen 1999). House III was divided into three sections of almost equal size, where the middle part consisted of a byre with space for about 12-16 animals (cattle). Belonging to the first generation of long-houses in Denmark, in which, once in a while, a fixed indoor space for cattle appears, the Legård houses demonstrate the importance of animal husbandry in the Early Bronze Age (Fokkens 1999; Rasmussen 1999).

With the exception perhaps of house I, all other houses at the Legård site were chronologically later, i.e. from the Early Bronze Age period III and the Late Bronze Age. They were all smaller, with no specific space for cattle. The decreasing size of houses during the Bronze Age in Thy follows the same general development as in the rest of Southern Scandinavia (Tesch 1993; Løken 1998) – and even in the Netherlands the same trend is clearly seen (Roymans & Fokkens 1991). In the later phases of the Bronze Age byres also occur once in a while among the Danish houses (in Thy a house with a byre from Late Bronze

Age period IV is known from Bjerre site 4), but they do not appear as a regular part of the Danish farm until the Early Pre Roman Iron Age.

The Legård site is typical of the conditions of preservation for Danish Bronze Age sites: Only the subsoil parts of structures with post-holes and pits are preserved, while floor layers and additional culture layers with refuse etc. have been ploughed up a long time ago. Better conditions are sometimes to be found in sandy locations, where drifting sand may have protected house sites. Since a situation of this type existed at Bjerre in northern Thy, a considerable part of the Bronze Age household excavation-work of the Thy Project was focused here, even though it was about 25 km outside the original catchment area of the project.

Bjerre

The Bjerre sites are situated on an uplifted Littorina sea floor immediately south of the Hanstholm Headland (fig. 10B). During the Late Neolithic period the marine deposits were no doubt still too wet to be used for agriculture and habitation, but in period II of the Early Bronze Age the first settlements were established. The exploitation of the area continued until Late Bronze Age period V, when a rise in the groundwater table around 800 BC followed by an increased sand drift made further habitation in this wetland area impossible (Sv.Th.Andersen personal communication; Clemmensen et al. 2001). This development, leading to the abandonment of the Bjerre

Fig. 9. The Early Bronze Age houses III and IX from Legård, Sønderhå parish.

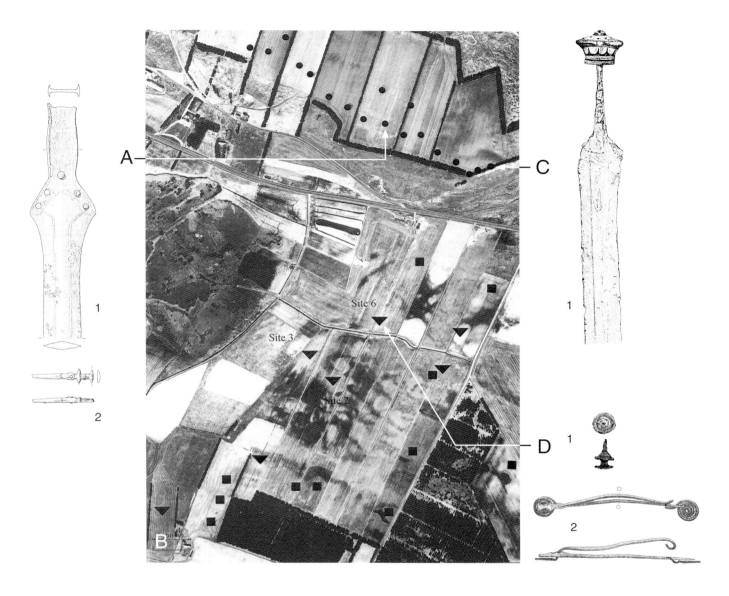

Fig. 10. A: Early Bronze Age burial find from barrow sb. nr. 15, Vigsø parish. 1: Bronze sword, 2: Part of a bronze fibula (after Aner/ Kersten 2002). B: Aerial photo of the Bjerre area. Closed circle: Barrow. Triangle: Site from Early Bronze Age. Square: Site from Late Bronze Age. C: Bronze sword from barrow sb. nr. 11, Vigsø parish. D: Bronze objects from Bjerre site 6. 1: Double button, 2: Fibula. (C & D: Drawing Walter Rommenhöller).

plain, is closely related to a general climatic change in North-West Europe (Van Geel & Renssen 1998), and it is most likely that an overexploitation of the Bronze Age landscape during the previous centuries added to the consequences of this climatic change.

Within a timespan of about 700-800 years a restricted number of farms used the area of the ancient sea bed for agriculture and cattle- and sheep raising (Bech 1991; 1993; 1997; Bech & Mikkelsen 1999; see also Earle et al. 1998). On two of the sites the TAP conducted excavations during five field seasons. Together with results from previous rescue work in the area, the Bjerre sites yielded detailed new knowledge of Bronze Age household conditions and land use and furthermore gave an

Fig. 11. Early Bronze Age house at Bjerre site 6 (after Earle et al. 1998).

procuring insight into the problems of getting proper timber for the houses and fuel for the fire places.

At Bjerre site 6, the TAP excavations uncovered a 25 m long and 8 m wide house from the Early Bronze Age per. II (fig. 11). Three out of four 14C-dates (K-7122, 7123 and 7125) make the house almost contemporary with the Legård houses, mentioned above, while a fourth resulted in a dating to the Late Neolithic (K-7124), which is evidently too old. Two bronze objects from the site, a fibula and a double button (fig. 10D), belong, according to the standard chronology of Danish burial finds, to late period II and period III. One of the 14C-dates (K-7122) indicates that the use of the house could perhaps have lasted a few decades into period III as well, and this would fit with the dating of the double button.

It is evident than in the construction of the Legård houses a large quantity of timber would have had to be used, not only for the inner construction but also for the bole walls with horizontal timbers between the vertical wall posts. Contrary to that, the Bjerre house gives the impression of a scarcity of wood. Due to the high ground water table at site 6 a high proportion of the wood used for the walls and the inner posts of the house was actually preserved. Bottom parts of the posts, some with clearly visible cut marks from the bronze axe used, tell us about the type of wood. It was mainly oak wood (*Quercus sp.*), but willow (*Salix sp.*) was also used and, surprisingly, there were even two pieces of wood from larch trees (*Larix*) (Christensen 1999). As the nearest places where larch trees grew at that time were the Alpine regions or Siberia

(Christensen 1999), the Bronze Age inhabitants had no doubt found the larch wood drifting ashore on the North Sea Coast, one or two kilometres away from the site. As the size of timber in the house was modest, and even crooked branches came into use in the wattle and daub walls, the evidence for scarcity of proper trunks is striking and reflects regional variance within Thy, where Bjerre, no doubt, had less tree vegetation and a more open and wind-exposed environment than the inland Sønderhå region.

Analyses of the fuel used at Bjerre site 6 and the Late Bronze Age site 7 tell the same story of shortage of wood-resources, with a large variety of species used, including sea buckthorn (*Hippopae rhamnoides*).

Due to the preserved bone material, the wear from use on the flint tools, and the archaeo-botanical material, the Bronze Age farm Bjerre site 6 has given an almost unique insight into many aspects of daily life – including even evidence of special activities such as the collecting of amber. 69 unworked pieces of amber, packed tightly together in a ball about the size of an adult's fist, were buried just inside the house near the northern wall line. Perhaps the amber had been kept in a small bag. In addition, 85 small pieces of unworked amber were found, most of them in the western end of the house, where the living quarters were.

Although amber did not play any significant role at all in the Danish Bronze Age – at least not as a source for amber beads and other ornaments (Jensen 1965; 2000) – it is obvious that amber collecting on a regular basis was also a part of daily life at the sites near the North Sea coast of Thy, both in the Early and in the Late Bronze Age. A comparison of the large amount of unworked amber from the Late Bronze Age site 7 (about 1800 pieces) with the more modest number from site 6 gives indications of an increase in collection of amber during the Bronze Age (Earle 2001). The absence of small amber pieces and amber dust in the light fractions of the many flotations from the two sites makes it clear that production of amber beads or other amber objects did not take place at all, in contrast to what is documented from a Late Neolithic site at Sønderhå (Earle et al. 1998) and from a

number of other Neolithic sites along the North Sea coast of Thy (Hirsch & Liversage 1987). It seems that the Bronze Age farmers at Bjerre did not use the amber themselves, but most probably collected it for trade-like external exchange systems.

To which segment of Bronze Age society did the inhabitants of the house at site 6 belong? The big Legård halls no doubt had chieftain status (Earle et al. 1998; Kristiansen 1998), but can the same be said of the 25 m long house at site 6? When it was first uncovered it held the prize as the longest Bronze Age house in Viborg county (Bertelsen et al. 1996) – and it was therefore thought to be the residence of one of the Bronze Age chiefs of Thy (Earle et al. 1998). Since then a number of new Bronze Age houses have turned up with sizes very near or even surpassing the length of this house, so the chieftain status attributed to the head of household at site 6 may well be thrown into question.

About half a kilometre from site 6, at the edge of the Hanstholm Headland, where the sea bed is 40 metres below, there is a row of Bronze Age burial mounds (fig. 10A). Among the few grave finds known from the barrows are two with Early Bronze Age swords (fig. 10A1 + C), one of which was even accompanied by a fibula resembling the one from site 6 (fig. 10A2). Taking the many bronze swords from the Early Bronze Age period III in Thy into consideration (Aner & Kersten 2002), it is evident that all males with bronze swords were not necessarily "chieftains" (Kristiansen 1984). So even if the head of the household at site 6 was buried with a sword in one of those graves, he could also represent a more humble segment of Bronze Age society than that of a "chieftain" (Fokkens 1999).

The fieldwork phase of the Thy Archaeological Project has now been concluded and a final publication of the Bronze Age research is in preparation. This has been a low budget project compared to e.g. the Ystad Project in Sweden (Berglund 1991). During the period of fieldwork 1991-1998 just over 2.5 mill. DKK was spent, with about 40% from Danish funding and the rest mainly from the United States (National Science Foundation (grant SBR-9207082)). Although the long-term perspective has not been as long as originally planned, it was nevertheless long enough to support models for the long-term economic and social development of Thy from about 2600 BC - 500 BC (Earle 1997, 2001). As a project involving many participants from different research traditions it has resulted not only in the implementation of new procedures, but also in many discussions of the interpretation of the project data. Last but not least, the strong combination and integration of archaeological fieldwork with pollen and archaeo-botanical studies places the project within a broader development in Scandinavia moving towards the closer integration of natural sciences and archaeology in diachronic settlement studies.

Notes

1. In the years 1991-1993 TASP surveys were led by Nick Thorpe, University College, London (now King Alfred's College, Winchester) and in 1994-1997 by Jørgen Westphal, University of Aarhus, Institute of Prehistoric Archaeology, Moesgård, Denmark.
2. Although the western coastline of Thy in the Atlantic and Early Sub-boreal Period was about 5 km inland compared to the present sea shore (Jessen 1920), the inland character of the Sønderhå area in the Neolithic and Early Bronze Age is based on the fact that already in the middle of the Atlantic Period coastal barriers blocked up the connection between Lake Ove and the North Sea (Andersen 1994).
3. Sites on fig. 7A: 1: THY 2983, 2: THY 2981, 3: Sb. nr. 17-18, 4: THY 2978, 5: THY 3425 (sb. nr. 114), 6: THY 2965 (sb. nr. 26).
4. Sites on fig. 7B: 1: THY 2982, 2: THY 2985, 3: Sb. nr. 2-3, 4: THY 3460, 5: THY 1690 (sb. nr. 105), 6: Sb. nr. 101, 7: THY 2001 (sb. nr. 107), 8: THY 3855 (sb. nr. 118), 9: THY 2918 (sb. nr. 111), 10: THY 2004 (sb. nr. 37), 11: Sb. nr. 88 + 93.
5. Sites on fig. 8A: 1: THY 3493, 2: THY 3500, 3: THY 3701, 4: THY 3702, 5: THY 3495, 6: THY 3488, 7: THY 3489, 8: THY 3490, 9: THY 3499, 10: THY 3491, 11: THY 3451 (sb. nr. 266), 12: THY 3453 (sb. nr. 268), 13: THY 3455 (sb. nr. 270), 14: THY 3458 (sb. nr. 272), 15: THY 2456 (sb. nr. 263).

6. Sites on fig. 8B: 1: THY 2456 (sb. nr. 263), 2: THY 3450 (sb. nr. 265), 3: THY 3452 (sb. nr. 267), 4: THY 3454 (sb. nr. 269), 5: THY 3456.

References

Andersen, Sv. Th. et al. 1983: Environment and Man. Current Studies in Vegetational History at the Geological Survey of Denmark. In: *Journal of Danish Archaeology* 2, 1983, 184-196.

Andersen, Sv. Th. 1994: Pollenanalyser fra Ove Sø. In: *Geobotaniske Undersøgelser Af Kulturlandskabets Historie,* DGU Kunderapport nr. 18, København, 30-33.

Andersen, Sv. Th. 1995a: History of Vegetation and Agriculture at Hassing Huse Mose, Thy, Northwest Denmark, since the Ice Age. In: *Journal of Danish Archaeology* 11, 1992-93, 57-79.

Andersen, Sv. Th. 1995b: Pollenanalyser fra Ove Sø. In: *Geobotaniske Undersøgelser Af Kulturlandskabets Historie.* DGU Kunderapport nr. 12, København, 36-55.

Andersen, Sv. Th. 1999: Pollen analyses from Early Bronze Age Barrows in Thy. In: *Journal of Danish Archaeology* 13, 1996-97, 7-17.

Aner, E. & Kersten, K., 2002: *Die Funde der älteren Bronzezeit des nordischen Kreises in Dänemark, Schleswig-Holsten und Niedersachsen* XI, Thisted Amt. Neumünster.

Bech, Jens-Henrik & Anne-Louise Haack Olsen 1985: Nye gravfund fra enkeltgravskulturen i Thy. *MIV* (Museer i Viborg Amt), Viborg, 36-47.

Bech, Jens-Henrik 1991: Et bronzealderlandskab ved Bjerre i Nordthy. Om arkæologiske udgravninger forud for en planlagt motorbane. *MIV* (Museer i Viborg Amt) 16, Viborg, 41-48.

Bech, Jens-Henrik 1993: Settlements on the raised sea-bed at Bjerre, northern Thy. In: S. Hvass & B. Storgård (eds.). *Digging into the Past. 25 years of Danish Archaeology*, Herning, 142-143.

Bech, Jens-Henrik 1997: Bronze Age Settlements on raised sea-beds at Bjerre, Thy, NW-Jutland. In: J.J. Assendorp (ed.). *Forschungen zur bronzezeitlichen Besiedlung Mittel- und Nordeuropas.* Internationales Symposium vom 9.-11. Mai 1996 in Hitzacker. Internationale Archäologie 38, Espelkamp, 3-15.

Bech, Jens-Henrik 1998: Thy Projektet. In: Mogens B. Henriksen (ed.): *Bebyggelseshistoriske projekter. Deres betydning, bearbejdning og publikation.* Rapport fra et bebyggelseshistorisk seminar på Hollufgård den 9. april 1997. Skrifter fra Odense Bys Museer 3, 1998, Odense, 57-65.

Bech, Jens-Henrik & Martin Mikkelsen 1999: Landscapes, settlement and subsistence in Bronze Age Thy, NW Denmark. In: C. Fabech & J. Ringtved (eds.) *Settlement and Landscape*. Proceedings of a conference in Århus, Denmark May 4-7 1998, Højbjerg, 69-77.

Berglund, Bjørn E. (ed.): *The cultural landscape during 6000 years in southern Sweden – the Ystad Project*. Ecological Bulletins 41, Copenhagen.

Bertelsen, J.B et al. 1996: *Bronzealderens bopladser i Midt- og Nordvestjylland* . De arkæologiske museer i Viborg amt, Skive, 1996.

Christensen, Kjeld 1999: Artsbestemmelse m.v. af bygningstømmer fra bronzealderbopladsen "Bjerre plads 6" i Thy. *NNU rapport* nr. 13, 1999, København, 1-33.

Clemmensen, Lars et al. 2001: Large-scale aeolian sand movement along the west coast of Jutland, Denmark in late Subboreal-early Subatlantic time – a record of climatic change or cultural impact ? In: *GFF* vol. 123, Stockholm, 193-203.

Earle, Timothy 1997: *How chiefs come to power. The political Economy in Prehistory*. Stanford University Press, Stanford.

Earle, Timothy et al. 1998: The political Economy of Late Neolithic and Early Bronze Age Society: the Thy Archaeological Project. In: *Norwegian Archaeological Review* 31, No. 1, Oslo, 1-28.

Earle, Timothy 2001: The Bronze Age economy of Thy: Finance in networked chiefdoms. In: Timothy Earle (ed.): *Bronze Age Economics: The First Political Economies*. Westview Press, Denver Col.

Fokkens, Harry 1999: Cattle and martiality: changing relations between man and landscape in the Late Neolithic and the Bronze Age. In: C. Fabech & J. Ringtved (eds.). *Settlement and Landscape*. Proceedings of a conference in Århus, Denmark May 4-7 1998, Højbjerg, 35-43.

Glob, Peter Vilhelm 1944: Studier over Den Jyske Enkeltgravskultur. *Årbøger for nordisk Oldkyndighed og Historie* 1944. København, 1-283.

Hirsch, Klaus & David Liversage 1987: Ravforarbejdning i yngre stenalder. In: *Nationalmuseets Arbejdsmark* 1987, København, 193-200.

Hvass, Steen 1986: En boplads fra enkeltgravkulturen i Vorbasse. In: C. Adamsen & K. Ebbesen (eds.). *Stridsøksetid I Sydskandinavien*. Beretning fra et symposium 28.-30. Oct. 1985 i Vejle. Arkæologiske Skrifter 1, Forhistorisk Arkæologisk Institut, København, 325-335.

Jensen, Jørgen 1965: Bernsteinfunde und Bernsteinhandel der jüngeren Bronzezeit Dänemarks. *Acta Archaeologica* 36, København, 43-86.

Jensen, Jørgen 2000: *Nordens Guld. En bog om oldtidens rav, mennesker og myter*. København.

Jessen, Axel 1920: *Stenalderhavets Udbredelse i det nordlige Jylland*. DGU II. række, nr. 35. København.

Kelertas, Kristina 1997: *The Changing political economy of Thy, Denmark. The paleobotanical Evidence*. Unpublished doctoral dissertation. Department of Archaeology, University of California, Los Angeles.

Kristiansen, Kristian 1984: Krieger und Häuptlinge in der Bronzezeit Dänemarks. Ein Beitrag zur Geschichte des bronzezeitlichen Schwertes. *Jahrbuch des Römisch-Germanisches Zentralmuseums vol. 31,* Mainz, 187-208.

Kristiansen, Kristian 1998: The Construction of a Bronze Age Landscape. Cosmology, Economy and Social Organisation in Thy, Northwestern Jutland. In: B. Hänsel (ed.). *Man and Environment in European Bronze Age*, Kiel, 281-92.

Kristiansen, Kristian 1999: Symbolic structures and social institutions. The twin rulers in bronze age Europe. In: A. Gustafsson, & H. Karlsson (eds.). *Glyfer och arkeologiska rum – en vänbok till Jarl Nordbladh*, Göteborg, 537-552.

Liversage, David 1988: Mortens Sande 2 – a Single Grave Camp site in Northwest Jutland. In: *Journal of Danish Archaeology* 6, 1987, 101-124.

Løken, Trond 1998: Hustyper og sosialstruktur gjennom bronsealder på Forsanmoen, Rogaland, Sørvest-Norge. In: T. Løken (ed.). *Bronsealder i Norden – Regioner og interaksjon*. Foredrag ved det 7. nordiske bronsealder-symposium i Rogaland 31. august-3. september 1995. AMS-Varia 33, Arkeologisk museum i Stavanger, 107-121.

Mathiassen, Therkel 1948: *Studier over Vestjyllands Oldtidsbebyggelse*. Nationalmuseets Skrifter, Arkæologisk-Historisk Række II. København.

Mikkelsen, Martin 1991: Metode og prioritering i forbindelse med lokalisering og udgravning af bronzealderbosættelser. In: *AUD* (Arkæologiske udgravninger i Danmark) 1991, 33-42.

Mikkelsen, Martin & Kristian Kristiansen 1996: *AUD* 1996, 168.

Mikkelsen, Martin & Kristian Kristiansen 1997: *AUD* 1997, 148.

Mikkelsen, Martin forthcoming: *Bebyggelsen i bronzealder og tidlig ældre jernalder i Østthy*. Publication by Jutland Archaeological Society, Højbjerg, in preparation.

Odgaard, B. V. and P. Rasmussen 2000: Origin and temporal development of macro-scale vegetation patterns in the cultural landscape of Denmark. *Journal of Ecology*, 88, 733-748.

Olsen, Anne-Louise Haack & Bech, Jens-Henrik 1996: Damsgård. En overpløjet høj fra ældre bronzealder per. III med stenkiste og ligbrændingsgrube. *Kuml* 1993-94, 155-198.

Rasmussen, Marianne 1999: Livestock without bones. The long-house as contributor to the interpretation of livestock management in the Southern Scandinavian Early Bronze Age. In: C. Fabech & J. Ringtved (eds.). *Settlement and Landscape.* Proceedings of a conference in Århus, Denmark May 4-7 1998, Højbjerg, 281-290.

Rosenberg, Gustav: *Hjortspringfundet.* Nordiske Fortidsminder III,1. København.

Rostholm, Hans 1986: Lustrup og andre bopladsfund fra Herning-egnen. In: C. Adamsen & K. Ebbesen (eds.). *Stridsøksetid I Sydskandinavien.* Beretning fra et symposium 28.-30. Oct. 1985 in Vejle. Arkæologiske Skrifter 1, Forhistorisk Arkæologisk Institut, København, 301-317.

Roymans, Nico & Harry Fokkens 1991: Een overzicht van veertig jaar nederzettingsonderzoek in de Lage Landen. In: Fokkens, Harrt & Nico Roymans (eds.). *Nederzettingen uit de bronstijd en de vroege ijzertijd in de Lage Landen.* NAR (Nederlandse Archeologische Rapporten) 13, Amersfoort, 1-19.

Steinberg, John 1996: Ploughzone sampling in Denmark. Isolating and interpreting site signatures from disturbed contexts. *Antiquity* 70, 368-392.

Steinberg, John 1997: *The Economic Prehistory of Thy, Denmark*: A study of the Changing Value of Flint Based on a Methodology of the Plowzone. Unpublished doctoral dissertation. University of California, Los Angeles.

Tesch, Sten 1993: *Houses, Farmsteads, and Long-term Change. A regional Study of Prehistoric Settlements in the Köpinge Area, in Scania, Southern Sweden.* Lund.

Thorpe, Nick 1997: From Settlements to Monuments: Site Succession in Late Neolithic and Early Bronze Age Jutland, west Denmark. In: G. Nash (ed.). *Semiotics of Landscape: Archaeology of Mind*, BAR International Series 661, 1997, Oxford, 71-79.

Van Geel, Bas & Hans Renssen 1998: Abrupt Climatic Change around 2,650 BP in North-West Europe: Evidence for Climatic Teleconnections and a Tentative Explanation. In: A.S.Issar & N. Brown (eds.). *Water, Environment and Society in Times of Climatic Change*, 1998, Kluwer Academic Publishers, the Netherlands, 21-41.

Vedsted, Jacob 1986: *Fortidsminder og kulturlandskab.* En kildekritisk analyse af tragtbægerkulturens fundmateriale fra Norddjursland. Djurslands Museum og Forlaget Skippershoved. Ebeltoft.

Strukturveränderungen einer Siedlungskammer im westlichen Odergebiet
– die "Neuenhagener Oderinsel"

Eike Gringmuth-Dallmer

1. Methodischer Ansatz, Finanzierung und praktische Durchführung des Projektes

Das deutsch/polnische Gemeinschaftsprojekt "Mensch und Umwelt im Odergebiet in ur- und frühgeschichtlicher Zeit", kurz genannt Oderprojekt, hatte das Ziel, im Rahmen einer Längsschnittuntersuchung eine möglichst komplexe Erforschung der Mensch-Umwelt-Beziehungen in einem Bereich etwa 50 km beiderseits der Oder vorzunehmen (Gringmuth-Dallmer 1997a). Der zeitliche Rahmen bewegte sich zwischen Mesolithikum und Mittelalter. Der besondere Schwerpunkt der Fragestellung lag auf der *aktiven* Einflußnahme des Menschen auf seine Umwelt. Dieser Gesichtspunkt kommt m.E. in den meisten siedlungsarchäologischen Arbeiten zu kurz, wo er zwar verbal genannt wird, in der praktischen Durchführung aber fast immer nur die Reaktion des Menschen auf die natürlichen Verhältnisse untersucht wird – teilweise mit einer bis ins Perverse getriebenen Perfektion.

Die Untersuchungen erfolgten auf drei Ebenen:

1. großräumige vergleichende Untersuchungen der einzelnen Perioden;
2. die intensive interdisziplinäre Untersuchung von Siedlungskammern als wichtigstem Teil des Projektes;
3. die Bearbeitung einzelner Problemkreise, z.B. des frühesten Eisens.

Die deutschen Aktivitäten, über die hier berichtet werden soll, wurden von der Volkswagen-Stiftung über einen Zeitraum von 6 Jahren (1993-1999) mit einem Betrag von 2,3 Millionen DM gefördert, die beiden hauptamtlich beschäftigten Archäologen waren feste Mitarbeiter des Deutschen Archäologischen Instituts (DAI), von dem sie bezahlt wurden. Organisation und Ablauf des Unternehmens können hier nicht dargestellt werden, sondern es seien nur drei aus meiner Sicht besonders wichtige Tatsachen erwähnt:

1. Die Zahl der direkt für das Projekt angestellten Mitarbeiter war relativ gering: eine Archäologin und ein Archäologe, eine Palynologin mit wissenschaftlich-technischer Assistentin, ein Grabungstechniker und je eine halbe Stelle für eine Fotografin und eine Zeichnerin, hinzu kamen eine wissenschaftliche Hilfskraft und für drei Jahre eine Doktorandin. Außerdem waren vier Naturwissenschaftler des DAI einbezogen.
2. Vor allem im Bereich der Geowissenschaften arbeitete auf freiwilliger und unentgeltlicher Basis eine größere Anzahl hochqualifizierter Spezial-

isten mit, ohne die die vielleicht wichtigsten Ergebnisse des Projektes nicht hätten erzielt werden können.

3. Es bestand eine intensive Zusammenarbeit mit verschiedenartigen geistes- und naturwissenschaftlichen Instituten mehrerer Universitäten. Allein an vier Universitäten entstanden Dissertationen, Diplom- und Magisterarbeiten sowie in größerem Umfang Seminararbeiten, die direkt aus dem Projekt hervorgingen und deren Ergebnisse in den inzwischen erscheinenen Abschlußband[1] einflossen. Grabungen, technische Aufarbeitung und Redaktionsarbeiten wurden zum weit überwiegenden Teil mit studentischen Hilfskräften durchgeführt.

Die drei genannten "Säulen" haben sich als außerordentlich effektiv erwiesen, wie hoffentlich das im folgenden vorzustellende Beispiel belegt. Es betrifft die Untersuchung einer Siedlungskammer (oben Punkt 2).

2. Der Untersuchungsraum

Die Neuenhagener Oderinsel, etwa 50 km nordwestlich von Frankfurt/Oder gelegen, bildet den westlichen Ausläufer eines weichselkaltzeitlichen Endmoränenzuges. Sie wird im Norden, Westen und Süden vom ehemaligen Hauptstrom der Oder umflossen, der Mitte des 18. Jh. mit einem Durchstich bei Hohensaaten seine ursprüngliche Funktion verlor. Während sich der Norden und der Osten nur wenige Meter über den Meeresspiegel erheben, steigt das Gelände im Süden und Westen bis auf über 80 m an (Abb. 1).

Wie die geologische Karte zeigt, bezieht sich die Insellage nicht nur auf das Verhältnis zur Oder, sondern auch auf die Geologie, indem sich der Kern aus Beckensand und -ton zusammensetzt, umgeben von Auelehm (Schlick), der in den meisten ur- und frühgeschichtlichen Perioden Überschwemmungsgebiet und damit nicht zu besiedeln war. Daraus ergibt sich, daß die Insel einerseits von der Aue und andererseits von so kargen Sanden bedeckt war, daß man sich

wundert, hier überhaupt Spuren prähistorischer Ansiedlungen zu finden.

3. Der Besiedlungsablauf

Dieser Eindruck täuscht jedoch. Die Oderinsel weist eine Vielzahl archäologischer Fundplätze auf, die im Rahmen einer Magisterarbeit von M. Zabel (1999) aufgearbeitet wurden. Danach liegen eindeutige Besiedlungsnachweise für das Spätneolithikum, die späte Bronze-/frühe Eisenzeit, die römische Kaiserzeit und die Slawen vor. Der Schwerpunkt der Besiedlung liegt durchweg im Westteil der Landschaft.

Daß dieses Bild nicht allzusehr durch den Forschungsstand verzerrt ist, zeigt zum einen ein Pollendiagramm aus dem Großen Krebssee inmitten der Insel, das nach Aussage der Bearbeiterin S. Jahns (1999; 2000) die regionale Situation widerspiegelt, also wohl die der ganzen Landschaft. Seine Datierung erfolgte mittels ^{14}C/AMS, also völlig unabhängig von der Archäologie. Das verstärkte Auftreten der Siedlungszeiger in den genannten Perioden spricht dafür, daß der Forschungsstand durchaus repräsentativ ist.

Eine zweite Korrelation konnte M. Zabel zwischen der Besiedlung und den Spiegelschwankungen der Ostsee feststellen. Er schreibt: "Steigt der Ostseespiegel, so geht insgesamt die Zahl der Fundstellen auch in vernässungsgeschützten Arealen zurück. ... Ob daraus auch ein Vorhandensein von Siedlungen in der Aue abgeleitet werden kann, muß offenbleiben," im vorliegenden Fall "ist dies eher unwahrscheinlich" (Zabel 1999, 61).

4. Analyse der Siedlungsplatzwahl mittels GIS

Eine wichtige Fragestellung bestand in der Analyse der Siedlungsplatzwahl. M. Zabel hat mit Hilfe einer Hauptkomponentenanalyse im Rahmen eines Geographischen Informationssystems (GIS) eine Quali-

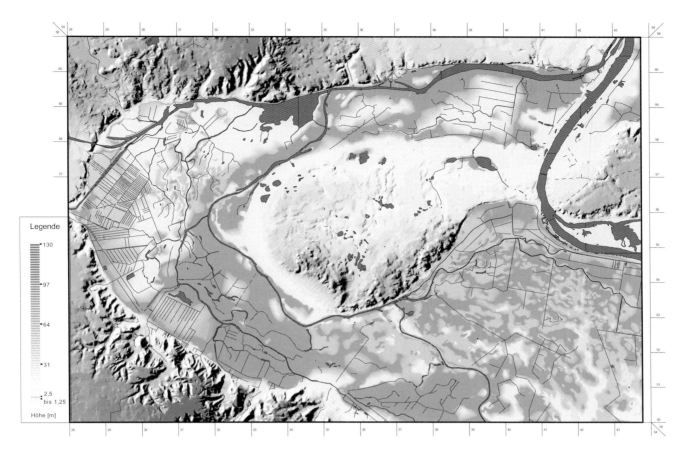

Abb. 1: Neuenhagener Oderinsel und Umland, Höhenmodell und Gewässernetz (Realisierung M. Zabel)

tätsbewertung der Siedlungsstandorte vorgenommen. Als Grundlage dienten die Einzelvariablen Höhe, Wasserentfernung, Boden, Neigung und Exposition. Mit der Wahl bestimmter Landschaftspunkte und somit auch bestimmter komplexer Landschaftsmerkmale, repräsentiert durch die Fundplätze der archäologischen Gruppen, treten dabei Vorstellungen von Besiedlungsattraktivität hervor. Weiterhin verfolgt er die Frage, inwieweit gewisse Prioritäten erkennbar sind und welche Landschaftsvariable bei einer Gruppe dominiert. Dabei zeigten sich sowohl zeitliche Unterschiede als auch solche zwischen Siedlungen und Gräberfeldern, wie kurz an den beiden am stärksten vertretenen Perioden gezeigt sei.

Im Vergleich zu den vorangegangenen Besiedlungsphasen weist die Lausitzer Kultur als erste Gruppe eine gewisse Unabhängigkeit von der Höhenlage auf. Eine größere Rolle spielen Neigung, Boden und Exposition. Bei den Gräberfeldern weisen hingegen die einzelnen Faktoren eine relativ unspezifische Verteilung auf. Daraus wird auf ein definiertes Konzept der bronzezeitlichen Kulturlandschaft geschlossen, nach dem die Wahl der Siedlungsbereiche streng definierten Regeln folgte – eine Formulierung, die mir überzogen erscheint – während die Gräberfelder außerhalb bzw. am Rand des attraktiven Siedlungsbereiches angelegt wurden, ohne derartigen festen Regeln zu folgen.

In der frühen Eisenzeit (Göritzer Gruppe) macht sich dann eine starke Fixierung auf die Einhaltung bestimmter Höhenpositionen und Wasserentfernungen bemerkbar, obwohl das Verbreitungsbild dem der Lausitzer Kultur recht ähnlich ist und in etwa die gleichen Areale genutzt werden. Als Erklärung bietet sich die statistische Verteilung der Höhenwerte beider Siedlungsphasen an. Für die Lausitzer Kultur liegt das Häufigkeitsmaximum bei 5-10 m NN, in der Göritzer Gruppe bei 15-20 m NN, woraus eine Verlagerungstendenz zu höheren Standorten abzuleiten ist. Der Bezug zu holozänen Transgressionsvorgängen im Odermündungsgebiet ist hier deutlich.

Entsprechende Berechnungen hat Zabel auch für die anderen Zeiten vorgenommen, auch wenn die statistische Sicherheit dort noch geringer ist. Auf eine nähere Darstellung sei hier verzichtet.

5. Die Grabung Neuenhagen

Im Zentrum der Insel wurden 1996/97 im Rahmen des Projektes Teile einer früheisenzeitlichen Siedlung der Göritzer Gruppe (etwa 7. Jh. v.Chr.) untersucht.[2]

Auf der L-förmig angelegten Fläche, die den Fundplatz auf 95 Meter in Nord-Süd- und auf 35 Meter in Ost-West-Richtung erschloß, wurden insgesamt knapp 700 m² ausgegraben. Der untersuchte Abschnitt zerfällt in zwei unterschiedlich strukturierte Bereiche. Während im Norden und in der Mitte die früheisenzeitliche Siedlungsschicht mit Gruben, Pfostenlöchern, zu vermutenden Produktionsstätten und Hausresten direkt der modernen Pflugschicht unterlagert, ist sie im Süden und Westen von einer bis zu 70 cm starken Auflage bedeckt. In die Kulturschicht selbst waren hier Pfostenlöcher eingetieft

(Gringmuth-Dallmer 1997b, Abb. 11). Für die Rekonstruktion eines ganzen Gebäudegrundrisses war die Fläche zu klein, jedoch wurde eine Doppelreihe kleiner Pfostenlöcher entdeckt, die offensichtlich von einem Zaun herrühren und zumindest ein Haus im Süden begrenzen.

Ein von den Bodenkundlern analysiertes und gemeinsam mit den Archäologen interpretiertes Profil in diesem Bereich läßt in nuce die gesamte Entwicklung des Platzes rekonstruieren (Abb. 2). Der an der Basis des Profils lagernde, in sich nochmals gegliederte Sand (g, h) ist in seinen unteren Teilen deutlich geschichtet, d.h. äolisch hierher verfrachtet worden, in seinem Oberteil (f) jedoch völlig unstrukturiert, was dafür spricht, daß er kurzzeitig – zwischen einem Mal und 5 Jahren – bearbeitet worden ist, also acker- oder gartenbaulich genutzt wurde. Nach dieser Nutzung begann die eigentliche Besiedlung des Platzes, die sich in der dunkelgrauen bis tiefschwarzen Siedlungsschicht (e) niederschlägt, in die auch die erfaßten Gebäude eingetieft waren. Sie wird ihrerseits von einem bis zu 70 cm starken Paket lehmigen, z.T. humosen Sandes überlagert (b-d). Es ist stellenweise nochmals dreigegliedert, ohne daß sich klare Abgrenzungen ausmachen ließen. Zwei dieser "Unterschichten" gehören wiederum zusammen. Das Paket wird als Auftragsboden interpretiert. Sollte diese Ansprache stimmen, so läge hier die älteste bekannte derartige Bildung im nordostdeutschen Raum vor. Sie entspricht etwa

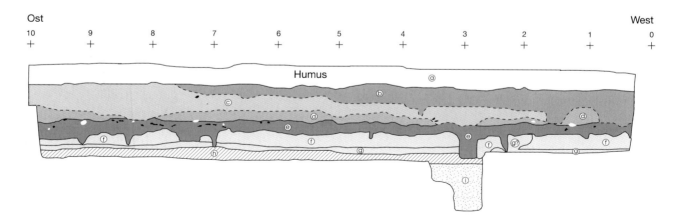

Abb. 2: Neuenhagen, Kr. Märkisch-Oderland, Fpl. 10. Südprofil bei L 51/f0. b-d Auftragsboden; e Kulturschicht; f unstrukturierter Sand; g-h geschichteter Sand; i Geschiebemergel (Realisierung E. Schultze)

den frühesten Plaggenböden Nordwestdeutschlands, die O. Harck (1987, 23 ff.) aus Archsum publiziert hat, hier allerdings schon in die mittlere Bronzezeit zu datieren. Und sie liefert genau das, was wir gezielt suchen wollten: ein Zeugnis für die bewußte, aktive Gestaltung der Umwelt durch den Menschen.

Genau an der Stelle, wo die Kulturschicht in das aufliegende Paket eintaucht, d.h. am Beginn des Auftragsbodens, kamen der auffallendste Befund und der herausragendste Fund zutage. Es handelt sich um eine massive Setzung sehr grober, dickwandiger Scherben von etwa 80 cm Durchmesser und 30 cm Tiefe. Sie ist annähernd kreisrund, die Scherben sind teilweise nach außen gewendet. Obenauf liegt ein völlig aus dem Rahmen fallendes, sehr fein gearbeitetes Etagengefäß (Gringmuth-Dallmer 1997b, Abb. 13, 14). Die Fundumstände – die feine Tasse auf der groben Scherbensetzung – lassen kaum eine andere Deutung als eine kultische zu. Und es fällt natürlich auf, daß dieses Gebilde genau dort errichtet wurde, wo mit dem künstlichen Bodenauftrag begonnen wurde. Das dürfte sicher kein Zufall sein.

Beobachtungen in anderen Teilen der Grabung gestatten, die Entwicklung noch weiter zurückzuverfolgen. Der pleistozäne Sand im Liegenden des beschriebenen Profils wird von einer in weiten Bereichen der Siedlung anzutreffenden grauen Schicht überlagert, die vereinzelt Scherben, aber keine Befunde enthält. Die Scherben zeigen, daß sie zu einem bestimmten Zeitpunkt die Oberfläche dargestellt haben muß, vermutlich ist sie als Weideland anzusprechen. Das setzt vorhergehende Rodung voraus. Diese Oberfläche wurde später von dem beschriebenen äolischen Sand überweht, der durch Ackerbau oder Überweidung freigesetzt wurde. Bohrungen, bei denen u.a. Scherben zum Vorschein kamen, lassen darauf schließen, daß ein entsprechender Zyklus schon einmal in noch früherer Zeit stattgefunden hat (Bork et al. 1998, 49 ff.; Schatz 2000, 82 ff.).

Das von N. Benecke (Berlin) bestimmte Tierknochenmaterial – pflanzliche Großreste mit Ausnahme von Holzkohle konnten trotz systematischen Schlämmens aller Grubeninhalte leider nicht geborgen werden – entspricht dem in dieser Zeit zu erwartenden: Es dominiert das Rind, gefolgt von Schwein und Schaf/Ziege. Die Jagd spielt eine geringe Rolle. Trotzdem ist infolge der äußerst ungünstigen naturräumlichen Ausstattung mit bestimmten wirtschaftlichen Umstrukturierungen zu rechnen. So ist es sicher kein Zufall, daß sich neben zahlreichen Fischresten unter den insgesamt nur wenigen Kleinfunden ein Angelhaken und ein Netzsenker befanden. Erwähnt seien in diesem Zusammenhang auch drei Bruchstücke tönerner Tierplastiken (Gringmuth-Dallmer 1997b, Abb. 12), von denen allerdings nicht sicher ist, ob sie von selbständigen Figuren oder von Gefäßrändern herstammen.

Chronologisch gehört fast das gesamte Material in die Stufe Göritz I (7. Jh.), einzelne Funde belegen ein Auslaufen in Göritz II.

Zum Abschluß der Kurzvorstellung der Grabung sei noch auf eine Beobachtung hingewiesen, die einen wichtigen Aspekt der Interpretation von Siedlungsstrukturen betrifft. Unter der sehr zahlreichen Keramik der Siedlung waren in größerem Umfang blasig aufgequollene Stücke, die entweder von Fehlbränden stammten oder sekundär ins Feuer gelangt waren. Im ersten Fall würden sie eine Produktion am Ort belegen. Die mineralogischen Untersuchungen erbrachten kein ganz eindeutiges Ergebnis, J. Riederer (1998, 23) hält aber Fehlbrand für am wahrscheinlichsten. Vergleichbare Keramik ist bisher aus der Göritzer Gruppe nicht beschrieben worden. Wenn das so ist, sei der vorsichtige Schluß gestattet, daß nur in einzelnen Siedlungen Töpferei betrieben wurde. Das aber würde eine funktionale Differenzierung der ländlichen Siedlungen bedeuten, die für die Gesamtstruktur der Landschaft wichtig wäre. Diese kurze Andeutung eines weiterführenden Problems möge jetzt genügen.

6. Die Entwicklung der Siedlungsstruktur auf der Oderinsel

In Kenntnis der Grabungsergebnisse von Neuenhagen und des Pollendiagramms vom etwa 2,5 km entfernten Großen Krebssee sei nun die Entwicklung

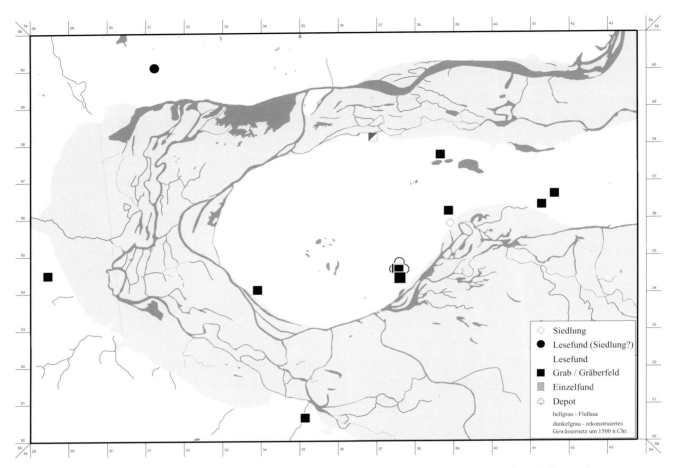

Abb. 3: Neuenhagener Oderinsel und Umland, Besiedlung der vorrömischen Eisenzeit (nach Zabel 1999).

der Siedlungsstruktur auf der Oderinsel unter Be-rücksichtigung der anthropogenen Siedlungsfaktoren aufgerollt – die Analyse von Zabel galt ja ausschließ-lich den naturräumlichen Faktoren.

Der menschliche Einfluß beginnt nach den Radio-karbondaten des Pollendiagramms mit einer relativ kurzen Phase um die Wende zum 4. Jahrtausend B.C. Eine intensivere Besiedlung ist dann um 3200 B.C. mit einer typischen Landnam-Phase nach Iver-sen greifbar, die ca. 1.000 Jahre lang dauerte. Archä-ologisch ist dieser Zeitraum kaum faßbar, lediglich einige Einzelfunde von Steingeräten liegen vor.

Vor diesem siedlungsgeschichtlichen Hintergrund sind die beiden begrabenen Schichten in Neuenha-gen zu betrachten, die vor der Hauptbesiedlungszeit zweimal die Anwesenheit des Menschen nachweisen. Die jüngere gehört ins Mittelneolithikum, die ältere

entweder in den ältesten pollenanalytisch belegten Abschnitt oder in einen älteren mittelneolithischen Horizont. Das Fehlen eindeutiger Befunde läßt darauf schließen, daß die ergrabenen bzw. erbohrten Horizonte nicht den Bereich der Siedlung, sondern den der Wirtschaftsflächen dokumentieren. Die menschliche Tätigkeit führte zu einer weitgehenden Entblößung der Oberfläche von der Vegetation und in ihrer Folge zu Dünenbildung, die ein weiteres Ver-bleiben unmöglich machte.

Die ausgedehnten Sandablagerungen, die die bei-den unteren Bewirtschaftungshorizonte bedecken, haben zu einer Kontroverse zwischen den Boden-kundlern und der Palynologin geführt. Während erstere meinten, ein solcher Materialtransport setze große Freiflächen voraus, konnte S. Jahns solche in ihren Pollendiagrammen nicht entdecken. Inzwischen scheint das Problem geklärt zu sein, da die Bestimmung der Holzkohlereste aus den Siedlungsgruben durch R. Neef (Berlin) praktisch nur Kiefer erbracht hat, was für ein völliges Zurückdrängen der vorher hier befindlichen Laubwälder und damit für ein weitgehendes Ausräumen der Landschaft spricht. Die Erklärung für den Widerspruch könnte darin bestehen, daß der Westen stärker landwirtschaftlich genutzt war und, gemäß der Hauptwindrichtung, der Sand vornehmlich aus diesem Teil der Neuenhagener Oderinsel und dem angrenzenden Barnim stammte, während eine stärkere Bewaldung im Osten den Transport größerer Sandmassen unterband. Für eine solche Vorstellung spricht, daß der Westen tatsächlich fundreicher ist als der Osten (vgl. die Gesamtkartierung bei Jahns 1999, Abb. 3).

Ein erneuter Siedlungsschub setzt in der späten Bronze-/frühen Eisenzeit ein (Abb. 3). Das Gebiet weist jetzt eine so massive Besiedlung auf, daß, so meine These, angesichts der geringwertigen naturräumlichen Ausstattung als Begründung nur ein Bevölkerungsdruck in den Altsiedellandschaften möglich ist. Im polnischen Teil des unteren Odergebietes ist eine deutliche Zunahme der Fundplatzzahlen zu konstatieren (Wesołowski 1996, Abb. 2, 3), die deutsche Seite ist leider nicht aufgearbeitet. Betrachtet man jedoch die Kartierung eines zufällig vorgelegten einzelnen Typs, der Turbanrandteller (Horst 1972, Abb. 2), so scheint sich durchaus eine starke Besiedlung anzudeuten. Gleiches gilt für den Beginn der Eisenzeit, für Göritz I (Griesa 1982, Karte 2).

Ein Grund dafür, daß eine Besiedlung der Landschaft wieder möglich wurde, könnte in einem Anstieg des Wasserspiegels in der frühen Eisenzeit liegen, der für den unteren Oderlauf rekonstruiert wurde.[3] Wie bereits erwähnt, sieht jedoch M. Zabel Feuchtphasen als Zeiten der Entsiedlung an, d.h. Standorte in der Aue wurden aufgegeben. Gleichzeitig aber (das ist nun meine Interpretation) könnte sich die Bewirtschaftungsmöglichkeit der Sande auf der Oderinsel verbessert haben. Schwer einzuordnen in die Vorstellung von einem kühleren Klima ist allerdings der Umstand, daß während der Ausgrabungen in Neuenhagen mehrere Reste von Sumpfschildkröten gefunden wurden, die zum Überleben eine sommerliche Durchschnittstemperatur von 20-21°C benötigen.

Unabhängig von der Begründung im einzelnen können wir jetzt den Besiedlungsgang auf der Oderinsel anhand des vorhin gezeigten Grabungsprofils näher verfolgen. Zu Beginn der Eisenzeit wird der Platz kurzzeitig bewirtschaftet, bevor eine sehr intensive Besiedlung auf dem stärker als heute reliefierten Gelände einsetzt. Der tiefer gelegene Teil der Siedlung wird relativ bald aufgegeben und von einem Auftragsboden bedeckt, der in zwei Phasen entstanden ist.

Das Aufbringen des Auftragsbodens hat tief in das Landschaftbild eingeschnitten. Für die in ihrer Entstehung verwandte mittelalterlich/neuzeitliche Plaggendüngung liegen einige Berechnungen vor. Danach werden für einen Hektar zu düngenden Bodens jährlich rund zwei Hektar Heidefläche benötigt. Für die Regeneration abgeplaggter Heideflächen werden je nach Boden 8-40 Jahre veranschlagt. Das heißt bei einem Mittelwert von 20 Jahren, daß pro Hektar regelmäßig bewirtschaftetem Plaggenesch 40 ha Plaggenmatt zur Verfügung stehen mußten (Behre 1980, 35). Wenn diese Werte auch für das Mittelalter mit seiner zweifellos erheblich intensiveren Abplaggung gelten, so lassen sie doch auch für Neuenhagen auf einen erheblichen Bedarf an zu verwertendem Boden schließen, dessen Herkunft sogar wahrscheinlich gemacht werden konnte.

Eine Durchsicht der von Otto Braasch erstellten Luftbilder der Oderinsel ergab, daß unmittelbar östlich und nordöstlich der Siedlung teils längliche, teils unregelmäßige Verfärbungen auftreten, die sich durch einen geringeren Bewuchs als ihre Umgebung auszeichnen. Es erscheint gut möglich, daß das Material des Auftragsbodens hier gewonnen wurde, eine Deutung, der O. Braasch ausdrücklich zustimmt. Ein Nachweis ist jedoch letztlich nur aus der Untersuchung dort anzulegender Aufschlüsse zu gewinnen. Die zahlreiche Keramik im Neuenhagener Auftragsboden und sein Humusgehalt deuten darauf hin, daß neben dem aus der Umgebung herangeschafften Material auch Dung aus der Siedlung verwendet wurde.

Mit dem Ende der Phase Göritz I läuft die intensive Besiedlung des Platzes weitgehend aus, die verbliebene Bevölkerung verläßt ihn in der Phase Göritz II. Legt man eine Besiedlungszeit von etwa 100 Jahren zugrunde, so fällt die Größe der von der Siedlung in Anspruch genommenen Fläche auf, auch unter Berücksichtigung der aus den "begrabenen" Hausresten zu erschließenden Tatsache, daß sie nie als Ganzes bewohnt wurde.

Warum aber wurde der Platz aufgegeben? Der Bodenkundler Th. Schatz (2000) hat die These aufgestellt, die anthropogenen Bodenumlagerungen hätten ein solches Ausmaß angenommen, daß die Menschen zum Abzug gezwungen wurden. Das erscheint im vorliegenden Fall durchaus plausibel, ist aber, trotz gleichgerichteter Beobachtungen an anderen Plätzen, kaum zu verallgemeinern. Denn in Göritz II setzt ein allgemeiner Besiedlungsrückgang ein, Göritz III weist nur noch eine sehr kleinräumige Verbreitung auf (Griesa 1982). Es müssen also zumindest auch andere, weiträumiger wirkende Faktoren eine Rolle gespielt haben, deren Ergründung Sache der Spezialisten für diese Zeit ist.

Betrachten wir noch kurz die weitere Entwicklung, bei der sich archäologischer und pollenanalytischer Befund wiederum weitgehend decken. Für die jüngere vorrömische Eisenzeit fehlen Besiedlungsspuren, aus der römischen Kaiserzeit sind lediglich zwei Gräberfelder bekannt, die sich aber gut im Pollendiagramm niederschlagen, da sie am Rand der beiden Krebsseen liegen. Die Völkerwanderungszeit zeigt die übliche Besiedlungslücke.

Die dann einsetzende slawische Besiedlung bietet eine direkte Parallele zu der der späten Bronze-/frühen Eisenzeit. Bekannt sind sieben Fundplätze. Lediglich von zwei Plätzen liegen vereinzelte mittelslawische Scherben vor, ansonsten gehören alle Funde in die spätslawische Zeit nach 1000 (Gringmuth-Dallmer 1997b, 580). Diese geradezu explosionsartige Vermehrung der Fundplätze ist im gesamten Gebiet westlich der Oder zu beobachten und läßt auch hier den Schluß zu, daß ein Bevölkerungsdruck eine stärkere Besiedlung des kargen Gebietes bewirkt hat. Vermutlich Mitte des 14. Jh. setzt dann der Landesausbau im Rahmen der hochmittelalterlichen Ostsiedlung ein, der sich auch sehr

deutlich im Pollendiagramm niederschlägt und die unmittelbare Grundlage für das heutige Siedlungsbild der "Oderinsel" gelegt hat.

7. Schlußbemerkung

Betrachten wir abschließend die Forschungen auf der Neuenhagener Oderinsel unter dem Gesichtspunkt diachroner Siedlungsverlagerungen, so scheinen mir vor allem zwei Aussagen wichtig:

1. – diese Aussage gilt für jede Art siedlungsarchäologischer Forschung – konnten auch in gering reliefierten Landschaften Erosions- und Akkumulationsvorgänge das archäologische Fundbild so verzerren, daß allein aus der Fundverbreitung keine weitreichenden Schlüsse gezogen werden sollten.

2. bestätigen die Untersuchungen einerseits die Notwendigkeit kleinräumiger interdisziplinärer Forschungen. Andererseits hat sich wiederum gezeigt, daß die Interpretation der erschlossenen Vorgänge nicht ohne die Berücksichtigung großräumiger Entwicklungen möglich ist.

Literatur

Behre, K.-E. 1980: Zur mittelalterlichen Plaggenwirtschaft in Nordwestdeutschland und angrenzenden Gebieten nach botanischen Untersuchungen. In: Beck, H., D. Denecke & H. Jankuhn (Hrsg.), *Untersuchungen zur eisenzeitlichen und frühmittelalterlichen Flur in Mitteleuropa und ihrer Nutzung, T. 2*, Göttingen, 30-44.

Bork, H.-R., H. Bork, C. Dalchow, B. Faust, H.-P. Piorr & Th. Schatz 1998: *Landschaftsentwicklung in Mitteleuropa*. Gotha/Stuttgart.

Brose, F. 1994: Das untere Odertal: Talentwicklung, Nutzung und Wasserbau. In: J. H. Schroeder (Hrsg.), *Führer zur Geologie von Berlin und Brandenburg 2. Bad Freienwalde – Parsteiner See*, Berlin, 152--157.

Griesa, S. 1982: *Die Göritzer Gruppe. (= Veröffentlichungen des Museums für Ur- u. Frühgeschichte Potsdam 16)*.

Gringmuth-Dallmer, E. 1997a: Das Projekt "Mensch und Umwelt im Odergebiet in ur- und frühgeschichtlicher Zeit«. *Archäologisches Nachrichtenblatt 2*, 309-315.

Gringmuth-Dallmer, E. 1997: Das Projekt "Mensch und Umwelt im Odergebiet in ur- und frühgeschichtlicher Zeit«. Eine Zwischenbilanz. *Ber. RGK 78*, 5-27.

Harck, O. 1987: Archäologisches zur Kenntnis des vor- und frühgeschichtlichen Ackerbaus. In: G. Kossack u.a., *Archsum auf Sylt, T. 2: Landwirtschaft und Umwelt in vor- und frühgeschichtlicher Zeit*, Mainz, 1-50.

Horst, F. 1972: Die uckermärkisch-westpommersche Gruppe der jüngeren Bronzezeit. *Mitteilungen des Bezirksfachausschusses für Ur- und Frühgeschichte Neubrandenburg 19*, 16-20.

Jahns, S. 1999: Pollenanalytische Untersuchungen am Großen Krebssee, Ostbrandenburg. Ein Beitrag zur Siedlungs- und Vegetationsgeschichte der Neuenhagener Oderinsel. *Germania 77*, 639-661.

Jahns, S. 2000: Late-glacial and Holocene woodland dynamics and land-use history of the Lower Oder valley, north-eastern Germany, based on two, AMS 14C dated, pollen profiles. *Vegetation Hist. Archaeobotany 9*, 111-123.

Riederer, J. 1998: Materialanalysen an archäologischen Keramiken aus Brandenburg. *Archäologie in Berlin und Brandenurg 1997*, 22-23.

Schatz, Th. 2000: *Untersuchungen zur holozänen Landschaftsentwicklung Nordostdeutschlands. (= ZALF-Bericht 41)*. Müncheberg.

Wesołowski, S. 1996: Stan badań nad osadnictwem kultury łużyckiej Pomorza Zachodniego. In: L. Leciejewicz & E. Gringmuth-Dallmer (red.), Człowiek a środowisko w środkowym i dolnym nadordzu – Mensch und Umwelt im mittleren und unteren Odergebiet, Wrocław, 81-96.

Zabel, M. 1999: *Die urgeschichtliche Besiedlung der Neuenhagener Oderinsel*. Ungedr. Magisterarbeit FU Berlin.

Anmerkungen

1. Forschungen zu Mensch und Umwelt im Odergebiet in ur- und frühgeschichtlicher Zeit, hrsg. E. Gringmuth-Dallmer/L. Leciejewicz, Mainz 2002. Die im folgenden behandelten Untersuchungen sind dort ausführlicher dargestellt.

2. Erster zusammenfassender Bericht bei Gringmuth-Dallmer 1997b, 17ff.

3. Brose 1994. Wiederabdruck der dort vorgelegten Kurve bei Gringmuth-Dallmer 1997b, Abb. 6.

Central Europe

Diachronic micro-regional Studies of Settlement on the Loess Uplands of south-eastern Poland in the Bronze Age

Sławomir Kadrow & Jacek Górski

Analysis of all publications devoted to metal objects from the Bronze Age found in Poland, and their chronology, brings to light a very interesting phenomenon. The territory of Poland is divided into two parts. In the western part of our country there are numerous finds of metal artefacts, including hoards, elements of grave furnishings, and stray finds. In the eastern part, however, there are only single finds of this kind. This asymmetry is especially striking among finds from the Early Bronze Age (fig. 1). As regards finds from later periods the number of metal remains increases slowly in the Vistula river basin. Nevertheless, it is too small to serve as a basis for developing a serious, independent and sufficiently detailed relative chronology of the areas in question. Again, comparing chronologies for the western and eastern part of Poland one can observe the same asymmetry as in the case of the number of metal objects. The "western" chronologies usually represent sequences of narrow units of time (phases, subphases, or horizons), whereas the "eastern" ones are only very general (fig. 2).

After more than thirty years of very intensive investigations (excavations and surface surveys) in SE Poland, especially on the loess uplands (cf. Kruk 1973; Machnikowie 1973; Rydzewski 1986; Górski 1997; Kadrow 1997) it is clear that the scarcity of metal artefacts in the described areas is not caused by the lack of proper research projects. It seems to reflect a real prehistoric situation. No wonder that attempts to import various systems of 'metal' chronologies from the outside, i.e. from the Carpathian Basin, the Upper Danube areas, Bohemia, or from Southern Scandinavia, have failed. An urgent need for a local chronology (or chronologies) therefore arose. The only way to provide this was to use the potential evidence of the extremely rich pottery assemblages from the large settlements that had existed over long periods. On the one hand pottery offers great possibilities to develop a very 'fine' chronology, because of its variations over time. On the other hand, however, there are wide variations in pottery that occur in the spatial dimension. Pottery used to evolve in a quite different ways even in locations not too distant from each other. Instead of one system (as in the case of metal chronology), one has to develop many 'local' pottery chronologies inside any one region.

Pottery chronologies based only on typological considerations have almost always turned out to be false, in part, or as a whole. They must therefore be controlled by external factors such as stratigraphy or radiocarbon dating. In the context of the Bronze Age archaeology of SE Poland, only large so-called 'multicultural' settlements which have been excavated to a sufficient degree can serve as a basis for constructing reliable chronologies. In order to reach results of this kind a special analytical programme was developed (Kadrow 1991a; 1991b). Several assumptions were adopted in this research programme. First, that archaeological evidence from large settlements could furnish data that would permit the reconstruction

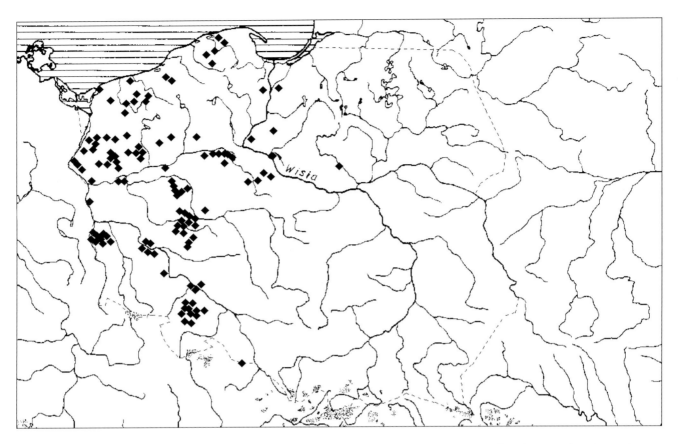

Fig. 1. Metal hoards from the Early and Middle Bronze Age in Poland; 1 – hoards dated to the period BrA2 and BrA2/BrB1, 2 – hoards dated to BrB1-BrB2 and BrC, 3 – the 'western' loess uplands of Małopolska (distribution of hoards based on: Blajer 1990; 1999).

of the spatial organisation of the settlement and the chronological differentiation of the stages of its development. Second, that the features discovered could be ordered to produce reconstruction of aspects of the original building complexes (subsequently referred to as 'house clusters'). Third, that the analysis of depositional processes in pit fills would allow for the isolation of sufficiently homogeneous artefact assemblages related to successive stages of development of the settlement. This would facilitate recognition of stratigraphic divisions within the house cluster sequences as well as the reconstruction of settlement plans corresponding to successive stages of development. The volume of pottery, its representative character and stratigraphical context, were used as basic criteria for establishing cultural and chronological affiliation (Kadrow 1991a: 641).

At first, the programme mentioned above was adopted to analyse the Early Bronze Age settlement at Iwanowice, the 'Babia Góra' site (Kadrow 1991a; 1991b; Kadrow & Machnik 1993), then it was tested again to analyse pottery materials from the Trzciniec culture (Early Bronze Age) from the settlement at Kraków, the 'Kopiec Wandy' (Mogiła 55) site (Górski 1993; 1994).

General information on the loess uplands of SE Poland

The loess-covered areas of Poland belong to the loess zone that runs along a parallel of latitude from the Atlantic coast of France to the Ural Mountains. They

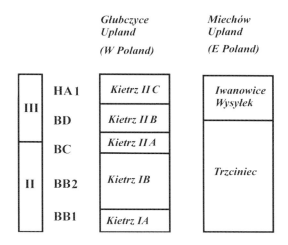

		Głubczyce Upland (W Poland)	Miechów Upland (E Poland)
III	HA1	*Kietrz II C*	*Iwanowice Wysyłek*
	BD	*Kietrz II B*	
	BC	*Kietrz II A*	
II	BB2	*Kietrz I B*	*Trzciniec*
	BB1	*Kietrz I A*	

Fig. 2. Chronology of the Early and Middle Bronze Age in western and eastern parts of Poland (based on Gedl 1982).

can be further subdivided into several areas of varying size. In the Polish southern uplands three such areas may be distinguished: the "Lublin" in the east, the "Sandomierz" in the middle and the "Kraków" area in the west (Kruk 1997, 18-33). In the piedmont region there are two areas: the Carpathian and the Sudeten area (fig. 3).

The uplands part of the "Kraków" (Cracow) loess area – the Loess Uplands of Western Małopolska (Little Poland) – covers some 2 500 square km (fig. 4). More than 70% of this area has a loess cover. Only the upper parts of some hills, steeper slopes and the bottoms of deeper valleys are free of loess. The depth of the loess stratum does not exceed 20 m. The loess cover reproduces the relief beneath it. The uplands under discussion are divided into two subregions: the

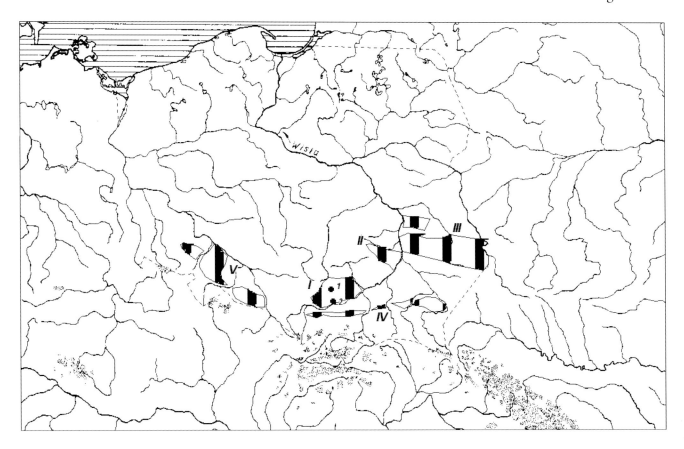

Fig. 3. Distribution of loess soils in Poland; a – typical loess soils, b – periglacial deposits (silty and clayey) with thin patches of eolian loesses, I – 'Kraków' loess, II – 'Sandomierz' loesses, III – 'Lublin' loesses, IV – Carpathian loesses, V – Sudeten loess; 1 – Iwanowice, the 'Babia Góra' site, 2 – Kraków-Nowa Huta, the 'Kopiec Wandy' site (after Kruk 1997).

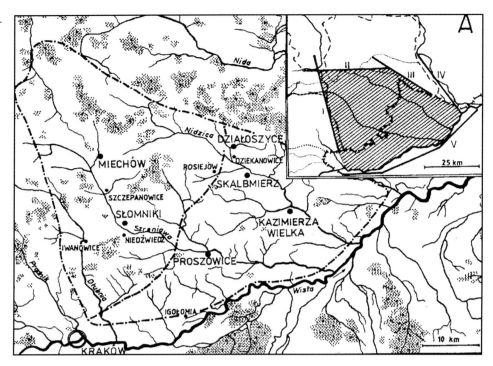

Fig. 4. Loess Uplands of Western Małopolska;
A – the "investigation field" and its borders; 1 – Iwanowice, the 'Babia Góra' site, 2 – Kraków-Nowa Huta, the 'Kopiec Wandy' site (after Kruk 1997).

Miechów Uplands and the Proszowice Plateau (fig. 4). The region under discussion is an uplands area, dipping towards the south-east. The most highly elevated parts are in the west with the highest areas rising a little over 400 m. above sea level. Among the main rivers are the Dłubnia, Szreniawa, Nidzica and Nida, which belong to left-bank tributaries of the Wisła (Vistula) river (fig. 4). The western part of the region, belonging to the basins of the Dłubnia and upper Szreniawa, has a low density of river network. This is the result of a high soil permeability. The basins of the lower Szreniawa, Nidzica and Nida are much better developed. The upper part of the main rivers of the area have relatively steeply sloping beds (2.5-5.0%; c. f. Kruk 1973: 11-18).

The soil cover of the Loess Uplands of Western Małopolska is not very diversified. Soils formed from material other than loess occupy small areas. The most commonly occurring are brown loess soils. A slightly smaller area is occupied by chernozems, forming several large patches in the southern part of the Miechów Uplands and Proszowice Plateau.

The character of the vegetation in the region is determined by the loess cover, alluvial sediments

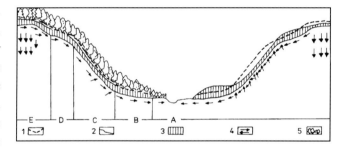

Fig. 5. Landscape zones on the Loess Uplands of Western Małopolska; 1 – natural shape of the slope, 2 – present shape of the slope, 3 – thickness of the soil profile, 4 – direction and intensity of the ground water movements, 5 – vegetative cover; A – bottom of the valley, B – terrace over the bottom of the valley, C – slopes, D – edge of the watershed, E – watersheds (after Kruk 1973; 1980).

and cretaceous rock formations such as gypsums and limestones that in some places appear on the surface. The vegetation of the Loess Uplands of Western Małopolska is greatly diversified. It consists of e.g. meadows and xerothermic scrubs, light xerothermic oak forests and forests growing on dry ground. In some places they create a landscape of a park-like character that is unique in Poland and resembles the forest-steppe of south-eastern Europe. The existence of this vegetation in our region is edaphic and results from anthropogenic transformations.

On the basis of a reconstruction of a potential vegetation (fig. 5) in the environment of the loess uplands (Kruk & Przywara 1983) one can describe the natural landscape of the area in question in frames of five zones: (A) an alluvial zone; very damp low-lying lands covered by alder and marshy multi-species forests – this zone is very productive for agriculture; (B) a valley terrace above the flood plain covered by dry multi-species forests of linden and hornbeam – since only a low level of agricultural technology was needed to produce high crop yields, this zone had great economic potential; (C) dry slopes of the uplands which separate the lower zone in the valleys from the uplands (upper zone) – clusters of oak in linden and hornbeam forests, giving a topography which would have hindered both settlement location and agricultural production there; (D) very dry edges of uplands covered by multi-species forests of linden, hornbeam and oak – great economic potential but not as high as zone B; (E) the very dry zone of uplands covered by oak forests with unfavourable conditions (lack of water) for stable settlement – this zone may have been utilised for agriculture and for stock-breeding.

Settlement studies in Western Loess Uplands in Małopolska

At the end of 1960's the Cracow Branch of the Institute of Archaeology and Ethnology (Polish Academy of Sciences) started work on a research project examining settlement patterns in the western part of Little Poland during Neolithic and the Early Bronze Age. In order to do this, a relatively small, compact area along three left tributaries of an upper Vistula River was chosen (fig. 4). This territory was thoroughly examined by means of archaeological surface surveying. Nearly all the sites preserved up till now were recorded in their full topographical context. This survey enabled settlement patterns to be identified for various chronological and cultural units. It was observed that changes in settlement patterns depended mainly on changes in socio-economic systems, and not on climatic ones (Kruk 1973).

In a sense the studies on the settlement system in the Metal Ages were a continuation of the Neolithic work. They were conducted within the same region. This time, however, they were focused almost exclusively on the geography of settlements (Rydzewski 1986). Again they were based first of all on results of field surveys. Thanks to these investigations we know of more than 1000 settlement-related locations (settlements, cemeteries, hoards, stray finds) covering the time from the beginning of the Bronze Age to the beginning of the Iron Age (more than 350 sites from the Mierzanovice culture, more than 260 sites from the Trzciniec culture, and more than 500 sites from the Lusatian culture).

As a result of studies of the geography of the settlement from the Metal Ages, an outline of settlement systems of the main archaeological cultures was drawn up. The traces of the Mierzanowice culture appear rather irregularly throughout the region. One can perceive four zones of concentrations: (a) along the upper basin of the Dłubnia river, (b) in the vicinity of Kraków-Nowa Huta, (c) in the lower section of the Szreniawa river, and (d) in the middle section of Nidzica (fig. 6). In these zones settlement traces appear in the form of small groups. They usually occupy areas of about 4-5 km^2 and consist of 2-4 settlement points. In their vicinity numerous stray finds occur. Almost all stable settlements were located in the upper zones of the landscape, especially in the D zone (Rydzewski 1986: 132-140).

The appearance of the Trzciniec culture introduces some changes in the picture of settlement on the loess uplands (Rydzewski 1986: 140-147). The area under occupation was larger and the settlement network closer in comparison with the Mierzanowice culture. We can see three main settlement zones located along the rivers Dłubnia, Szreniawa and Nidzica (Fig. 7). Within these zones there appear to be clearly separated micro-regions, consisting of two or (mostly) three settlements (in reality 2-5) covering an area of 2-6 km^2.

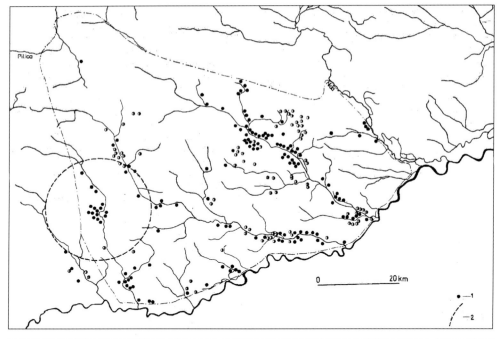

Fig. 6. Spatial distribution of settlement locations of the Mierzanowice culture on the Western Loess Upland in Małopolska; 1 – settlement locations, 2 – circle 10 km around Iwanowice, the 'Babia Góra' site-1; (after Kadrow 1997b).

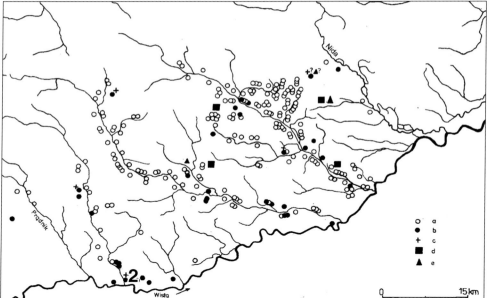

Fig. 7. Spatial distribution of settlements from the Trzciniec culture on the Western Loess Upland in Małopolska; a–e – various kinds of settlement locations; 2 – Kraków-Nowa Huta, the 'Kopiec Wandy' site (after Górski 1997).

The majority of the settlements were located on prominent river terraces, but larger sites were also located in the naturally isolated parts of the land (landscape zone B). A smaller proportion of the settlements existed on the edges of the highland (zone D).

The proper colonisation of the loess uplands began with the appearance of the Lusatian culture population in this area (fig. 8). We can observe the essential increase in the intensity of settlement. The Lusatian culture enlarged its areas of habitation, occupying sites even at a distance from the main rivers. The Vistula terrace was especially intensively settled in this period. Units, consisting of 3-4 settlements, covering areas of 5-6 km² formed larger agglomerations covering an area of 15-20 km². In these cases the number of settlements in the agglomerations exceeded 10. Settlements

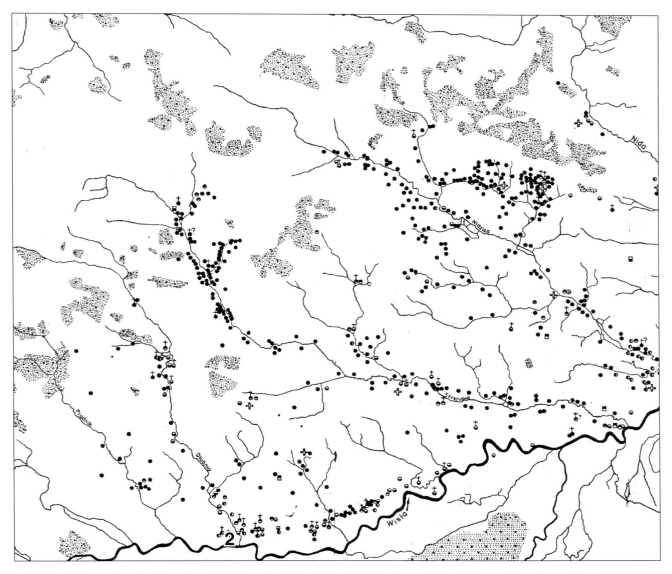

Fig. 8. Spatial distribution of settlements of the Lusatian culture on the Western Loess Upland in Małopolska; a–e – various kinds of settlement locations; 2 – Kraków-Nowa Huta, the 'Kopiec Wandy' site (after Rydzewski 1997).

were located almost exclusively on the wide river terraces (zone B). The higher landscape zones were very rarely occupied (Rydzewski 1986: 147-153).

Analyses of some better recognized settlement micro-regions allowed us to draw up a more detailed picture of the Mierzanowice culture settlement system (cf. Kadrow 1995: 28-55; Kadrow, Machnik, Machnik 1995). The settlement network of the Mierzanowice culture is distinctly agglomerated (fig. 9). Settlement locations are concentrated in some places

and create more or less stable micro-regions which are at a distance of more than 10 km from one another. Formally one can distinguish single finds, camp-sites, settlements, graves and cemeteries. Functionally we can determine them as places for the exploitation and processing of flint, short-lived subsidiary settlements connected with some forms of seasonal economic activities and long-term 'main' settlements, where the people of the Mierzanowice culture used to live permanently. At those places there are traces of dwellings and household devices in the form of various pits sunken into the ground (Kadrow 1991: 72-78). These settlements were accompanied by cemeteries (fig. 10), where their dead were buried. The sizes of the micro-regions and the duration of their evolutions depended on local environmental, economic, social, cultural and political factors. Some of them evolved during the whole Mierzanowice culture, i.e. about 700 years.

The long-term 'main' settlements, inhabited through many building phases, together with the associated cemeteries, were located on the exposed relief areas in the upper landscape zone (D) of the loess

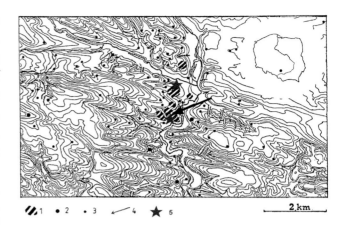

Fig. 10. The Iwanowice micro-region in the Early Bronze Age; 1 – stable settlements from the Mierzanowice culture, 2 – settlement traces from the Mierzanowice culture, 3 – single finds (mainly flint artefacts) probably connected with the Mierzanowice culture, 4 – Iwanowice, the 'Babia Góra I/II' site, 5 – the Early Bronze Age cemeteries.

uplands. These were at the edges of the large valleys (e.g. Iwanowice, Babia Góra I/II and Góra Klin), or small valleys (e.g. Szarbia, site 9 and Mierzanowice site I/IV). Smaller settlements inhabited only during one building phase (e.g. Iwanowice, Babia Góra III site) were located in the upper landscape zones as well. Other settlement locations lie both in the upper (D and E), and lower parts (zone B) of the loess uplands landscape.

There are a few spectacular deviations from the "rules" of site-location mentioned above (e.g. Pleszów site IV/20). All of these deviations concern the locations of the 'main' settlements or big cemeteries on the terraces (zone B) above the flood plains of the great Vistula valley. However, parts of the vast terraces had been in agricultural exploitation for so long in the Early Bronze Age that they had been ecologically transformed, so that – one can presume – they closely resembled those landscapes which were preferred by the populations of this time (i.e. the relatively open landscapes of the uplands). Probably for settlers the most important feature was the character of the vegetation rather than any formally understood topography.

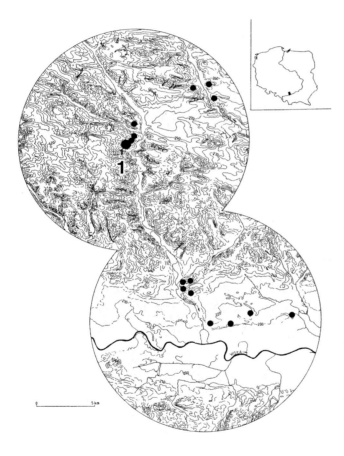

Fig. 9. Settlement network of the Mierzanowice culture on the areas 10 km around the 'Babia Góra' site at Iwanowice (1) and the 'Kopiec Wandy' site at Kraków-Nowa Huta; black circles – stable settlement locations from the Mierzanowice culture.

78

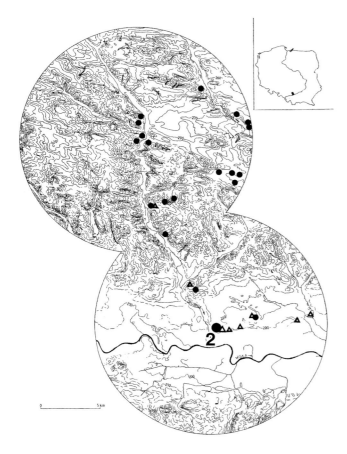

Fig. 11. Settlement networks from the Trzciniec and Lusatian cultures on the areas 10 km around the Kraków-Nowa Huta, the 'Kopiec Wandy' site (2) and Iwanowice, the 'Babia Góra' site; black circles – stable settlement locations of the Trzciniec culture, and triangles – stable settlement locations from the Lusatian culture from its early phase.

It seems, however, that on the loess areas described here the population of the Trzciniec culture continued the most essential features of the Mierzanowice culture settlement system (fig. 11). The most important in this case were the long-term, 'main' settlements, inhabited through many successive building phases. One of them is the Kraków-Kopiec Wandy site. Until now, the existence of such settlements was recorded only, in the whole range of the Trzciniec culture, on the loess uplands of the western part of Małopolska (Górski, Kadrow 1996: 16-20).

The second step of this project was to excavate some previously selected settlements and their micro-regions. One of them was the Neolithic settlement complex at Bronocice (Kruk & Milisauskas 1985; Milisauskas & Kruk 1984; 1989). Another was the Iwanowice micro-region, dated mainly to the Early Bronze Age (Machnikowie 1973; Machnikowie & Kaczanowski 1987).

Iwanowice, the 'Babia Góra' site

The whole Iwanowice micro-region, investigated during 1967-1981, consists of a few settlements, two cemeteries and many stray finds (fig. 10). The Babia Góra settlement complex (the settlement – cf. Kadrow 1991a; 1991b, and the cemetery – cf. Kadrow & Machnikowie 1992) is among the biggest and most extensively investigated of all the settlements in the area under discussion.

The village of Iwanowice is situated in the Iwanowice Basin unfolding itself at the place where the Dłubnia River and its largest tributary – the Minożka – join. The Dłubnia valley is flat-bottomed and the widest part of it is more than 500 m wide (fig. 10). The Iwanowice Basin is situated in a loess uplands environment. The fringes of the valley create hill slopes – (the core of this is Babia Góra) – with relative heights rising 40 m above the valley bottom in some places. The bottom of the valley has a height of 266 m at the south-eastern edge of the Babia Góra promontory.

Babia Góra is on a plateau situated on the western edge of the Dłubnia River valley at the village of Iwanowice (fig. 12). It is located some 20 km north of Cracow (50°12'45" N Lat. and 19°58'30" E Long.).

The area covered by Babia Góra I and II is about 520 m long and 230 m wide (fig. 12). Babia Góra III, separated from other parts of the site by a shallow depression occupies the south-eastern slope of the next promontory. The surface of Babia Góra is about 16 hectares – Babia Góra I and II covering approximately 8 hectares and Babia Góra III also covering approxi-

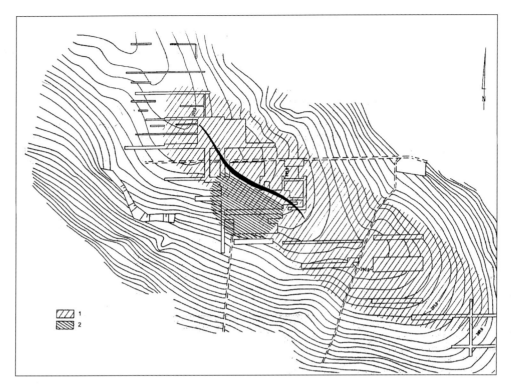

Fig. 12. Iwanowice, the 'Babia Góra I/II' site; 1 – settlement, 2 – cemetery.

mately 8 hectares. The traces of the Mierzanowice culture settlement are limited to 4.5 hectares (Babia Góra I – 1.5 hectares, Babia Góra II – 2 hectares, and Babia Góra III about 1 hectare).

There were 199 settlement features which were qualified as belonging to the Mierzanowice culture (fig. 13a). Nearly all the graves – among the 156 discovered in the local cemetery – are also connected with the Early Bronze Age. Within the framework of an interdisciplinary analytical project more than 11,000 of pottery fragments, 33,000 flint artefacts, a few thousand animal bones, 500 palaeobotanical samples, etc. were analysed.

A prolonged human occupation and subsequent economic use of the site have brought about an erosion of its surface. Because of this, and above all because of the nature of the prehistoric building activities, the so-called culture layer survives only in relic form. Conclusions concerning the spatial form of the settlement and its evolution therefore had to be sought through a multi-aspect analysis of settlement features deeply sunk into the ground.

Among the 199 Mierzanowice culture features there are: trapeze-shaped features (104, i.e. 52.26%), rectangular features (26, i.e. 13.06%), hemispherical features (67, i.e. 33.67%) and two ditches (fig. 14; cf. Kadrow 1991b: 19-38). Trapeze-shaped features (T-features) contained stratified fills with a cone-shaped deposit at the bottom. T-features showed a significant degree of similarity as to shape and size. Generally, the volume of the fill ranged from 2 to 3 cubic metres. There are no post-holes, nor any visible house structures or other building forms.

The onset of depositional processes in a T-feature can be linked to the discontinuation of the pit's original function as a multiple-use container, cellar, storage pit, etc. While in use, the pit was presumably covered by a kind of roofing or a lid. After its removal, the destruction of the pit set in. Within a relatively limited period of time a stratified, cone-shaped deposit formed at the pit bottom (fig. 15a) following the caving-in of the soil from around the pit edge. Later, wedge-shaped slides of natural loess from the upper parts of the pit occurred (fig. 15b). Thus, a layer of

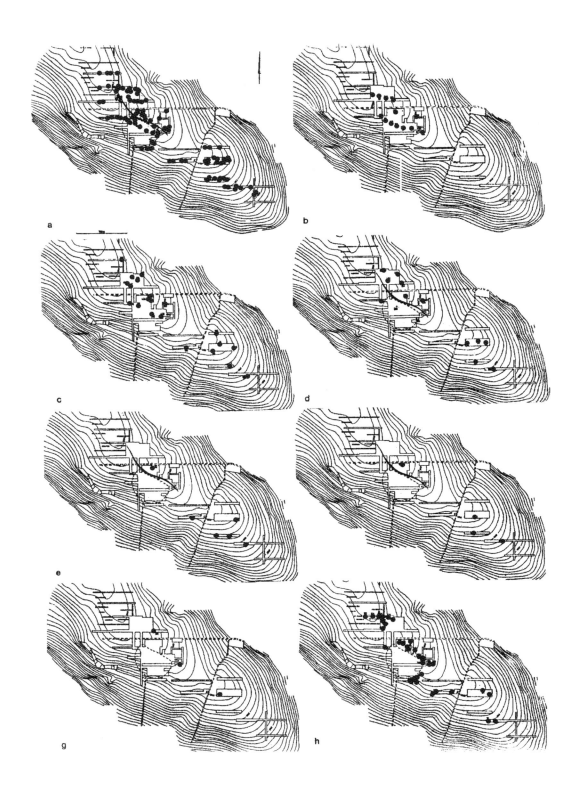

Fig. 13. Iwanowice, the 'Babia Góra I/II' site; a – all features belonging to the Mierzanowice culture, b – features dated to 1st building phase, c – features dated to 2nd building phase, d – features dated to 3rd building phase, e – features dated to 4th building phase, f – features dated to 5th building phase, g – features dated to 6th building phase, h – features dated to 7th building phase.

(usually) sterile loess formed, burying the cone-shaped deposit and effectively sealing it from contamination by surface material deposited at a later date. The wedge-shaped collapse of loess considerably widened the pit opening, causing a further filling in of the pit. The result was a large hollow in the upper part of the pit (fig. 15c). The first two stages of destruction of a T-feature occurred fairly rapidly. The final filling up of the hollow must have been much slower, possibly spanning several centuries. The mouth of the pit continued to widen as the earth accumulated in the hollow (fig. 15d). Under favourable conditions a certain type of stratified formation built up within the pit (cf. Boelicke et al. 1976; Boelicke et al. 1981).

The undisturbed processes of deposition described above resulted in the formation of a system of stratification recurring in all T-pits. At the same time they produced a specific accumulation of artefacts inside

	T-feature	R-feature	H-feature
Kopiec Wandy	43	12	45
Babia Góra	48	15	37

Fig. 14. Frequency of the main categories of features on the 'Babia Góra' site at Iwanowice and on the 'Kopiec Wandy' site at Kraków-Nowa Huta.

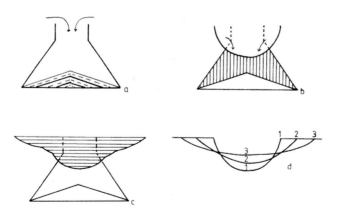

Fig. 15. Depositional processes in T-feature fills; a – formation of the cone-shaped deposit, b – collapse of soil from around the pit edge, c – formation of the hollow, d – filling of the hollow.

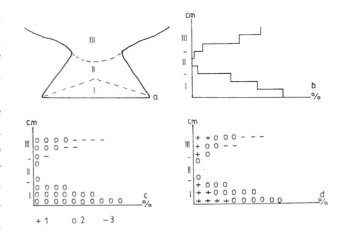

Fig. 16. Patterns of pottery deposition in fills of various kinds of features; a – stratified structure of T-feature, b – percentage distribution of pottery in T-feature with stratified fills in various layers, c – deposition of chronologically defined pottery in fills of T-feature with stratified fills which are sunk into the ground in previously unoccupied areas (1 – pottery older than time of functioning of the feature, 2 – pottery from the time of function of the feature, 3 – pottery later than the time of funtion of the feature), d – deposition of chronologically defined pottery in fills of T-features with stratified fills which are sunken into the ground in previously occupied areas.

the fill (fig. 16). Each feature was typically found to contain pottery fragments from 20 to 40 vessels. The percentage of entire vessels represented by sherds in these pits averaged 15-20%. The percentage of surviving sherds in other pits is significantly lower.

T-features are discussed at length here as they played a key role in the progress of the research programme. They alone contained compact artefact material in their cone-shaped deposits, 41 of them yielding numerous, representative and relatively homogenous pottery assemblages. A detailed description of pottery fragments using 126 traits (technological, morphological and decorative) helped to group pottery assemblages into 12 types, referred to as pottery sets. The sets are thought to reflect the diachronic and synchronic variability of ceramic material. What is more important, however, is that this classificatory

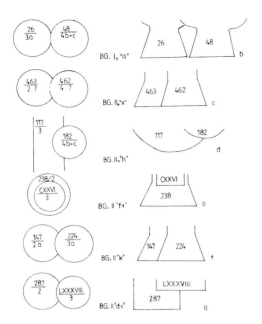

Fig. 17. Iwanowice, the 'Babia Góra' site; selected lay-outs of vertical stratigraphy between features of the Mierzano-wice culture.

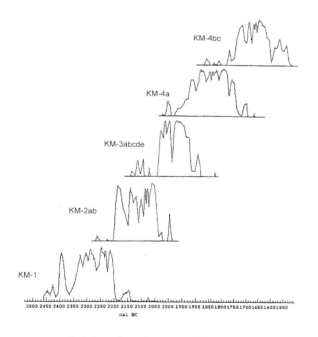

Fig. 18. Probability distributions of the summed up radiocarbon dates (in frames of stylistic pottery phases) of the Mierzanowice culture from the 'Babia Góra' site at Iwanowice (with the exception of 14C dates for pottery sets 4a, which are based on dates from Szarbia Zwierzyniecka; cf. Baczyńska 1994).

procedure establishes the temporal relationships between the identified pottery sets. Furthermore, their evident correlation with the four main stages of development of the Mierzanowice Culture identified by Jan Machnik (1984; 1989), justifies the categorisation of pottery sets into four basic groups: (1 – Protomierzanowice phase), (2a, 2b – early phase), (3a, 3b, 3c, 3d, 3e – classic phase) and (4a, 4b, 4b-c, 4d – late phase). For the purpose of further analysis of pottery fragments a chronological scheme specific to the Babia Góra site was constructed on the basis of the conclusions provided by the analyses of vertical and horizontal stratigraphy.

Vertical stratigraphic analyses conclusively document the early, classical and late stages in the chronological sequence of the Mierzanowice Culture at Babia Góra, Iwanowice, as represented by pottery groups 2, 3 and 4, respectively (fig. 17). What is characteristic of the stratigraphic situation is the complete absence of vertical stratigraphy between pottery groups ascribed to one stage in Machnik's classification, namely, between sets 3a and 3b, 2a and 2b, 4a and 4b, etc. This could indicate the lack of significant chronological differentiation of sets within these stages. Analyses of horizontal stratigraphy and radiocarbon dating helped to answer this question.

The point of departure for the horizontal stratigraphic analyses was to establish the existence of a specific spatial relationship between pottery sets of the same kind. T-features containing pottery assemblages from the same set never occurred close to one another (cf. Kuna 1991: 334-337). It became apparent that the minimum distance between two such pits was not less than 10 m. This observation led to the following hypothesis: only a single pit existed at a given time within a radius of 10 m. If true, then every other T-feature found within this area would have to be earlier or later. To complete the chronological sequence of pottery sets, radiocarbon dates were used (Table 1; Fig. 18), and certain premises following from the 'logic' of the evolution of pottery-making at Babia Góra. Ultimately, shortest time intervals were obtained, identifiable on the basis of pottery analysis (fig. 19). The 'shortest time interval' was understood

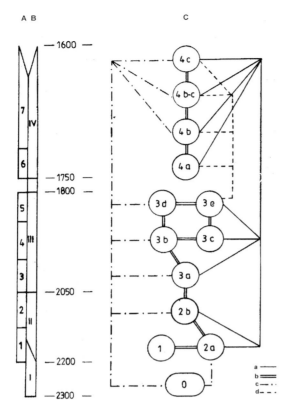

shape – with a longer axis of 130 m and a shorter one of 60 m (fig. 13b). In the second building phase (*c.* 2130-2050 cal BC) the features still form a closed but this time oval spatial pattern (Kadrow 1991b, 80-81): The settlement zone widens towards Babia Góra I and in a north-west direction. The whole occupied area forms an axial structure (350 x 60 m) oriented NW-SE with a surface of about 1.2 hectares (fig. 13c). There are traces of settlements from the same time on the Babia Góra III site. In the third building phase (c. 2050-1970 cal. BC) the area of occupation nearly equals that of the previous phase, but it is slightly smaller. The settlement retracted e.g. from the NW site outskirts. The central ditch appeared at the same time (fig. 13d). At this time Babia Góra II was divided into two functionally different parts: a settlement and a cemetery (Kadrow 1991a: 648). The boundaries of this division generally align with the above mentioned ditch. The hub of settlement move to Babia Góra I (fig. 13d). Regular forms of settlement were not duplicated there. In the fourth

Fig. 19. Iwanowice, the 'Babia Góra' site. Chronological systems for the Mierzanowice culture; A – building phases, B – phases of stylistic pottery evolution, C – sequence of pottery sets; a – relations between pottery sets based on vertical stratigraphy, b – on horizontal stratigraphy, c – on radiocarbon dates, d – on typological and stylistical considerations.

to correspond to a building phase defined as an objectively existing complex of contemporary features – in other words, the remains of a settlement from a certain time interval. Additionally the whole chronological system as described was positively tested using the methods of correspondence analysis (fig. 20; cf. Kadrow 1997a).

At the beginning of the permanent Mierzanowice culture settlement, (first building phase, *c.* 2200-2130 cal. BC) a spatial distribution of trapeze-shaped features (house clusters) shows a very regular pattern (Kadrow 1991a, 647-648). The features form a lens

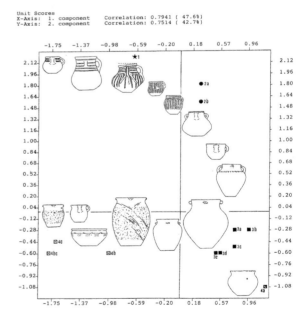

Fig. 20. Chronological arrangement of the Mierzanowice culture pottery sets from the 'Babia Góra' site at Iwanowice based on correspondence analysis (details in Kadrow 1997a).

building phase (*c.* 1970-1880 cal. BC) the tendency toward relative diminishment of the settlement size together with concentrating its hub at Babia Góra I (fig. 13e) became more pronounced (Kadrow 1991b: 82). In the fifth building phase *(c.* 1880-1800 cal. BC) this trend was continued (fig. 13f). Four evolutionary streams can be detected here: (1) gradual decrease of number of features (2) maintenance of an axial spatial structure, (3) non-occupation of the terrain south of the ditch at Babia Góra II, but at the same time maintenance of the hub of settlement at Babia Góra I, (4) an increase of minimal distances between trapeze-shaped features – to 30 m (fig. 19). Together with the end of this phase, the central ditch ceased to function (Kadrow 1991b: 83). In the sixth building phase (c. 1750-1700 cal. BC) the only significant change in hitherto existing tendencies was the return of settlement to Babia Góra II (fig. 13g). A different picture of spatial distribution of trapeze-shaped features is presented in the seventh building phase (*c.* 1700-1600 cal. BC). Features were agglomerated in a few places on the plateau of Babia Góra I and II and in the cemetery surroundings (fig. 13h). In this phase one house cluster was represented by partly contemporary trapeze-shaped features. The main characteristics of this time are as follows: (1) axial spatial distribution of agglomerated features, with an addition of two "arms" surrounding the cemetery, (2) minimal distances of about 50 m between agglomerated features, (3) minimal surfaces of 1000 m² for these agglomerated (4) a distinct increase in the number of features created by the agglomerations in comparison with the 4th, 5th and 6th building phases, (5) settlement and cemetery zones consequently excluded each other, (6) vertical stratigraphy proves that the ditch did not exist in this time. Its profile was considerably reduced, and its area was a place of intensive occupation (Kadrow 1991b: 84-86).

Changes can also be observed in the numbers of features of separate building phases. The increase in minimal distances between features is a linear function (fig. 21). This process can be interpreted in two ways: (1) as a gradual loosening up of house clusters;

	1	2	3	4	5	6	7	8
Kopiec Wandy	14	9	15	14	19	23	25	27
Babia Góra	6	9	12	16	18	41	21	

Fig. 21. Minimal distances between T-features with stratified fills in the sequence of building phases on the 'Babia Góra' site at Iwanowice and on the 'Kopiec Wandy' site at Kraków-Nowa Huta.

or (2) as a gradual enlarging of the area of house clusters. There is clear interdependence between the decreasing number of trapeze-shaped features and the increase in the minimal distances between them. Indirectly, there is an interdependence between a decreasing degree of regularity in terms of spatial distribution of these features and the above mentioned tendencies. In the early Mierzanowice culture phase (building phases 1-2) a relatively densely populated settlement (with many house clusters), placed within a small area, was covered by densely located dwellings (with very short distances between house clusters) in accordance with a precisely defined and regular plan (lense-shaped or oval). At the end of the classic phase (in the 5th building phase) a depopulated settlement (few house clusters), covering an extremely large area, was made up of scattered dwellings (with large distances between house clusters) in a more or less axial pattern. A different model is presented by the spatial distribution of houses in the 7th building phase. There was relatively dense grouping of large and numerous house clusters, covering a remarkable area of the settlement in an axial distribution (Kadrow 1991a: 647-649).

Some radiocarbon dates show the existence of settlement forms in the time directly preceding the first building phase (the so-called '0' phase). This period is dated to 2300-2200 cal. BC. The characteristic feature of the settlement in this period is the lack of any kind of pits. The archaeologically detectable traces of these settlement forms consisted of potsherds, which although not numerous, were technologically specific (parts of cups and jars with jutting out rims, ornamented with triple lines of cord imprints). A

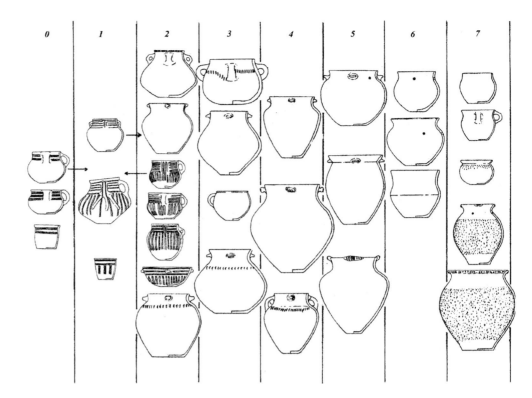

Fig. 22. A scheme of the Mierzanowice culture pottery evolution on the 'Babia Góra' site at Iwanowice against the background of the sequence of stylistic pottery phases (I-IV) and building phases (0-7).

lack of features, and a random spatial distribution of pottery fragments and other remains, including an imported piece of pottery of the Nyirseg culture, pointed to a different type of use of the site terrain at this time in comparison with the later functioning of the permanent settlement. This was probably an incursion by relatively limited groups of people, leaving few material traces. These people did not construct permanent dwellings and did not dig deep features closely connected with them. A transition from an incursion to stable settlement forms was tightly correlated with a transition from the proto-Mierzanowice phase (so-called Chłopice-Veselé) to the early Mierzanowice culture phase, also reflected in stylistic pottery changes (Kadrow 1991b: 85-86).

Because all the pottery sets from the 'Babia Góra' site at Iwanowice have already been completely described and published in Polish (Kadrow 1991b), and a selection of them also in German (Kadrow & Machnik 1993), in this article we would like to show only the general scheme of Mierzanowice culture pottery evolution (fig. 22).

Kraków-Nowa Huta, the 'Kopiec Wandy' site (Mogiła 55)

The site is situated on the edge of the left bank of the Vistula river terrace (50°04'13"N Lat., 20°04'15"E Long.) about 350 m east of the Dłubnia river and 2 km north of the Vistula (fig. 23). It was discovered already in 1910. In the following few years 16 pits were explored. In 1962 large rescue excavations (4.6 hectares) in advance of the construction of steelworks and a tramway line were led by Stanisław Buratyiski. During these investigations, which continued until 1966, numerous features were excavated which are dated from the Early Neolithic to the Middle Ages. There are more than 200 pits from the Trzciniec and Lusatian cultures among them.

It is impossible to estimate the whole surface of the investigated site. It is situated on the industrial area, which was heavily transformed in the 1950s and 60s. Probably its surface was larger than 8 hectares. However, the traces of the Trzciniec and Lusatian culture were limited to an area of a little more than 4 hectares.

One can assume that the greater part (up to 80%) of settlements belonging to the cultures in question was excavated. It must be stressed, however, that the rescue character of the excavations on this site resulted in exploration of some features in great haste. Therefore, unlike the 'Babia Góra' site at Iwanowice, in many cases there are imperfections in the records of field evidence.

About 210 features dug into the virgin soil belonged to the Trzciniec and Lusatian Cultures (fig. 24). Because of the poor state of documentation only half of these features could be described in detail (Górski 1993). Due to the shape of their profiles three groups of features were distinguished (fig. 14): trapeze-shaped (T-features – 49.5%), rectangular-shaped (R-features – 11.4%) and hollow-like (H-features – 29.5%). Additionally, several pits had combined shape, for example trapeze and rectangular (6.9%). Two pits had irregular profile, one feature was described as a ditch (1%). The filling found in features was either homogenous or multilayer. Pit dimensions (depth, bottom-diameter) were connected with the shape of profile and type of the filling.

Analysis of the co-occurrence of 27 attributes of ceramics from bottom parts of T-features or R-features served as a basis for differentiation of the investigated materials. Some of the attributes occurred with each other, and some occurred separately (Górski 1994: 74-79). On the basis of the detailed analysis of morphological, technological and ornamental variables the assemblages of pottery named Al, A2, A3, B, C, C-D and D have been distinguished (Górski 1994: 81-91; 1998; 1999). They signify successive stylistic phases of pottery evolution. They could be dated to the time between the transition from Periods I/II (or BrA2/BrB1) of the Bronze Age and to the beginning of Period IV (or HaA) of the Bronze Age. Assemblages of type A (fig. 25) represent classic materials of the Trzciniec culture linked to the end of Period I and the earlier part of Period II of the Bronze Age (or from the end of BrA2 to the end of BrB). They correspond to pottery known from barrow-cemeteries and phase Ia in the settlement at Jakuszowice (Górski 1991b: 71-72, 75). At that time Trans-Carpathian contacts are marked in the materials of the described culture for the first time.

The B-type assemblages (fig. 25) are dated to the end of Period II of the Bronze Age (or BrC). The most typical of them are vessels (usually amphorae) ornamented with vertical plastic motives. At the beginning of Period III of the Bronze Age (or BrD) ceramics decorated with vertical grooves (C-type assemblages) occurs and this is the last stage of stylistic development of the Trzciniec culture pottery (fig. 25). Assemblages of B and C types could be synchronized with phases Ib and II of the settlement at Jakuszowice (Górski 1991b: 72-74, 76).

About the middle of Period III of the Bronze Age (or the beginning of HaA) new settlements representing the early phase of the Lusatian culture were founded. New settlers came here most probably from Upper Silesia (Ged1 1982: 21-22; Rydzewski 1992: 181, fig. 3). Vessels of 'Silesian' type occur also in our site in the late Trzciniec culture context (assemblages of type C-D; fig. 25). There are also features with pure early Lusatian materials (assemblages of type D; fig. 25). This demonstrates the adaptation of attributes of the Lusatian culture by the Trzciniec culture population.

Dispersion of features with stylistically similar materials led to the observation of some spatially regular structures. They have been defined as building-phases

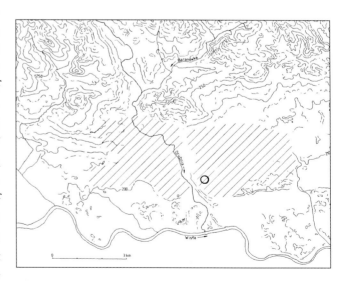

Fig. 23. Location of the 'Kopiec Wandy' (Wanda Barrow) site at Kraków Nowa Huta (Acc. to Bober 1993).

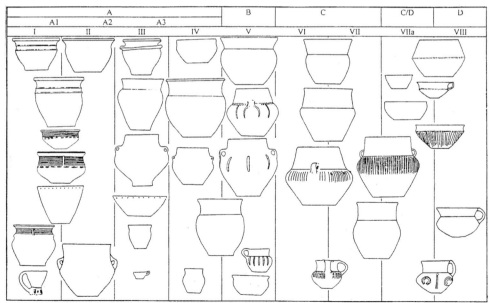

Fig. 24. The 'Kopiec Wandy' site at Kraków-Nowa Huta. Spatial distribution of all features belonging to the Trzciniec and Lusatian cultures.

Fig. 25. A scheme of the evolution of the pottery of the Trzciniec and Lusatian cultures (A-D) on the 'Kopiec Wandy' site at Kraków-Nowa Huta against the background of the sequence of building phases (I-VIII).

88

(cf. the chapter devoted to Iwanowice, the 'Babia Góra' site). The majority of these spatial structures have regular lentoid shape (fig. 26). Those structures consist of T- and R-features. In particular building-phases those pits are located at a similar distance from each other (fig. 21) and the area covered by them equals the areas of successive settlements (fig. 26). Pits containing chronologically similar pottery were not located close to each other. This was typical of the Trzciniec stage of the development of this site, which ends in the VIIth building-phase. Almost every pit from that phase is accompanied by a feature containing early Lusatian vessels (fig. 26g). In the next phase (fig. 13) there were no regular patterns of the feature distribution. Only two concentrations of pits along with several lesser groups or particular features can be distinguished. In phases I-VIIa each pit can be treated as the indirect relics of a household (cf. Kadrow 1991b: 73-75). It is possible to assume that an average of 10-15 households existed simultaneously. This conclusion is similar to results from the Mierzanowice culture settlement at Iwanowice (Kadrow 1991b: 87-90). It is important that each building-phase covered different part of the site (fig. 26a).

The VIIIth phase (fig. 26h) represents a 'stabilisation' in the settlement pattern. This is reflected in a different spatial distribution of features, which created particular clusters. In this phase there were only two households on the site but they existed for a relatively long time; the other households were abandoned earlier.

Through analysing ceramic assemblages in successive building-phases one can observe real evolution trends in pottery (Figs. 27-37). In general they follow stylistic changes which were common to the whole area of the Trzciniec culture settlement on the 'western' loess uplands (fig. 24).

Analysis of the Bronze Age materials from the 'Kopiec Wandy' site (Mogiła 55) at Krakow Nova Huta produced extensive information connected mainly with chronological differentiation of the Trzciniec culture pottery (fig. 25). A huge area uncovered during excavations enabled us to use horizontal planigraphy in the investigation of settlement patterns. This led to the discovery of regular settlement structures, and consequently to a reasoned view of the size and shape of the settlement (fig. 26). The appearance of the Lusatian culture in the neighbourhood of Cracow influenced the Trzciniec settlement, and this can be seen not only in new attributes in pottery, but also in changes relating to how the settlement space was arranged.

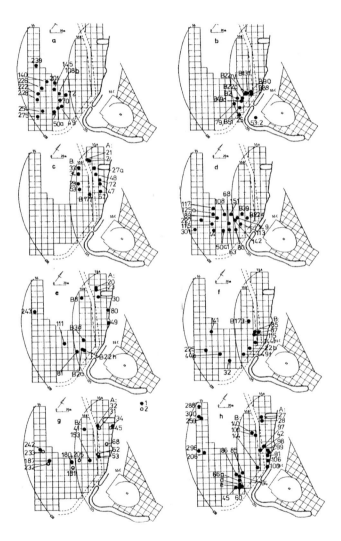

Fig. 26. The 'Kopiec Wandy' site at Kraków-Nowa Huta. Spatial distribution of features dated to: a – 1st building phase, b – 2nd building phase, c – 3rd building phase, d – 4th building phase, e – 5th building phase, f – 6th building phase, g – 7th(1) and 7ha(2) building phases, h – 8th building phase.

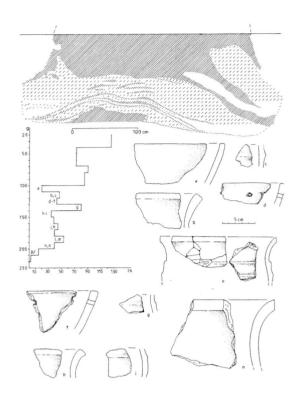

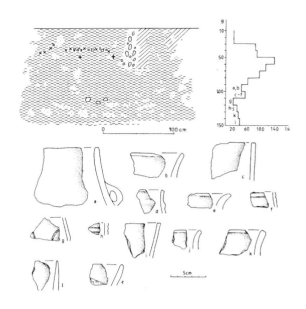

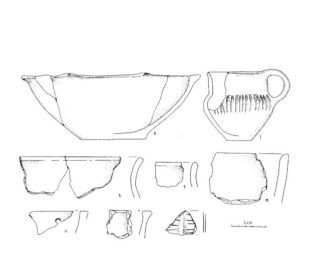

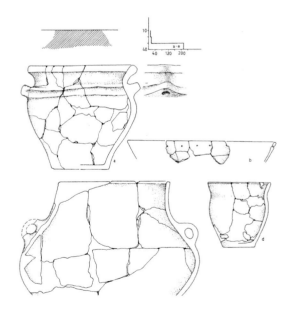

Fig. 29. The 'Kopiec Wandy' site at Kraków-Nowa Huta. Feature No 25 representing pottery sets from building phase II (drawn by A. Piwowarczyk).

Fig. 27. The 'Kopiec Wandy' site at Kraków-Nowa Huta. Feature No 228 representing pottery sets from building phase I (drawn by A. Piwowarczyk).

Fig. 28. The 'Kopiec Wandy' site at Kraków-Nowa Huta. Feature No 228 representing pottery sets from building phase I (drawn by A. Piwowarczyk).

Fig. 30. The 'Kopiec Wandy' site at Kraków-Nowa Huta. Feature No B34 representing pottery sets from building phase III (drawn by A. Piwowarczyk).

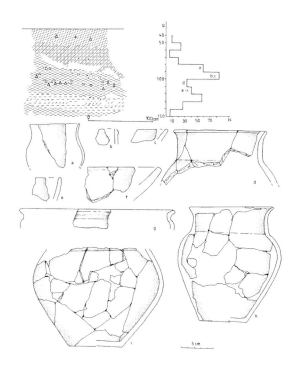

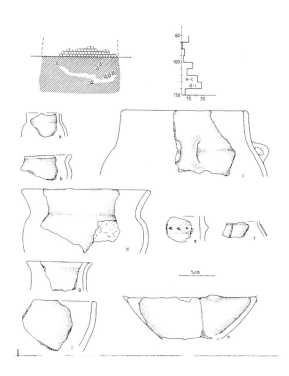

Fig. 31. The 'Kopiec Wandy' site at Kraków-Nowa Huta. Feature No 68 representing pottery sets from building phase IV (drawn by A. Piwowarczyk).

Fig. 33. The 'Kopiec Wandy' site at Kraków-Nowa Huta. Feature No B38 representing pottery sets from building phase V (drawn by A. Piwowarczyk).

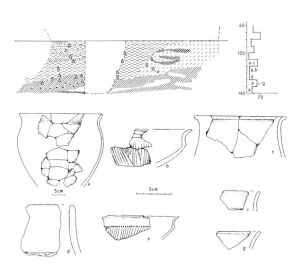

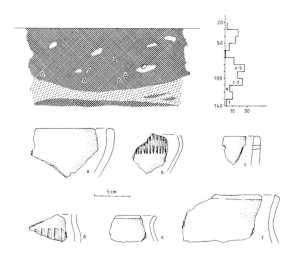

Fig. 32. The 'Kopiec Wandy' site at Kraków-Nowa Huta. Feature No 111 representing pottery sets from building phase V (drawn by A. Piwowarczyk).

Fig. 34. The 'Kopiec Wandy' site at Kraków-Nowa Huta. Feature No 141 representing pottery sets from building phase VI (drawn by A. Piwowarczyk).

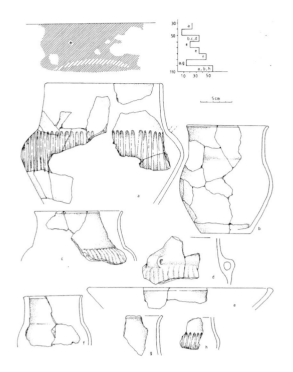

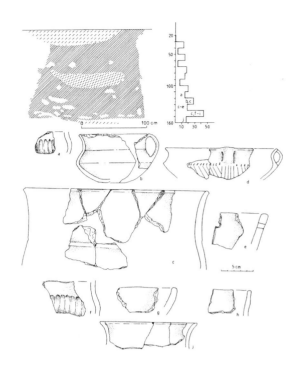

Fig. 35. The 'Kopiec Wandy' site at Kraków-Nowa Huta. Feature No 385 representing pottery sets from building phase VII (drawn by A. Piwowarczyk).

Fig. 37. The 'Kopiec Wandy' site at Kraków-Nowa Huta. Feature No 85 representing pottery sets from building phase VIII (drawn by A. Piwowarczyk).

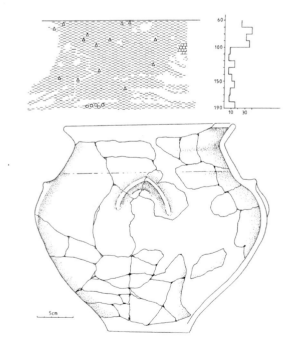

Fig. 36. The 'Kopiec Wandy' site at Kraków-Nowa Huta. Feature No A52 representing pottery sets from building phase VIIa (drawn by A. Piwowarczyk).

Synchronization of chronological sequences at Iwanowice, the 'Babia Góra' site and at Kraków-Nowa Huta, the 'Kopiec Wandy' site

According to Jan Machnik the sequences of the Mierzanowice culture and of the Strzyżów culture were parallel with phases I-IV of the Unetice culture, i.e. synchronous with phase A1 of the Bronze Age after Reinecke (Machnik 1967: 194). In the following stage of the Early Bronze Age, i.e. in phase A2 after Reinecke, the earlier stage of the Trzciniec culture – contemporaneous to the classic phase of the Unetice culture – was attested in the territory of Małopolska. Within the frames of absolute chronology the end of the Mierzanowice culture and the beginning of the Trzciniec culture was placed around 1600 conv. bc (Machnik 1967: 237), i.e. around 1900 cal. BC. A similar chronological position has been attributed by

Czech and Slovak archaeologists to the other components of the so-called Epi-Corded Circum-Carpathian Cultural Circle, i.e. to the Nitra and Kotśany groups (e.g. Točik 1963; Bátora 1989). Discoveries at Szarbia Zwierzyniecka (Baczyńska 1985) resulted in a certain "rejuvenation" of the Mierzanowice culture, following the clarification of the late phase of the culture in question, called the Szarbia Phase (Machnik 1984). In the monograph on the Szarbia cemetery site an extension of the duration of the Mierzanowice culture for a period of at least 100 years has been postulated (Baczyńska 1994: 50). The long series of radiocarbon dates from the Babia Góra Site at Iwanowice (Kadrow 1991a; 1991b: 57-61) allows us to move the end of the culture in question (in the form of the Giebułtów group) to an even later time-frame – 1400/1350 conv. bc, i.e. 1650/1600 cal. BC.

In the light of the "metal chronology", during the long and important period corresponding generally with classic and late phases of the Únětice culture, Małopolska appears practically uninhabited. In this situation we had to leave the "beaten track" of typological- stylistic analyses of metal artefacts and turn our hopes to the increase in the number of radiocarbon dates and to local sequences of pottery evolution as recorded at Iwanowice and Kraków-Nowa Huta. In the territory in question there are even seven sepulchral objects with such dates – one grave from Miernów (Kempisty 1978) and six graves from Żerniki Górne (Kempisty & Włodarczyk 1996). On the basis of these the beginning of the Trzciniec culture in Little Poland can be set to c. 1800 BC (Table 2), that is contemporary with the beginning of the late phase of the Mierzanowice culture (Kadrow, Machnik 1997). Thus, during a period of at least 200 years, i.e. between 1800 and 1600 BC, we should take into account the coexistence of these two cultures in Małopolska.

There is a complete lack of radiocarbon dates from the 'Kopiec Wandy' site at Kraków-Nowa Huta and, at the same time, a lack of common stylistic elements in pottery assemblages from that site and from the 'Babia Góra' site at Iwanowice. However, the A1 type of the Trzciniec culture pottery, recorded in the early

graves at Miernów and Żerniki Górne suggests that they were contemporary to the 7th building phase at Iwanowice and to the 1st building phase at Kraków-Nowa Huta. Another possibility for estimating the absolute chronology of the sequence of building phases at Kraków-Nowa Huta arises from the knowledge that the pottery sets from the 5th building phase were contemporary to period Br C after Reinecke. Thanks to dendrochronological analyses in Denmark one can date this period to c. 1400-1350 BC (Randsborg 1992, 105). There were some bronze pins inside the features dated to the 8th building phase. They belong to the type of *Nadel mit verdicktem Kolbenkopf* variant *Pleszów* and *Trzebnik*. This type of pin is dated to the beginning of the HaA1 period, and so to the 12th century BC. The average duration of one building phase at Iwanowice equals 60-70 years, and we assume the same value for one such phase on the 'Kopiec Wandy' site. The sequence of all building phases could last 500, or more probably 600 years. This calculation fits very well with the assumption that the 1st building phase should be dated to the 17th century BC, the 5th building phase to the 1st half of the 14th century, and the last phase to the 1st[t] half of the 12th century BC. Accepting these proposals we could synchronize sequences of building phases on the two sites (fig. 38).

The problem of culture change on the Western Loess Uplands in Małopolska

In the period between 1800-1700 cal. BC the non-loess areas of western Małopolska and adjacent areas to the west became a target for the first groups of people of the Trzciniec culture coming from the north. Most probably these people carried with them the pottery of type A1 assemblages. They went to the areas that were not of interest to the people of the Mierzanowice culture. During this time in the upper landscape zones of the Western Loess Uplands the network of stabilized micro-regions of the Mierzano-

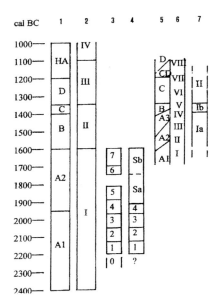

Fig. 38. Synchronization of sequencies of building phases at Iwanowice, the 'Babia Góra' site and at Kraków-Nowa Huta, the 'Kopiec Wandy' site; 1 – Reinecke's chronological system, 2 – Montelius/Kostrzewski chronological system, 3 – sequence of building phases at Iwanowice, the 'Babia Góra' site, 4 – reconstructed chronology at Mierzanowice, site I/IV, 5 – sequence of the Trzciniec pottery assemblages on the Western Loess Uplands in Małopolska, 6 – building phases at Kraków-Nowa Huta, the 'Kopiec Wandy' site, 7 – chronology of the Trzciniec culture settlement at Jakuszowice.

wice culture prevailed. Between these meso-regions, in the Nida valley and to the East of it, the settlements of the Trzciniec culture (Miernów, Żerniki Górne) became a major factor. Due to positively different economic models the people of the cultures in question exploited environmentally different areas and remained practically isolated one from another.

At the end of the period in question (i.e. c. 1800-1700 BC) the area where Kraków-Nowa Huta now is could have been a place where the communities of both cultures came into contact. It is possible that the first substantial acculturation of the local people of the Mierzanowice culture with newcomers of the Trzciniec culture took place then. It seems that such an acculturation process applied to the communities of the classic

phase of the Mierzanowice culture on the Dłubnia river, that lasted there till around 1800-1750 BC (Kadrow 1991b: 50-61). There is evidence of the adoption by the people of the Trzciniec culture of some technological elements of the late classic Mierzanowice culture, and – even more importantly – of the model of big settlement sites typical for that stage of the latter culture. Around 1700-1650 BC there already existed on the loess areas near Kraków a stable network of large settlement sites of both Mierzanowice and Trzciniec cultures (fig. 39), mutually respecting each other's rights. Close to the end of the coexistence of both communities (i.e. c. 1650-1600 BC) the Trzciniec elements prevailed decidedly east of the Dłubnia valley (fig. 39). The Mierzanowice culture settlement network in the form of the Giebułtów group survived for a while on the areas west of this river, also extending into southern Kraków-Częstochowa and the foreland of the Moravia Gates.

The story of the occupation of the loess zone of western Małopolska by the people of the Trzciniec culture illustrates perfectly one of the models of cultural changes proposed by David Clarke (1968; cf. also Kadrow 1995; fig. 39). During the initial stage (1900/1800-1700 BC) the first groups of the Trzciniec cultures moved into areas around the domains of the Mierzanowice culture people. The latter concentrated in settlement micro-regions populated by local groups. Local ties seem to be more important for them than kinship. The Mierzanowice culture groups prevailed on the loess areas. Non-loess areas were the domain of the Trzciniec culture group. As they lacked permanent dwelling sites because of their mobility, kinship ties formed the main basis of their organisational structure.

The second stage of the coexistence began more or less between 1800 and 1700 BC. During this time the peoples of the Mierzanowice and Trzciniec cultures came into contact with each other – probably accidentally – in the area of present day Kraków-Nowa Huta. It is not of significance for us whether this contact resulted from common or conflicting interests of the two communities. What is important is that the Trzciniec culture people were transformed as a result of this event. Adopting some social and organisational ideas from the Mierzanowice culture they began to form local communities, stabilizing their settlement network. Large, long lasting settlement sites – so typical of the Trzciniec culture in western Małopolska – originated in this period. In consequence, the influence of the Trzciniec culture communities augmented considerably, resulting in an increasing transformation of the Mierzanowice culture communities towards the "Trzciniec-like" cultural pattern. Around 1700 BC the first micro-regional units of the Trzciniec culture began competition with corresponding units (i.e. with local groups) of the Mierzanowice culture (fig. 39).

The last stage of coexistence of the Mierzanowice and Trzciniec cultures on the loess areas of western Little Poland began in the 17th century BC. The acculturation process encompassed all the micro-regions of the Mierzanowice culture in the loess area to the West of the Dłubnia river. Local communities of that culture west of the river (the Giebułtów group) resisted this process, probably because of their links with the Věteřov culture (Kadrow & Machnik 1997). In the years 1650-1600 BC the Trzciniec culture micro-regional structure was already dominant in western Little Poland (fig. 39). The Mierzanowice culture in the form of the Giebułtów group found asylum in the area west of the Dłubnia river.

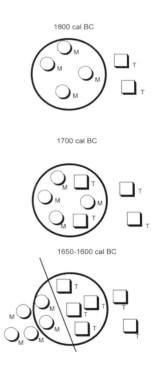

Fig. 39. Models of culture change on the Western Loess Uplands in Małopolska in BA2; rings with letter 'm' – settlement microregions of the Mierzanowice culture, squares with letter 't' – micro-regions (larger squares) and traces of transient penetrations (smaller squares) of the Trzciniec culture, large ring – Western Loess Uplands in Małopolska.

Bibliography

Baczyńska B. 1985: Fundstelle der jüngeren Phase der Mierzanowice-Kultur in Szarbia, Gemeinde Skalbmierz. In: *L'eneolithique et le debut de l'age du bronze dans certains regions de l'Europe.* Kraków, 123-132.

Baczyńska B. 1994: *Cmentarzysko kultury mierzanowickiej w Szarbi, woj. kieleckie. Studium obrządku pogrzebowego.* Kraków (English Summary).

Bátora J. 1989: Anfänge der Bronzezeit in der Südwestslowakei, *Das Äneolithikum und die früheste Bronzezeit (C14 3000-2000 b.c.) in Mitteleuropa: Kulturelle und chronologische Beziehungen. Acta des XIV Internationalen Symposiums Prag-Liblice, 20-24.10.1986 (Praehistorica* 15). Praha, 207-212.

Bober J. 1993: Osada kultury ceramiki promienistej w Krakowie-Nowej Hucie-Mogile w rejonie Kopca Wandy. Część I – materiały. *Materiały Archeologiczne Nowej Huty* 16, 7-53 (English summary).

Boelicke U. & R. Kuper, H. Löhr, J. Lüning, W. Schwellnus, P. Stehli, A. Zimmermann 1976: Untersuchungen zur neolitischen Besiedlung der Aldenhovener Platte. *Bonner Jahrbücher* 176, 299-317.

Boelicke U. & D. Von Brandt, R. Drew, J. Eckert, J. Gaffrey, A.J. Kalis, J. Lüning, J. Schalich, W. Schwellnus, P. Stehli, J. Weiner, M. Wolters, A. Zimmermann 1981: Untersuchungen zur neolithischen Besiedlung der Aldenhovener Platte. *Bonner Jahrbücher* 181, 251-285.

Blajer W. 1990: *Skarby z wczesnej epoki brązu na ziemiach polskich.* (= *Prace Komisji Archeologicznej PAN O/Kraków* 28). Kraków (German summary).

Blajer W. 1999: *Skarby ze starszej i środkowej epoki brązu na ziemiach polskich..* (= *Prace Komisji Archeologicznej PAN O/Kraków* 30). Kraków (German summary).

Clarke D.L. 1968: *Analytical Archaeology.* London.

Gedl M. 1982: Periodyzacja i chronologia kultury łużyckiej w zachodniej Małopolsce. In: M. Gedl (ed.), *Południowa strefa kultury łużyckiej i powiązania tej kultury z południem*. Kraków – Przemyśl, 11-33 (German summary).

Górski J. 1991: *Osada kultury trzcinieckiej w Jakuszowicach, cz. I. (Badania w Jakuszowicach 1)*. Kraków (German summary).

Górski J. 1993: Osada kultury trzcinieckiej i łużyckiej w Nowej Hucie-Mogile, stan. 55. Analiza materiałów. Część I. *Materiały Archeologiczne Nowej Huty* 16, 55-102 (English summary).

Górski J. 1994: Osada kultury trzcinieckiej i łużyckiej w Nowej Hucie-Mogile, stan. 55. Analiza materiałów. Część II. *Materiały Archeologiczne Nowej Huty* 17, 65-113 (English summary).

Górski J. 1997: Kultura trzciniecka. In: K. Tunia (ed.) *Z archeologii Małopolski. Historia i stan badań zachodniomałopolskiej wyżyny lessowej*. Kraków, 219-245 (English summary).

Górski J. 1998: The Foundations of Trzciniec Culture taxonomy in Western Małopolska. *Baltic-Pontic Studies* 6, 7-18.

Górski J. 1999: Die Beziehungen zwischen dem westlichen Kleinpolen und dem Gebiet der Slowakei in der klassischen Phase der Trzciniec-Kultur (ausgewählte Aspekte). In: J. Bátora & J. Peska (eds.) *Aktuelle Probleme der Erforschung der Frühbronzezeit in Böhmen und Mähren und in der Slowakei*, Nitra, 251-265.

Górski J. & S. Kadrow 1996: Kultura mierzanowicka i kultura trzciniecka w zachodniej Małopolsce. Problem zmiany kulturowej. *Sprawozdania Archeologiczne* 48, 9-32 (English summary).

Kadrow S. 1991a: Iwanowice, Babia Góra site: spatial evolution of an Early Bronze Age Mierzanowice Culture settlement (2300-1600 BC). *Antiquity* 65, 640-650.

Kadrow S. 1991b: *Iwanowice, stanowisko Babia Góra, cz. I. Rozwój przestrzenny osady z wczesnego okresu epoki brązu*. Kraków (English summary).

Kadrow S. 1995: *Gospodarka i społeczeństwo. Wczesny okres epoki brązu w Małopolsce*. Kraków (English summary).

Kadrow S. 1997a: Korrespondenzanalyse und neue Aspekte der Chronologie der frühbronzezeitlichen Siedlung in Iwanowice bei Krakau (Polen). In: J. Müller, A. Zimmermann (eds.) *Archäologie und Korrespondenzanalyse; Beispiele, Fragen, Perspektiven. (= Internationale Archäologie* 23). Espelkamp, 137-146.

Kadrow S. 1997b: Kultura mierzanowicka i kultura pucharów dzwonowatych. In: K. Tunia (ed.) *Z archeologii Małopolski. Historia i stan badań zachodniomałopolskiej wyżyny lessowej*. Kraków, 185-208 (English summary).

Kadrow S. 2000: Wczesnobrązowa wytwórczość metalurgiczna w stylu wierzbowego liścia. In: J. Rydzewski (ed.) *150 lat Muzeum Archeologicznego w Krakowie*. Kraków, 141-153 (German summary).

Kadrow S., Machnik & J. Machnik 1995: Early Bronze Age settlement on 'Babia Góra' site at Iwanowice against the background of the contemporary settlement network in an upper Vistula River basin (SE Poland). *Memoires Museo Civico Storia Naturale Verona, Sez. Scienze Uomo* 4, 203-220.

Kadrow S. & J. Machnik 1993: Zur Chronologie der Frühbronzezeit: Iwanowice bei Krakau, Fundplatz "Babia Góra". *Praehistorische Zeitschrift* 68.2, 201-241.

Kadrow S. & J. Machnik 1997: *Kultura mierzanowicka. Chronologia, taksonomia i rozwój przestrzenny*. Kraków (English summary).

Kadrow S., A. & J. Machnikowie 1992: *Iwanowice, stanowisko Babia Góra, część II. Cmentarzysko z wczesnego okresu epoki brązu*. Kraków (English summary).

Kadrow S. & D. Makowicz-Poliszot 2000: Tiergräber der Mierzanowice Kultur auf der Fundstelle "Babia Góra" in Iwanowice, Gm. *loco*, Wojewodschaft Małopolska. In: S. Kadrow (ed.) *A Turning of Ages. Jubilee Book Dedicated to Professor Jan Machnik on His 70th Anniversary*. Kraków, 257-300.

Kempisty A. 1978: *Schyłek neolitu i początek epoki brązu na Wyżynie Małopolskiej w świetle badań nad kopcami*. Warszawa.

Kempisty A. & P. Włodarczak 1996: Chronologia absolutna cmentarzyska w Żernikach Górnych. In: *Concordia. Studia ofiarowane Jerzemu Okuliczowi-Kozarynowi w sześćdziesiątą piątą rocznicę urodzin*, Warszawa, 127-140.

Kruk J. 1973: *Studia osadnicze nad neolitem wyżyn lessowych*. Wrocław (English summary).

Kruk J. 1980: Remarks on Studies Concerning the Geography of Settlement of Prehistoric Communities. In: R. Schild (ed.) *Unconventional Archaeology*. Wrocław, 17-32.

Kruk J. 1997: Zarys fizjografii. In: K. Tunia (ed.) *Z archeologii Małopolski. Historia i stan badań Zachodniomałopolskiej Wyżyny Lessowej*. Kraków, 11-46 (English summary).

Kruk J. & S. Milisauskas 1985 *Bronocice. Osiedle obronne ludności kultury lubelsko-wołyńskiej (2800-2700 lat p.n.e.)*. Wrocław (English summary).

Kruk J. & L. Przywara 1983: Roślinność potencjalna jako metoda rekonstrukcji naturalnych warunków rozwoju społeczności pradziejowych. *Archeologia Polska* 28, 19-50 (English summary).

Kuna M. 1991: The structuring of prehistoric landscape. *Antiquity* 65(247), 332-347.

Machnik J. 1967: *Stosunki kulturowe na przełomie neolitu i epoki brązu w Małopolsce (na tle przemian w Europie Środkowej)* (= *Materiały do prahistorii ziem polskich, cz. III, z. 1*). Warszawa

Machnik J. 1984: Frühbronzezeitliche Kulturen in Kleinpolen. In: N. Tasić (ed.) *Die Kulturen der Frühbronzezeit des Karpatenbeckens und des Nordbalkans.* Beograd, 341-376.

Machnik J. 1989: Neue Angaben für die Periodisierung der Frühbronzezeit in Kleinpolen. *Das Äneolithikum und die früheste Bronzezeit (C14 3000-2000 b.c.) in Mitteleuropa: Kulturelle und chronologische Beziehungen. Acta des XIV Internationalen Symposiums Prag-Liblice, 20-24.10.1986 (Praehistorica 15).* Praha, 275-279.

Machnikowie A. & J. 1973: Wczesnobrązowy zespół osadniczy na "Babiej Górze" w Iwanowicach, pow. Miechów, w świetle dotychczasowych badań wykopaliskowych. In: J. Machnik (ed.) *Z badań nad neolitem i wczesną epoką brązu w Małopolsce. (Prace Komisji Archeologicznej PAN O/Kraków 4).* Kraków, 141-158.

Machnikowie A., J. & K. Kaczanowski 1987: *Osada i cmentarzysko z wczesnego okresu epoki brązu na 'Górze Klin' w Iwanowicach.* Wrocław (German summary).

Milisauskas S. & J. Kruk 1984: Settlement organization and the appearance of low level hierarchical societies during the Neolithic in the Bronocice microregion, Southeastern Poland. *Germania,* 62, 1-30.

Milisauskas S. & J. Kruk 1989: Economy, migration, settlement organization, and warfare during the late Neolithic in Southeatern Poland. *Germania* 67, 77-96.

Randsborg K. 1992: Historical Implications. Chronological Studies in European Archaeology c. 1200-500 B.C.. *Acta Archaeologica.* 62, 89-108.

Rydzewski J. 1986: Przemiany stref zasiedlenia na wyżynach lessowych zachodniej Małopolski w epoce brązu i żelaza. *Archeologia Polski* 31, 125-194 (English summary).

Rydzewski J. 1997: Kultura łużycka. In: K. Tunia (ed.), *Z archeologii Małopolski. Historia i stan badań zachodniomałopolskiej wyżyny lessowej.* Kraków, 249-286 (English summary).

Tauber H. 1973: Copenhagen radiocarbon dates X, *Radiocarbon* 15, 86-112.

Točík A. 1963: Die Nitra-Gruppe. *Archeologicky rozhledy* 15, 716-774.

Włodarczak P. 1998: Groby kultury mierzanowickiej oraz kultury trzcinieckiej z Żernik Górnych. In: A. Kośko & J. Czebreszuk (eds.) *Trzciniec. System kulturowy czy interkulturowy proces?,* Poznań, 161-177 (English summary).

Kulturmobilität im Gebiet der Slowakei von der Mittleren bis zur Spätbronzezeit

Václav Furmánek

Die Besiedlung der Slowakei war in der jüngeren Urzeit in hohem Maße von den bestehenden Naturbedingungen beeinflußt. Am bedeutendsten von ihnen waren die geologischen Verhältnisse, das Geländerelief, die Hydrographie, pedologische Bedingungen und klimatische Gegebenheiten.

Das Gebiet der Slowakei befindet sich zwischen $47^0 50'$ – $49^0 05'$ nördlicher Breite und $16^0 50'$ – $22^0 30'$ östlicher Länge. Es gehört zum alpinen Gebirgssystem, für das hohe Gebirge und tiefe Becken kennzeichnend sind. Dominierend ist hier der Karpatenbogen, von welchem der Nordwestteil – die Westkarpaten – das Landschaftsgepräge bestimmt. Gekennzeichnet ist dieses durch ein gegliedertes Relief, verhältnismäßig große Unterschiede in der Überseehöhe und einem hohen Anteil von Hochländern. Nur im Südwesten und Südosten besteht mit größeren Niederungen eine nach Süden offene Landschaft.

Die Besiedlung der Slowakei konzentrierte sich in der Bronzezeit vor allem auf die Niederungen bis zu einer obere Grenze von rund 300 m über NN. Es waren dies drei Niederungen: die donauländische, die südslowakische und die ostslowakische. In ihnen wurden die urzeitlichen Sitze vor allem auf mäßig erhöhten Fluß- und Bachterrassen und Lößdünen errichtet. Erst in den jüngeren Abschnitten der Bronzezeit drang die Besiedlung in die Gebirgsbecken vor. Auch hier wurden Terrassen in der Nähe von Wasserläufen und auf sanften, günstig orientierten Hängen besiedelt. Später verschob sich die Besiedlung auch

auf Spornlagen und Gipfel von strategisch günstig gelegenen Bergen bis in die Überseehöhe von rund 1000 m.

Die hydrologischen Verhältnisse der Slowakei sind durch die Flußläufe der Hauptflüsse gegeben. Von Bedeutung waren sie nicht nur für die Wirtschaft, sondern auch für die Kommunikation. Beinahe das ganze Gebiet der Slowakei gehört zum DonauzuflußSystem und durch Vermittlung dieses Stromes inkliniert es nach Süden, zur Balkanhalbinsel und zum Einzugsgebiet des Schwarzen Meeres. Nur ein kleines Gebiet im Nordostteil des Landes gehört zum Zufluß des Poprad und des Dunajec und inkliniert nach Norden zum Ostseeraum. Das Gebiet des Donauzuflusses gliedert sich in zwei Teile. Es ist dies der westliche Teil, dessen Flüsse durch Vermittlung der March, Waag, Gran und Eipel direkt in die Donau münden, und der östliche Teil, der zum Einzugsgebiet der Theiß gehört. Diese Unterschiede beeinflußten und determinierten während der ganzen Bronzezeit die Kulturorientierung der urzeitlichen Besiedlung im Nordteil des Karpatenbeckens.

Die Flußtäler stellten die Hauptkommunikationsadern der urzeitlichen Slowakei dar. Entlang ihrer Läufe drang die Bevölkerung der einzelnen bronzezeitlichen archäologischen Kulturen tiefer in die gebirgigen Landschaftsteile vor. Blickt man auf die hydrologische Karte der Slowakei, ist zu sehen, daß der Großteil der slowakischen Flüsse von Norden nach Süden fließt. Das bedeutet, daß die natürliche

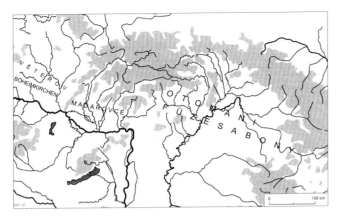

Abb. 1. Verbreitung der Kulturkomplexe Maďarovce-Věteřov-Böheimkirchen und Otomani-Füzesabony.

vorherrschende Bevölkerungsbewegung die von Süden nach Norden war. Die West-Ost-, bzw. Ost-Westtrasse war wesentlich weniger frequentiert (Furmánek & al. 1999, 155-156, Abb. 70).

Diese Bewegungen, Interaktionen, die Mobilität der urzeitlichen Gemeinschaften und die sich ändernde Besiedlungsdynamik werde ich versuchen, in den Hauptbesiedlungsregionen und in den verschiedenen Horizonten der Bronzezeit in der Slowakei zu dokumentieren: zu Beginn der mittleren Bronzezeit (Br B1), im Verlauf der mittleren Bronzezeit (Br B2-Br C), in

der jüngeren Bronzezeit (Br D-Ha A), in der Spätbronzezeit (HaB) und schließlich ganz im Endabschnitt der Spätbronzezeit (Ha B3).

Im Verlauf der älteren Bronzezeit gestaltete sich in der Slowakei eine kulturelle Bipartität, die in gewissen Aspekten interessanterweise sogar bis heute anhält. Die Südwestslowakei war von Trägern der Maďarovce-Kultur besiedelt, die Bestandteil des großen mitteleuropäischen Kulturkomplexes Věteřov-Maďarovce-Böheimkirchen war (Furmánek & al. 1999, 47), Er stand den zeitgleichen Kulturen im westlichen Teil Mitteleuropas nahe. In der Ostslowakei existierte damals die Otomani-Kultur. Sie bildete einen Bestandteil des Kulturkomplexes Otomani-Füzesabony (Ibid. 52), der in seinem Südostteil verhältnismäßig enge Kontakte zur Wietenberg-Kultur hatte (Boroffka 1994). Es muß betont werden, daß beide angeführten Kulturkomplexe (Věteřov-Maďarovce-Böheimkirchen und Otomani-Füzesabony) nicht unmittelbar benachbart waren (Abb. 1). Das bedeutet allerdings gar nicht, daß zwischen ihnen keine Kontakte bestanden hätten. Die Quantität und Qualität der Kontakte lassen sich wenigstens teilweise dank der gegenwärtig zur Verfügung stehenden archäologischen Quellen verfolgen.

Gleich einleitend muß gesagt werden, daß an der Wende der älteren zur mittleren Bronzezeit, bzw. zu

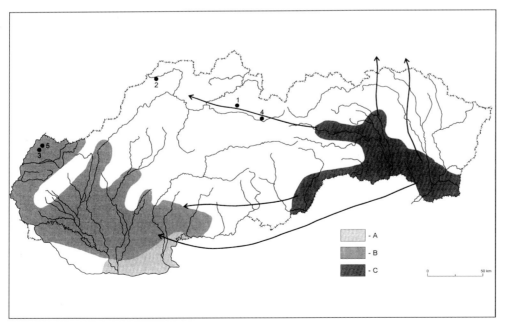

Abb. 2. Verbreitung A – der Nordpannonischen Kultur, B – der Maďarovce Kultur, C – der Otomani-Kultur in der Slowakei; Hauptrichtungen der Kulturströmung und die im Text angeführten Fundstellen: 1 Liptovská Sielnica – Liptovská Mara; 2 Makov; 3 Petrova Ves; 4 Podtureň; 5 Unín.

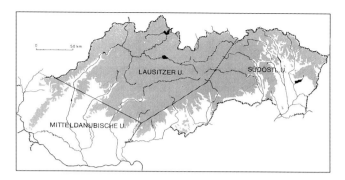

Abb. 3. Ausdehnung der drei urnenfelderzeitlichen Kulturkreise in der Slowakei: Kulturkomplex der mitteldanubischen Urnenfelder; Kulturkomplex der Lausitzer Urnenfelder; Kulturkomplex der südöstlichen Urnenfelder.

Beginn der mittleren Bronzezeit (Stufe Br B1) eindeutig eine Strömung von Osten nach Westen vorherrschte. Bis auf kleine Ausnahmen (Furmánek & Veliačik 1991, 35, Abb. 4) waren es Träger der Otomani-Kultur, die aus dem Osten nach Westen vordrangen (Abb. 2). Ob dieses Vordringen auch ethnisch und nicht nur kulturell zu verstehen ist, kann gegenwärtig schwer beurteilt werden. Keramik der Otomani-Kultur wurde auf Fundstellen der Maďarovce-Kultur schon seit langem konstatiert (Točík 1963). In letzter Zeit wurden diese Importe dreimal eingehender bearbeitet und interpretiert (Benkovsky-Pivovarová 1998; Marková 1998; Furmánek & Marková 1999). Diesen Blick erweitert gewissermaßen auch der neue Einzelfund einer bronzenen Nackenscheibenaxt des Typus A nach A. Mozsolics (1967, 34-40) vom Fundort Petrova Ves, der sich in der Nachbarschaft der bedeutsamen befestigten Siedlung der Maďarovce-Věteřov-Kultur (Studeníková 1982) in Unín befindet. Es kann also konstatiert werden, daß das Vordringen der Träger, bzw. die Einsickerung der materiellen Kultur der Otomani-Bevölkerung in die Südwestslowakei verhältnismäßig gut bekannt und nachgewiesen ist. Das Potential der Träger der Otomani-Kultur äußerte sich jedoch intensiv auch in den nördlichen Regionen der Karpaten. Eine Enklave der Otomani-Kultur in Südostpolen, d. h. nördlich des Karpatenbogens, wurde schon seit längerem konstatiert (Vladár 1977). Auch neue Grabungen bestätigen dies (Gancarski

1984; 1994). Einflüsse der Otomani-Kultur sickerten jedoch auch im Innern des Karpatenbogens westwärts bis in das obere Waagtal. Ein Beleg dessen ist nicht nur der typische bronzene herzförmige gerippte Koszider-Anhänger aus Podtureň (Furmánek 1980, 25, Taf. 13, 322), die besenstrichverzierte Keramik aus Liptovská Mara (mündliche Information von K. Pieta) und weitere nordslowakische Fundstellen, sondern auch der angebliche Hortfund von Bronzegegenständen des Koszider-Horizontes aus der Fundstelle Makov in der Nordwestslowakei (Bartík & Farkaš, 1997), d. h. sogar aus dem nordslowakisch-mährischen Grenzgebiet.

Im weiteren Verlauf der mittleren Bronzezeit und zu Beginn der jüngeren Bronzezeit änderte sich die kulturhistorische Situation in der Slowakei radikal. Die Slowakei teilte sich in drei Regionen (Abb. 3), in denen jeweils die kulturelle, wirtschaftliche und gesellschaftliche Entwicklung bis in die ausklingende Bronzezeit selbständig verlief (Furmánek & al. 1999, 70, Abb. 26). Determiniert waren diese Regionen durch geographische Gegebenheiten der Landschaft, die ältere Unterlage wie auch durch Kontakte mit den benachbarten archäologischen Kulturen. Der ebene Teil der Südwestslowakei war in der mittleren Bronzezeit von Trägern der Hügelgräberkulturen besiedelt und später erstreckte sich hier der Komplex der mitteldanubischen Urnenfelderkulturen. Die Nord- und Mittelslowakei war von Trägern der Lausitzer Kultur besiedelt und der Ost- und Südteil der Mittelslowakei war die Domäne der südöstlichen Urnenfelderkultur. In allen drei Regionen änderte sich in den einzelnen Bronzezeitepochen die Dichte der Besiedlung ausgeprägt (Abb. 4). Auch die gegenseitigen Kontakte waren in den verschiedenen Bronzezeitepochen unterschiedlich.

Die mitteldanubische und karpatische Hügelgräberkultur in der Südwestslowakei (Ibid. 59-69, Abb. 20) repräsentierten relativ geschlossene Kulturentitäten. Vorausgesetzt wird zwar (Veliačik 1983, 166), daß sie einen Anteil am Initiationsprozeß der Entstehung des slowakischen Zweiges der Lausitzer Kultur hatten (Abb. 5), jedoch fehlen markante Beweise, welche diese Hypothese bestätigen würden. In

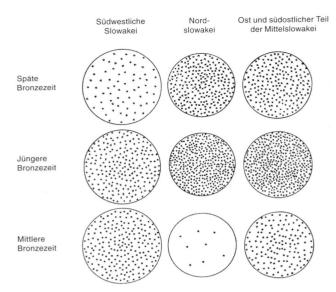

Südwestliche Slowakei   Nord-slowakei   Ost und südöstlicher Teil der Mittelslowakei

Späte Bronzezeit

Jüngere Bronzezeit

Mittlere Bronzezeit

Abb. 4. Schematische Darstellung der Besiedlungsdichte von der mittleren bis zur späten Bronzezeit in der Slowakei.

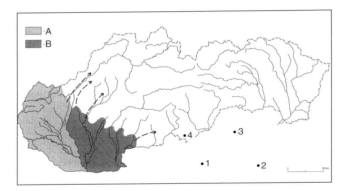

Abb. 5. Verbreitung A – der Mitteldanubischen Hügelgräberkultur, B – der Karpatischen Hügelgräberkultur in der Slowakei; Hauptrichtungen der Kulturströmung und die im Text angeführten Fundstellen: 1 Detek; 2 Egyek; 3 Halmaj; 4 Radzovce.

Mittel- und Nordmähren kann dies jedoch nachgewiesen werden. Es existieren sogar Beweise, daß die Bewölkerung der mitteldanubischen Hügelgräberkultur bis nach Nordmähren und Mährische Schlesien vordrang (Podborský & Koll. 1993, 273-274).

Interaktionen der Hügelgräberkulturen mit den südöstlichen Urnenfelderkulturen, und konkret mit der Pilinyer Kultur, existierten. Dies jedoch in der Slowakei nachzuweisen, ist gegenwärtig schwierig, vor allem wegen der Absenz von Geländegrabungen im Berührungsgebiet beider Kulturkomplexe. Konkrete Belege ein wechselseitigen Einwirkung wurden in den Formen und in der Verzierung der Keramik festgestellt (Furmánek 1977; Ožďáni 1986). Dies beglaubigen auch Fundstellen im Berührungsgebiet beider Kulturkomplexe in Ungarn. Ich denke vor allem an die Egyek-Kultur (Kovács 1966) und an die Gräberfelder Detek und Halmaj (Kemenczei 1968). Die Bronzeindustrie belegt einen bedeutenden Anteil der Bronzeverarbeitung der Pilinyer Kultur an jener der Hügelgräberkulturen (Ožďáni 1986). Der Bestattungsritus der mitteldanubischen und karpatischen Hügelgräber- und hügelgräberartigen Kulturen zeichnete sich durch Biritualität aus. Wenn auch die allmähliche Zunahme von Brandgräber auf Kosten der Körpergräber (Furmánek & Ožďáni 1990) mit den Veränderungen der mitteleuropäischen Religionsdoktrin zusammenhing, hat doch im wesentlichen der Einfluß der religiösen Bräuche der älteren Urnenfelderkulturen zur Intensivierung dieser Erscheinung beigetragen. Anderseits finden wir jedoch auf den Gräberfeldern der Pilinyer Kultur nirgends ein Körpergrab, nicht einmal in den Berührungsgebieten mit den Hügelgräberkulturen. Im Falle der ermittelten Hügelgrabkonstruktionen über manchen Brandgräbern auf umfangreichen Gräberfeldern der Pilinyer Kultur (z. B. Radzovce – Furmánek 1990) kann es sich um einem Einfluß aus dem hügelgräberbestattenden Milieu handeln (Furmánek 1977).

Auf der Grundlage der Hügelgräberkulturen entwickelten sich in der Südwestslowakei die Kulturen der älteren Phase der mitteldanubischen Urnenfelder (Furmánek & al. 1999, 70-81). In der jüngeren Bronzezeit bis zum Beginn der Stufe Ha A2 kennen wir die weiteste Verbreitung und grösste Dichte in den Sitzen der Bevölkerung (Romsauer & Veliačik 1987, 298, Abb. 1). In jener Zeit bestanden nachweisbare Kontakte mit der Lausitzer Kultur nur im westlichen Verbreitungsgebiet des Komplexes der mitteldanubischen Urnenfelderkulturen (im weiteren MUK). Jedoch während der Stufe Ha A1 ist im Waagtal eine 10-20 km breite unbesiedelte, man kann sagen,

Pufferzone zwischen diesen beiden Kulturkomplexen verfolgbar (Abb. 6). An ihrer Nordgrenze, aus der Sicht der Velatice-Kultur, demonstrierten die Träger der mitteldanubischen Urnenfelder ihre Kraft durch die Errichtung der ältesten Burgwallanlagen (Ducové – Veliačik 1997, 4-5) und prunkvoller Fürstenhügelgräber (Očkov – Paulík 1962). Zu Beginn der Stufe Ha A2 kam es im Bereich der MUK zur auffallenden Senkung der Dichte und Verbreitung der Besiedlung. Es existieren Hypothesen (Paulík 1993, 103-112), daß sich die Bevölkerung dieses Kulturkomplexes an den Stämmeverschiebungen der sogenannten bronzezeitlichen Völkerwanderung beteiligte. Aus archäologischen Quellen ist es evident, daß sich damals (Ha A2) zur Zeit der entstehenden Podoler Kultur und in ihrer weiteren Entwicklung das Besiedlungsausmaß der jüngeren Phase der MUF stark verkleinerte und die Anzahl der Fundstellen dramatisch abnahm. Die zusammenhängende Besiedlungsökumene der Lausitzer Kultur verschob sich nach Süden (Abb. 7). Sogar im archäologischen Material auf typischen Fundstellen der Podoler Kultur (Bratislava-Devín, Chotín) sehen wir bei der Keramik Einflüsse aus der Töpferei der Lausitzer Kultur. Damals tauchten

in der Südwestslowakei auch ausgeprägte Elemente aus dem Osten, aus dem Bereich Kyjatice-Kultur auf (Chotín, Kamenný Most, Malé Kosihy u. a.). Die allgemeine Situation war jedoch viel komplizierter. Untersucht wurden Fundstellen im Gebiet mit kompakter Besiedlung der lausitzischen Bevölkerung, in denen neben Komponenten dieser Kultur auch ausgeprägte Elemente der Podoler und der Kyjatice-Kultur erschienen, z. B. in Zlaté Moravce-Kňažice (Kujovský 1994). In jener Zeit entstanden auch, sowohl im Bereich der Lausitzer Kultur als auch der Podoler Kultur, neue Burgwälle, wahrscheinlich eine Reaktion auf die von Osten sich nähernde Gefahr. Ihre Gründungen, sofern wir es vorwiegend auf Grundlage von Geländeerkundungen und aus kleinen Sondagen konstatieren können, nahmen auch noch in der ausklingenden Bronzezeit zu (Veliačik 1996; 1997).

Der slowakische Zweig des Lausitzer Kulturkomplexes stellt eine seiner ältesten Äußerungen dar. Im ältesten Horizont erschienen lausitzische Denkmäler in der Slowakei nur isoliert und sporadisch (Furmánek & al. 1999, 83). Erst später, seit Beginn der jüngeren Bronzezeit, erlangte die Lausitzer Besiedlung der Nord- und Mittelslowakei ihre Intensität und das

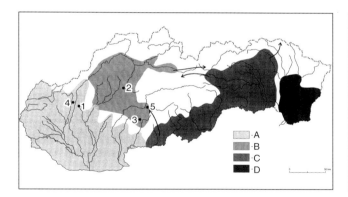

Abb. 6. Verbreitung der Kulturen des älteren Abschnittes der Urnenfelder in der Slowakei. A – Velatice- und Čaka-Kultur; B – Lausitzer Kultur; C – Pilinyer Kultur; D – Suciu de Sus-Kultur; Hauptrichtungen der Kulturströmung und die im Text angeführten Fundstellen: 1 Ducové; 2 Horná Štubňa; 3 Kráľovce-Krnišov; 4 Očkov; 5 Zvolen.

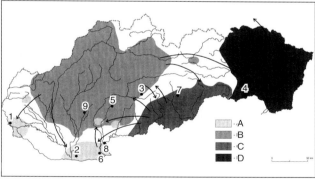

Abb. 7. Verbreitung der Kulturen des jüngeren Abschnittes der Urnenfelder in der Slowakei. A – Podoler Kultur; B – Lausitzer Kultur; C – Kyjatice-Kultur; D – Gáva-Kultur; Hauptrichtungen der Kulturströmung und die im Text angeführten Fundstellen: 1 Bratislava-Devín; 2 Chotín; 3 Detva; 4 Hraničná pri Hornáde-Kechnec; 5 Ilija; 6 Kamenný Most; 7 Kyjatice; 8 Malé Kosihy; 9 Zlaté Moravce-Kňažice.

größte Ausmaß (Ibid. Abb. 27). Vom Eindringen der Träger der Lausitzer Kultur in das spätbronzezeitliche Milieu des Kulturkomplexes MUL sprachen wir bereits (Abb. 7). Die Träger der Lausitzer Kultur schoben sich jedoch im Norden auch nach Osten in das Milieu der südöstlichen Urnenfelder vor (Abb. 7). Während in der mittleren und beginnenden jüngeren Bronzezeit die Zips mit Trägern der Pilinyer Kultur besiedelt war, wurde diese Region später von lausitzischer Bevölkerung bewohnt. Vereinzelt begegnet man Denkmälern der Lausitzer Kultur während der Spätbronzezeit sogar im Süden des Košicer Beckens (Abb. 7) auf der Fundstelle Hraničná pri Hornáde-Kechnec (Ibid. 88). Eine interessante Entwicklung weisen die Kontakte der Lausitzer mit den westlichen unter den südöstlichen Urnenfelderkulturen auf (Pilinyer und Kyjatice-Kultur). Obwohl eine Berührungsgrenze zwischen der Lausitzer und der Pilinyer Kultur über 180 km Luftlinie bestand, existieren auf ihr lediglich zwei bis drei natürliche Kommunikationsverbindungen (Furmánek 1988, 211, Abb. 1). Ende der mittleren und Anfang der jüngeren Bronzezeit hat namentlich der südliche Verbindungsweg aus dem Becken von Lučenec in das Zvolener funktioniert (Abb. 6). Belege seiner Benutzung sind die Bronzehortfunde von evident Pilinyer Herkunft in Zvolen Pustý hrad (Balaša 1946; Furmánek & Kuka 1973). Noch weiter im Norden fand man im lausitzischen Milieu ähnliche Depots auf den Fundorten Kráľovce-Krnišov (Mozsolics 1973, 141, Taf. 68) und Horná Štubňa (Veliačik 1983, Taf. 35, 1-6). Außer den erwähnten Hortfunden existiert im Milieu der Lausitzer Kultur in der Mittel- und Nordslowakei eine ganze Reihe von Bronzegegenständen, deren Pilinyer Provenienz evident ist (Furmánek 1988, 219-220). Belege einer entgegengesetzten Strömung sind selten (Demeterová 1977). Wesentlich komplizierter waren Kontakte zwischen der Lausitzer und Kyjatice-Kultur in der Jung- und Spätbronzezeit (Abb. 7). Es wurde bewiesen, daß sich die Lausitzer Kultur an der Genese der Kyjatice-Kultur beteiligte (Furmánek 1987). Andererseits drangen jedoch Träger der vollentwickelten Kyjatice-Kultur sowohl in das Verbreitungsgebiet der mitteldanubischen Urnenfelder als auch in den Be-

reich der Lausitzer Kultur vor (Abb. 7). Einen Beleg bilden Funde von sicherer Kyjaticer Provenienz auf den Burgwällen Detva-Kalamarka (Šalkovský 1994) und Ilija-Sitno (Žebrák 1987), und Spuren dieser Interaktionen erblicken wir auch im Keramikmaterial auf Gräberfeldern der Zvolener Gruppe der Lausitzer Kultur (Bátora 1979).

Der Komplex der südöstlichen Urnenfelderkulturen bildet die dritte Gruppe der Urnenfelder in der Slowakei. Von seinen Interaktionen mit den mitteldanubischen Urnenfelderkulturen sprachen wir bereits. Es verbleibt uns nur, die Interaktionaspekte zu erwähnen, von denen wir noch nicht sprachen, und die Kontakte zwischen den einzelnen Kulturen im Rahmen dieses Komplexes. In der älteren Phase dieses Komplexes (Abb. 6) war die Pilinyer Kultur dominant (Furmánek 1977). Die Suciu de Sus-Kultur reichte nur peripher in die Ostslowakei (Furmánek 1998). Aus der Sicht der Mobilität der Träger der Pilinyer Kultur ist die Enklave dieser Kultur in Südostpolen interessant (Dobrzańska & Rydzewski 1992). Bisher wurde angenommen, daß es sich um einen Kolonisationseinschlag aus der Ostslowakei handelte. In letzter Zeit zeigte es sich jedoch, daß das erwähnte Gebiet von Trägern der Otomani-Kultur besiedelt war, und so kann die Genese der Pilinyer Kultur auf dem Otomani-Substrat auch in dieser Region vorangenommen werden. Eine der bedeutendsten ostmitteleuropäischen und nordkarpatischen Kulturen war die Gáva-Kultur (Furmánek & al. 1999, 103-104). In der Slowakei nahm sie nicht nur den Bereich der Suciu de Sus-Kultur ein, sondern auch das östliche Verbreitungsgebiet der Pilinyer Kultur. Sie beteiligte sich auch an der Entstehung der Kyjatice-Kultur (Furmánek 1987). Ihre bedeutende Enklave konstatierte man auch in Südostpolen (Bazielich 1986), und das Vordringen weit nach Westen dokumentiert das Brandgrab aus der ostdeutschen Lokalität Zschornewitz (Agde 1939). Die vierte Kultur der südöstlichen Urnenfelder war die Kyjatice-Kultur (Furmánek & al. 1999, 101-103). Über ihre Genese, Kontakte mit der Lausitzer Kultur und dem Kulturkomplex MUK haben wir uns schon geäußert. Es sind noch einige Worte zu ihrem Ausklingen zu sagen. In ihren südli-

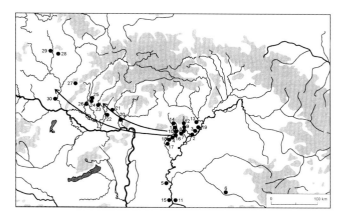

Abb. 8. Belege der nomadischen Einsickerung aus dem Theißgebiet in die Südwestslowakei, nach Niederösterreich und Mähren; 1 Aldebrő; 2 Ároktő-Dongóhalom; 3 Ároktő-Pélypuszta; 4 Boconád-Gosztonyi Tanya; 5 Csongrád; 6 Doboz-Maté erdő; 7 Dormánd-Hanyi puszta; 8 Füzesabony-Kettöshalom; 9 Füzesabony-Öregdomb; 10 Kál-Lengelő; 11 Lebő; 12 Maklár-Koszpérium; 13 Mezőcsát-Hörcsögös; 14 Sirok-Akasztőmály; 15 Szeged-Öthalom; 16 Tarnabod-Téglás; 17 Tarnaörs-Annakápolna; 18 Tarnaörs-Csárdamajor; 19 Tiszakeszi-Szódadomb; 20 Salka; 21 Želiezovce; 22 Maňa; 23 Ivanka pri Nitre; 24 Dvorníky-Posádka; 25 Dvorníky; 26 Sereď-Staré trhovisko; 27 Senica; 28 Podolí-Žuráň; 29 Brno-Obřany; 30 Stillfried. (Nach P. Romsauer 1997).

tet wurde, daß aber die Nomadengruppen die südslowakischen und nordungarischen Gebirge südlich umgingen (Abb. 8). Ihre ausgeprägte Anwesenheit zeigt sich erst in der Südwestslowakei, Niederösterreich und in Südmähren (Romsauer 1997, 1998).

Ende der Bronzezeit beobachten wir in der Slowakei eine Stagnation und ein Retardieren des wirtschaftlichen und gesellschaftlichen Niveaus der Urnenfelderbevölkerung. Der Untergang ihrer Zivilization wurde zur historischen Realität. Verursacht haben könnten dies verschiedene Faktoren. Erwogen wird eine verderbliche Folge der vernichtenden nomadischen Einfälle von Osten (Kossack 1980), über veränderte Klimabedingungen (Bouzek 1982; Jäger & Ložek 1982), über eine Erschöpfung der Rohstoffquellen u. a. Am wahrscheinlichsten jedoch handelte es sich um ein Zusammenwirken dieser und weiterer nicht identifizierbarer Faktoren, die einen Kollaps der Urnenfelderzivilisation verursachten. Der Untergang der einzelnen Komplexe oder Kulturen, bzw. ihr Aufgehen in der Zivilisation der Eisenzeit war nicht einheitlich und wies in den einzelnen Regionen einen differenzierten Verlauf auf (Stegmann-Rajtár 1992; Nebelsick 1994; Furmánek & al. 1999).

chen Verbreitungsgebieten ging sie schon in der Stufe Ha B1 unter (Kemenczei 1984, 56-57). Einer der Gründe dafür war der Druck nomadischer Ethnika, die wir in den archäologischen Quellen als Mezőcsát-Kultur oder Füzesabony-Mezőcsát-Typus kennzeichnen (Patek 1991). Gegenwärtig zeigt es sich jedoch, daß die Träger dieser Kultur in den Gebirgsgebieten Nordungarns (D. Matúz 1999) und im südlichen Teil der Mittelslowakei das Ende der Bronzezeit erlebten, vielleicht auch den Beginn der Eisenzeit. Es ist interessant, daß sich Körpergräberfelder der Mezőcsát-Kultur lediglich einige Dutzend Kilometer von den slowakischen Grenzen konzentrieren. Lange wurde angenommen, daß eine ähnliche Denkmälergruppe auch im Süden der Mittelslowakei gewesen sein könnte. Heute ist es schon beinahe sicher, daß diese Region durch den nomadischen Einfall total vernich-

Literatur

Balaša, G. 1946: Nález bronzového pokladu na Pustom hrade vo Zvolene. *Čas.MSS*, 36-37, 90-95.

Bartík, J. & Farkaš, Z. 1997: Nový sekeromlat s kotúčovitým tylom zo Slovenska. In: *AVANS v roku 1995*, Nitra, 24-25.

Bátora, J. 1979: Žiarové pohrebiská lužickej kultúry v oblasti Zvolena. *Slov. Arch.*, 27, 57-86.

Bazielich, M. 1986: Ze studiów porównawczych nad technolgią produkcji ceramiki kultury Gava z terenu Węgier oraz ceramiki tej kultury odkrytej w rejonie Krakówa-Nowej Huty. *Mat. Arch. Nowej Huty 10*, 59-71.

Benkovsky-Pivovarová, Z. 1998: Zum Zeitpunkt des Vorstosses der Otomani-Kultur in die Süd- und Westslowakei. *Východosl. Pravek 5*, 33-38.

Boroffka, N. 1994: *Die Wietenberg-Kultur*. Bonn.

Bouzek, J. 1982: Climatic changes and central European prehistory. In: *Climatic changes in Later Prehistory* (ed. A. Harding). Edinburg 1982, 179-191.

Demeterová, S. 1977: Nové nálezy ihlíc s guľovitou alebo dvojkónickou hlavicou a zosilneným kŕčikom zo Slovenska. *Slov. Arch. 25*, 449-462.

D. Matuz, E. 1999: A kyjaticei kultúra földvára Szilvásvárad-Töröksáncon. *Agria 35*, 5-84.

Dobrzańska, H. & Rydzewski, J. 1992: Elementy zakarpackie w materiałach kultury trzcinieckiej z osady w Mysławczycach, woj. Krakowskie. *Acta Arch. Carpathica 31*, 91-106.

Furmánek, V. 1977: Pilinyer Kultur. *Slov. Arch. 25*, 251-370.

Furmánek, V. 1980: *Die Anhänger in der Slowakei.* München.

Furmánek, V. 1987: Die Kyjatice-Kultur. In: *Die Urnenfelderkulturen Mitteleuropas.* Symposium Liblice 21.-25.10.1985. Praha, 317-324.

Furmánek, V. 1990: *Radzovce. Osada ľudu popolnicových polí.* Bratislava.

Furmánek, V. 1998: K problémům kultury Suciu de Sus na Slovensku. In: *Sborník Prací Fil. Fak. Brno M2* 1997, Brno, 155-167.

Furmánek, V. & Kuka, P. 1973: Bronzový depot piliňské kultury ze Zvolena. Arch. Rozhledy, vol. 25, 603-614, 667, 668.

Furmánek, V. & Marková, K. im Druck: Die westliche Peripherie der Otomani-Kultur in der Slowakei. In: *Die Otomani-Füzesabony-Kultur: Entwicklung, Chronologie, Wirtschaft.* Materialen der archäologischen Konferenz. Dukla, 27.-28.11 1997. Krosno 1999, 73-83.

Furmánek, V. & Ožďáni, O. 1990: Kontakte der Hügelgräberkulturen und des Kulturkomplexes der südöstlichen Urnenfelder. In: *Beiträge mitteleur. Bronzezeit.* Berlin-Nitra, 129-141.

Furmánek, V. & Veliačik, L. 1991: Anfänge der Urnenfelderkulturen in der Mittel- und Ostslowakei. In: *Die Anfänge der Urnenfelderkulturen in Europa.* Arch. Interregionalis, vol. 13. Warszawa, 29-46.

Furmánek, V. & Veliačik, L. & Vladár, J. 1999: *Die Bronzezeit im slowakischen Raum.* Rahden/Westf. 1999.

Gancarski, J. 1988: Wstępne sprawozdania z badań osady trzciniecko-otomańskiej na stanowisku nr. 29 w Jaśle, wojewódstwo Krośnieńskie. *Acta Arch. Carpathica 27*, 61-83.

Gancarski, J. 1994: Pogranicze kultury trzcinieckiej i Otomani-Füzesabony – grupa jasielska. In: *Problemy kultury trzcinieckiej.* Rzeszów, 75-104.

Jäger, K. D. & Ložek, V. 1982: Enviromental conditions and land cultivation during Urnfield Bronze Age in central Europe. In: Harding A. F. (ed.), *Climatic changes in Later Prehistory.* Edinburg, 168-178.

Kemenczei, T. 1968: Adatok a Kárpátmedenczei halomsíros kultúra vandorlásának kérdéséhes. *Arch. Ért. 95*, 159-187.

Kemenczei, T. 1984: *Die Spätbronzezeit Nordostungarns.* Budapest.

Kossack, G. 1980: "Kimmerische" Bronzen. Bemerkungen zur Zeitstellung in Ost- und Mitteleuropa. In: *Situla. Gabrovčev zbornik.* Lubljana, 109-144.

Kovács, T. 1966: A halomsíros kultúra leletei az Észak-Alföldön. *Arch. Ért.93*, 159-202.

Kujovský, R. 1994: Príspevok k poznaniu vzťahu lužických a stredodunajských popolnicových polí na Slovensku. *Slov. Arch.42*, 261-317.

Marková, K. 1998: K nálezom otomanskej kultúry na juhu stredného Slovenska. *Východosl. Pravek 5*, 39-50.

Mozsolics, A. 1967: *Bronzefunde des Karpatenbeckens. Depotfundhorizonte von Hajdúsámson und Kosziderpadlás.* Budapest.

Mozsolics, A. 1973: *Bronze- und Goldfunde des Karpatenbeckens. Depotfundhorizonte von Forró und Ópályi.* Budapest.

Ožďáni, O. 1986: Zur Problematik der Entwicklung der Hügelgräberkulturen in der Südwestslowakei. *Slov. Arch.34*, 5-96.

Patek, E. 1991: A Szabó János Győző által feltárt "preszkíta" síranyag. A Füzesabony-Mezőcsát típusu temetkezések újabb emlékei Heves megyében. In: *Agria 25-26.* Eger, 61-118.

Paulík, J. 1962: Das Velatice-Baierdorfer Hügelgrab in Očkov. *Slov. Arch. 10*, 5-96.

Paulík, J. 1993: *Bronzom kované dejiny.* Bratislava.

Podborský, V. und Koll. 1993: *Pravěké dějiny Moravy.* Brno.

Romsauer, P. 1997: *Juhozápadné Slovensko v prvej polovici I. tisícročia pred Kr.* Nitra (Unpublizierte Habilitationsarbeit).

Romsauer, P. 1998: Interakcie spoločenstiev s usadlým a jazdecko-nomádskym spôsobom života v I. tisícročí pred n. l. na západnom Slovensku. *Acta Nitriensiae l*, 83-104.

Romsauer, P. & Veliačik, L. 1987:Entwicklung und Beziehung der Besiedlung der Lausitzer und mitteldonauländischen Urnenfelder in der Westslowakei. In: *Die Urnenfelderkulturen Mitteleuropas.* Symposium Liblice 21.-25.10.1985. Praha, 295-304.

Šalkovský, P. 1994: *Hradisko v Detve.* Nitra.

Studeníková, E. 1982: Výskum v Uníne v roku 1981. In: *AVANS v roku 1981.* Nitra, 270-272.

Točík, A. 1963: Nálezy otomanskej kultúry na juho-západnom Slovensku. In: *Sborník III. Karlu Tihelkovi k pětašedesátinám.* Brno, 97-104.

Veliačik, L. 1983: *Die Lausitzer Kultur in der Slowakei.* Nitra.

Veliačik, L. 1996: Zur Frage der Kontaktzone der Besiedlung der Lausitzer und mitteldanubischen Urnenfelder in der Westslowakei: In: *Problemy epoki brązu i wczesnej epoki żelaza w Europie Środkowej.* Kraków, 503-512.

Veliačik, L. 1997: Praveké opevnené sídliská – predchodcovia stredovekých hradov. *Pamiatky Múzea 3/1997,* 2-5.

Vladár, J. 1977: Kultúrne kontakty karpatskej oblasti s územím Poľska v strednej dobe bronzovej. In: *Geneza kultury łużyckiej na terenie Nadodrza.* Wrocław, 225-226.

Žebrák, P. 1987: Die urzeitliche Burganlage von Sitno. In: *Die Urnenfelderkulturen Mitteleuropas.* Symposium Liblice 21.-25.10. 1985. Praha, 331-333.

Southern Europe

Late Bronze Age Lowland Settlements in Central Slovenia

– *Hamlets, Villages or Proto-urban Centres?*

Peter Turk

... For I suppose if Lacedaemon were to become desolate, and the temples and the foundations of the public buildings were left, that as time went on there would be a strong disposition with posterity to refuse to accept her fame as a true exponent of her power. And yet they occupy two-fifths of Peloponnese and lead the whole, not to speak of their numerous allies without. Still, as the city is neither built in a compact form nor adorned with magnificent temples and public edifices, but composed of villages after the old fashion of Hellas, there would be an impression of inadequacy. Whereas, if Athens were to suffer the same misfortune, I suppose that any inference from the appearance presented to the eye would make her power to have been twice as great as it is ...

Thucydides, *The Peloponnesian War*, 1.10.

1. Introduction

Since the year 1994 extensive archaeological fieldwork has been under way on the routes of the motorways that are being built all over Slovenia. In the past seven years over 60 new archaeological sites have been discovered and over half of them thoroughly excavated. There is no doubt that these rescue excavations along with preliminary field-surveys represent the biggest archaeological project ever executed in Slovenia. Its importance can be briefly described in the following observations:

1. The planning of the exact routes of the future motorways took fully into account the principle of not disturbing the already known archaeological sites. Besides, the investor (i.e. the Slovene government) agreed with the archaeological claim that all the planned routes should be extensively field-surveyed. In the case of discovery of a new potential archaeological site, an intensive field-survey was executed and small test trenches were dug. In this way the exact location, size and stratigraphy of the archaeological site could be defined. These basic processes ensured better planning of the rescue excavations. The pre-excavation activities were carried out under the supervision and co-ordination of the SAAS (*Skupina za arheologijo na avtocestah Slovenije*, i.e. *Group for Archaeology on the Slovenian motorways*).

2. The newly discovered archaeological sites were heavily endangered, due to the fact that the area under destruction was a very large one. The size of rescue excavations areas varied from 2,000 m² up to some 300,000 m². On the one hand this caused considerable organisational and scheduling problems for the excavators, though on the other hand it enabled the archaeologists to deal with large and extremely informative sections of the archaeological sites and their structures.

3. The overwhelming majority of the newly discovered and explored sites are settlements. This observation is even more important in the light of the fact that

we are dealing mostly with prehistoric lowland settlements, previously very poorly known in Slovenia. Among these new sites, settlements from the Bronze Age as well as from Neolithic and Eneolithic periods are numerous. On the other hand Iron Age and especially Hallstatt period settlements are decisively under-represented. The extremely large excavated areas within archaeological sites, sometimes with complicated but very informative and interesting building structures, as well as the great quantity and quality of the small finds that have come to light, confront archaeologists with the difficult task of publishing accurate site reports and, ultimately, modifying and revisiting the existing interpretations of the periods in question.

2. Dragomelj

2.1. Settlement

The village of Dragomelj is situated in the fully agrarian lowland landscape in the central Slovenian Ljubljana basin, some 10 km north-east of Ljubljana. The site entered the archaeological records in 1995 with the excavation of two Late Bronze Age hoards (see below, chapter 2.2). It is more appropriate for the purposes of this paper, however, to begin the presentation of this site with a summary of the recent excavations from 1997 and 2000. The site of Dragomelj is in fact situated on the route of the future Ljubljana-Maribor motorway and it was thus subject to extensive excavations, covering an area of some 12,000 m². Settlement remains from three different periods were documented. On the southern edge of the excavation area Late Neolithic traces of a local variant of the Lengyel culture were detected and on the northern edge early medieval settlement structures were encountered. Unlike these, the Urnfield culture settlement structures covered the whole excavation area.

It is worth mentioning that in the immediate vicinity another Urnfield culture settlement was excavated in the year 2000, namely the one in Podgorica south

Fig. 1: Digital ortho-photo picture of the village of Dragomelj with marked motorway route Ljubljana – Maribor and the extent of the archaeological excavations on the sites of Dragomelj (1) and Podgorica (2). Copyright: Geodetski zavod Slovenije, d.d.

of Dragomelj. The extent of both sites as well as their mutual spatial relationship is shown in fig. 1. The excavated area in the case of the Podgorica site is almost 2 hectares and in the case of Dragomelj it exceeds 1 hectare. In both sites the Urnfield culture settlement-remains cover the majority of the excavated area. As excavations took place only within the motorway route, it is obvious that the actual settlements covered substantially larger areas. In the case of Dragomelj, field-surveys proved that Urnfield culture ceramic sherds are to be found within an area of some 4 to 5 hectares. The distance between the sites is less than 400 m. The river Pšata flows through this rather

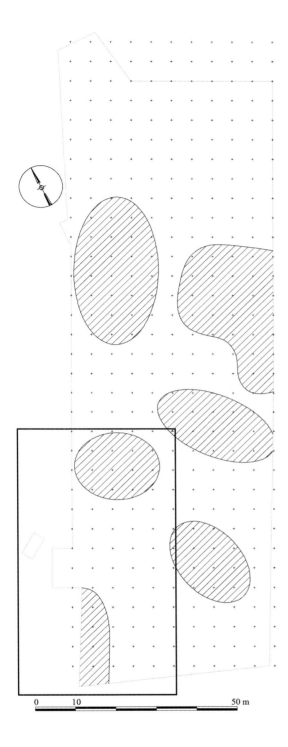

0 10   50 m

Fig. 2: Dragomelj. Excavation area in the year 2000. Marked areas represent intensive concentrations of Urnfield culture settlement structures (post-holes, storage-pits and pebble-pavements) which differ sharply from empty areas between them. Rectangle is enlarged in Fig. 3.

marshy area and separates the two sites. Preliminary analyses of the Podgorica ceramic forms equate this site with Dragomelj settlement in chronological terms. Ceramic finds from the latter settlement are comparable to later Urnfield culture (Ha B) hill-fort finds from central and south-eastern Slovenia (Dular 1994), though the radiocarbon analyses for some charcoal remains from the 1997 excavations in Dragomelj showed slightly earlier datings, to the Ha A and Ha B1 periods: [1]

1. 2990 +/- 40 BP, i.e. 1378-1060 cal. BC (2 sigma);
2. 2890 +/- 40 BP, i.e. 1200-928 cal. BC (2 sigma);
3. 2840 +/- 40 BP, i.e. 1116-904 cal. BC (2 sigma);
4. 2890 +/- 40 BP, i.e. 1200-928 cal. BC (2 sigma).

As the ceramic finds from the year 2000 excavations in no way differ from the ones from the 1997 excavations [2] there is good reason to believe that we are dealing with an extensive lowland open settlement from the early Urnfield culture and from the beginning of the late Urnfield culture. The life span of the settlement can thus be estimated at some 250-300 years at the most, but perhaps it covered an even shorter period of time. What can we say about building structures within this settlement?

The stratigraphy of the site under discussion is basically a simple one: under the layer of topsoil disturbed by modern agricultural activities there is a practically uniform Urnfield period culture layer with average small finds (mostly ceramic sherds, but also numerous loom-weights, spindle-whorls, whetstones, etc.). Visible settlement building and activity structures appear only at the interface with the natural soil (yellowish clay with pebbles) in the form of post-holes, storage-pits and other pits of unknown function, all cut into this geological layer, as well as some pebble-stone pavements.

Fig. 2 shows the intensity of settlement building and activity structures within the excavation area explored in 2000 (compare also enlarged area in fig. 3). The main characteristic of the Late Bronze Age phase settlement structures in Dragomelj is that areas with intensive remains of this kind cover some

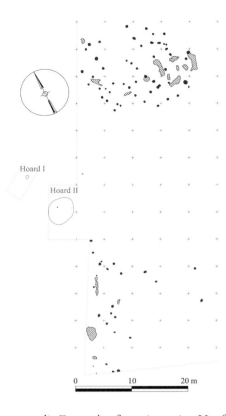

Hoard I

Hoard II

0   10   20 m

Fig. 3: Dragomelj. Example of two intensive Urnfield culture settlement structures (post-holes and storage-pits), possibly representing two homesteads, and the position of the two hoards between them.

300 to 800 m^2. They differ sharply from the more or less empty areas between them. Figs. 3 and 4 show, more accurately, what one such intensive settlement area looks like. Post-holes represent the most numerous category of settlement features. They are mainly organised so as to form parallel lines in the southeast – northwest direction, with a slight deviation to the north. They are obvious indicators of house plans. We can thus estimate that the houses were not more than 4 to 5 m wide and up to 7 to 8 m long. In many cases, however, it is hard to identify particular house plans with precision on the basis of numerous and sometimes confusing post-hole positions. This is very probably because there have been several building phases at the same location, but in some cases it is also because of poor preservation of post-holes and consequently lack of documentation of some of them. We can conclude, however, that the number of such house plans within one intensive settlement area ranges from three to six at the most. There are good reasons to believe that each of these areas with several houses represents a kind of homestead with residential as well as other outbuildings from the middle and the beginning of the late Urnfield culture in Dragomelj. It is hard to judge exactly whether these

Fig. 4: Dragomelj. View from northwest of the northern series of post-holes from fig. 3.

homesteads were contemporaneous or not. It is possible that at any given moment during the Dragomelj Late Bronze Age settlement life-span no more than a few such homesteads existed. But even if we postulate that the majority of homesteads were used at the same time, the fact still remains that – regarding the degree of complexity of the settlement under question – we are only dealing with so-called open dispersed settlement (Jockenhövel 1996, 210; comp. also Thrane 1996: 192f; Teržan 1999: 104f; Harding 2000: 57f). In fact, there are no defence structures documented at the periphery of the settlement. There are also no obvious signs of intentional house planning in the sense of regular symmetric combinations of houses with possible communications between them. The uniform southeast – northwest direction of houses is much more likely to be the result of the best possible insulation and orientation "against the prevailing wind" rather than "proto-urban house-planning".

The nearby contemporaneous settlement of Podgorica attests similar characteristics in its house structures: they are even much more sporadic than the ones at Dragomelj; they are likewise concentrated with large empty spaces between them. A general overview of structural features from both Urnfield culture sites shows dispersed farmsteads with large empty spaces (10-20 m and more) between them. If we deduce a similar situation also for unexcavated parts of both settlements outside the area of the future motorway, then a picture of two big lowland settlements appears (in the case of Dragomelj 4 to 5 hectares, in the case of Podgorica undoubtedly even more). The ratio of built to unbuilt space (comp. Harding 2000, ib.), however, weighs much in favour of the latter and attests very dispersed settlements.

What can we infer from these data about the Late Bronze Age population from the two settlements in question? Usually such dispersed farmsteads or hamlets are connected with family groups and their association with a village (Jockenhövel 1996: 211f; Harding 2000: 66f). In no way can a possible social stratification or a complex social grouping be inferred from these settlement data, nor can one speak about possible "proto-urban" indicators.[3] We can thus conclude, on the evidence of the remains of settlement building structures, that there was a small non-stratified population, shaped around basic nuclear family units, who lived here in the basin of the northern Ljubljana lowland region, in a simple self-sufficient way, around 1000 BC.

2.2. Hoards

Apart from and prior to the extensive rescue excavations that yielded the results just described, two hoards were excavated in Dragomelj in 1995 (Turk 1997: 2001:156f). They lay some 7 m apart at the very margins of the future rescue excavations (see their location in fig. 3) and represent two considerably different groups of bronzes. The first hoard – Dragomelj I – was partly documented in situ: it was deposited in a simple pit (fig. 5). It consists of copper and bronze semiproducts weighing in total over 84 kilos. There were 13 predominantly fragmented pick-shaped ingots cast in a one-piece mould and 39 predominantly well preserved plano-convex ingots in the hoard (selection in fig. 6).[4] Pick-shaped ingots of this type are frequently documented in hoards from northern Italy, the western Alps and the northern Adriatic hinterland (Turk 1997; 2000: 146f; Borgna & Turk 1998; see also Sperber 2000: 392f, Abb. 11, for up-dated distribution map). They are usually dated to the period of the transition from the early to late Urnfield culture and to the beginning of the latter (the horizons of Bronzo finale 2-3 in Italy and Ha B1 in Middle Europe). It seems significant that in this case from central Slovenia, as in the cases of many hoards with this type of ingot from northern Italy, e.g. in Porpetto, Bologna, Montagnana and Frattesina (Borgna & Turk 1998; Zannoni 1888, T. 25 a; De Min & Bietti Sestieri 1984; Bianchin Citton 1986; Arenoso Calipo & Bellintani 1994; Salzani 2000), the hoard was situated within the contemporary settlement. In all these hoards copper plano-convex ingots accompany the pick-shaped ingots, as is also the case in some other hoards, where the possible settlement

Fig. 5: Dragomelj. Hoard I in situ.

Fig. 6: Dragomelj. Selection of objects from the hoard I. National Museum of Slovenia.

context is not so clear.[5] Plano-convex ingots appear in hoards all over Europe from the Middle Bronze Age onwards, mostly in a fragmented state of preservation. Only at the transition to the late Urnfield culture and especially in early Ha B are they deposited in greater quantities and also completely preserved (Mozsolics 1984; Czajlik 1996; Turk 2000: 141f).

Objects from the second Dragomelj hoard were all documented in secondary positions in the topsoil due to recent deep ploughing. They were, however, mostly concentrated in an area of 20 m² seven metres away from the first hoard (see location of both hoards in fig. 3). The hoard Dragomelj II consists of 178 severely fragmented bronzes with a total weight of 5.8 kilos. This hoard is composed of totally different types of objects in relation to the first one: fragmented shaft-hole axes, small pieces of flat ingots and amorphous bronzes prevail; some fragments of winged and socketed axes, as well as of bronze sheet are also documented (selection of objects in fig. 7). As regards analogies and dating, shaft-hole axes from this hoard are of significant value: they are frequently documented on the Apennine peninsula in hoard contexts from the 11th to the 8th cent. BC (Carancini 1984: 196f). In recent years, however, a series of new discoveries attest their frequent appearance also in western and central Slovenia (Furlani 1996; Turk 2001: 162f)[6].

Regarding possible reasons for hoarding such a large quantity of bronze (and copper) material – the total weight of metal objects from both hoards exceeds 90 kilos – in the first report about the discovery (Turk 1997) a simple functionalistic explanation was given: both hoards should be understood in terms of provisional storage of objects within contemporaneous settlement; the objects were meant to be further metallurgically processed (as in the case of semi-manufactured ingots from hoard I) or remelted and recast (in the case of the supposedly unusable or badly cast and thus intentionally broken objects from hoard II). There are, however, some problems with this interpretation. In fact, the question arises: why would such a large quantity of metal items have remained unused for possible metallurgical activities? Instead,

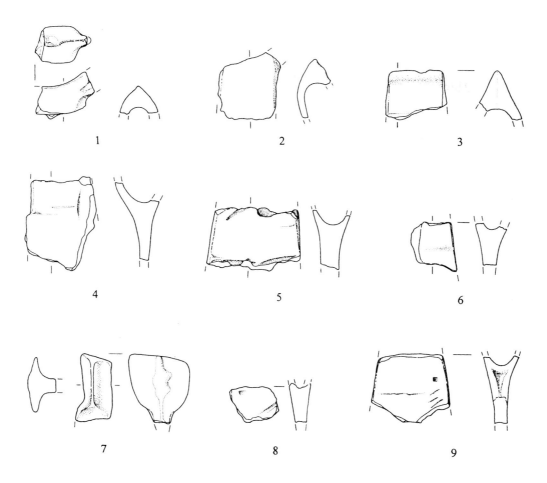

Fig. 7. Dragomelj. Selection of fragmented shaft-hole axes and a winged axe from the hoard II. Scale 1 : 2. National museum of Slovenia.

it remained in the ground after the Urnfield period settlement ceased to exist. Other possibilities of interpreting the bronze hoards from Dragomelj arose with the discoveries of new hoards at Kranj and Mengeš in northern Slovenia in 1998 (Turk 2001: 157f). On the one hand, their composition is closely related to the composition of the Dragomelj II hoard and on the other hand their specific site-circumstances speak much more in favour of votive interpretations, i.e. irreversible offerings.[7]

Whether the underlying motives for the hoarding were votive or secular, the fact remains that in the Dragomelj settlement more than 90 kilos of metal objects were discovered. Considering the complexity and length of time involved in the processes of mining and producing copper and bronze in the Urnfield culture period, such a quantity of metal items represents considerable wealth in itself. Such wealth is usually connected with much more complex and hierarchical societies than the one presented above (see part 2.1). The hoards themselves in a way contradict the picture of economic autarchy and lack of social stratification of the Dragomelj Urnfield culture settlement. This contradiction is reinforced by the fact that the numerous pick-shaped ingots and shaft-hole axes from the Dragomelj hoards hint at far-reaching contacts across local populations. It is worth mentioning that recent weight analyses of pick-shaped ingots revealed that their standard weight was a multiplication of an Eastern Mediterranean (Cypriot) Late Bronze Age weight unit.[8]

3. Conclusion

It is possible to state in summary that inhabitants of the Dragomelj Urnfield culture settlement possessed large quantities of objects which had specific "marked" value in broader European and Mediterranean regions. These objects were in economic terms internationally acknowledged currency. In addition, recent chemical analyses of the composition of identical types of objects from other Slovene hoards attest complex alloys of copper with considerable quantities of lead (in the case of shaft-hole axes) as well as nickel, antimony and arsenic (in the case of some examples of pick-shaped ingots) (Trampuž-Orel & Heath 1998; Trampuž-Orel et al. 1998). Obviously extensive metallurgical knowledge was invested in these complex alloys.

Expectations regarding the possible discovery of some traces of metallurgical activities in Dragomelj were considerable after the hoard excavations in 1995. Unfortunately, extensive settlement excavations in 1997 and 2000 have not yielded any direct evidence of such activity. On the other hand, in the nearby contemporaneous settlement of Podgorica (see above, part 2.1) two stone moulds for casting bronze objects were discovered. The first served for casting spearheads, the second for casting knives and ornaments in the form of wheel-shaped pendants and water-bird-shaped terminals. These extremely interesting discoveries hint at the possibility that in the case of the Dragomelj and Podgorica sites we are in fact dealing with a functionally unique settlement. The originally single settlement was probably partly destroyed by floods and alluvial accumulations of the river Pšata between them (fig. 1). Anyhow, within today's sites of Dragomelj and Podgorica distinctive areas were documented where on the one hand bronzes had been accumulated – for whatever reasons (in the case of Dragomelj), and on the other hand where there had been areas of metallurgical activities related to casting final objects (in the case of Podgorica). It is hardly likely that these activities served the local population alone. It is much more probable that they were a part of an extensive exchange network that – in accordance with the distribution areas of the pick-shaped ingots, the shaft-hole axes as well as the wheel-shaped pendants and the bird-shaped ornaments – covered regions at least from central Italy to the Pannonian plain.

The interesting hoards from Dragomelj and the mould finds from nearby Podgorica shed light on the population from both Urnfield culture settlements in a rather different way from what can be gained by isolated observation of building structures and their spatial organisation alone (see above chapter 2.1). The hoard finds and moulds discussed were prestigious in the sense that they would have conferred extraordinary status on their owners through possession of them. Alongside maintaining an obviously self-sufficient subsistence economy,[9] the settlements in question were evidently carrying out complex metallurgical (and ritual?) activities, which prove that they were important centres of metal production between the southern part of Middle Europe and the northern Mediterranean. Their inhabitants were thus active protagonists in a wider metallurgical community during the period of the 11th and 10th centuries BC.

The observations presented above allow the following conclusions to be drawn:

1. Experience of extensive prehistoric settlement excavations on the routes of the future motorways in Slovenia attests that no simple parallels can be drawn between settlement, the building structures of the settlement and the different levels of complexity of the prehistoric communities in question.
2. Sometimes precious and "lucky chance finds", as in the case of the Dragomelj hoards, can add considerably to the recognition of important technological and exchange aspects of the populations studied.
3. A series of questions regarding the internal relations of the inhabitants of the two settlements discussed remain unanswered. Among them a few can be listed:
a) Is the existence of the bronze accumulation area at Dragomelj on the one hand and the metallurgical area at Podgorica on the other a real indicator of a functional division within the settlement(s)? Is it possible that the recent destruction of the Drago-

melj settlement due to agricultural activities prevented us from learning more about this question?

b) What was the precise relation between the Late Bronze Age subsistence economy (agriculture, foraging, hunting) and metal production and long-distance exchange in the settlements under discussion? Was the latter the basic activity of the local population or was it perhaps just a short-term consequence of some chance "international" encounters?

c) How is it possible that such wealth as the two hoards from Dragomelj represent could be kept in a lowland village without any obvious defence structure?[10]

d) Is it possible that the unexplored nearby hillfort settlements represent the real paramount level of the lowland Urnfield culture villages?[11]

e) Is it – on the contrary – possible that big settlement complexes, such as Dragomelj and Podgorica, in fact represent real paramount sites (centres) within the larger – densely populated – cultural landscape and consequently consisted of larger communities, which defended themselves on small hillforts on their periphery?[12]

Apart from an accurate site report in preparation, the questions posed above present the guidelines for our future research into the Urnfield culture settlements in the northern Ljubljana basin.

Notes

1. The four analyses were executed by Groningen Laboratory (Centrum voor Isotopen Onderzoek, Faculteit der Wiskunde Natuurwetenschappen, Rijksuniversiteit Groningen, Nederlands) in 1998 (Analyses no. GrA10022, GrA10025, GrA10028 and GrA10030).
2. The Dragomelj excavations ended in spring 2001; selected charcoal samples will be additionally C14 dated in the near future.
3. Among such indicators, listed e.g. in Hänsel 1996: 241, the great majority do not fit in the case of the Dragomelj and Podgorica settlements.
4. The difference in the number and weight of objects from both hoards from Dragomelj between cited papers (Turk 1997: 2001, 156f) and the figures given here

is due to the pieces acquired more recently in 1999 and 2000.

5. The hoards from Madriolo in northeastern Italy (Borgna 1992) and Miljana in western Croatia (Vinski-Gasparini 1973: 216, T. 112; Dörfler et al. 1969) should be mentioned. It is indicative that in the case of Miljana a burned surface is reported in the vicinity of the hoard. Recent excavations and field surveys related to recently acquired and archaeologically documented Late Bronze Age hoards attest that hoards should be much more frequently connected to contemporaneous settlements than was previously supposed. This is e.g. the case in relation to the hoards from Saalfelden-Wiesersberg in western Austria (Krauß 1998/99, 120) and Mačkovac – Crišanj in northern Croatia (Vrdoljak 1997; Vrdoljak & Mihaljević 1999).
6. Both hoards from Dragomelj are analysed in detail in Turk 2000: 14f (this text is in preparation for publication).
7. The hoards from Kranj and Mengeš are treated in detail in Turk 2000: 38f, and are now being prepared for publication.
8. Pare 1999, 496f. The only completely preserved pick-shaped ingot from the hoard Dragomelj I (2844 g; see fig. 6) is almost exactly six times the weight of this unit of 475 g (Pare 1999, ib.). Cf. also Teržan 1996: 249f, for several other analogies from Slovene Late Bronze Age hoards with Eastern Mediterranean bronzes.
9. A considerable quantity of carbonated grain was gathered through wet sieving and flotation from both sites. This will be analysed during post-excavation work. Remains of animal bones were extremely rare at both sites. This is probably due to particularly acid earth in this area, which did not preserve these finds.
10. It is worth mentioning that the hoards from Kranj and Mengeš, with similar find composition as that of the Dragomelj II hoard, but of slightly later date, were both discovered within contemporaneous hillfort settlements (Turk 2001:157f).
11. A small trench was excavated in 2000 on the hillfort of Ajdovščina nad Dolskim at a distance of 2 kilomtres from Dragomelj. The excavations were headed by Mr. Primož Pavlin (Institute of Archaeology of the Slovene Academy of Sciences and Arts). They revealed remains of Urnfield culture layers that were obviously connected to the first building phases of the rampart.
12. A similar thesis was proposed by D. Svoljšak (1984) for the relation between the central lowland settlement

of Most na Soči and the peripheral hillfort settlements of the S. Lucia Early Iron Age group from western Slovenia.

Bibliography

Arenoso Calipo, C.M.S. & P. Bellintani 1994: Dati archeologici e paleoambientali del territorio di Frattesina di Fratta Polesine (RO) tra la tarda età del bronzo e la prima età del ferro. *Padusa 30*, 7-65.

Bianchin Citton, E. 1986: Rapporti tra Veneto ed Etruria mineraria nel Bronzo Finale e agli inizi dell'età del ferro. In: R. De Marinis (a cura di), *Gli Etruschi a nord del Po I.* Mantova, 40-51.

Borgna, E. 1992: *Il ripostiglio di Madriolo presso Cividale e i pani a piccone del Friuli – Venezia Giulia.* Roma.

Borgna, E. & P. Turk 1998: Metal Exchange and the Circulation of Bronze Objects between central Italy and the Caput Adriae (XI-VIIIth cent. BC): Implications for the Community Organisation. In: R. De Marinis et al. (eds.), *XIII U.I.S.P.P. Congress Proceedings, vol. 4 – Forlì*, 8.-14. September 1996 (1998), 351-364.

Carancini, G.L. 1984: *Le asce nell'Italia continentale II.* PBF IX/12. München.

Czajlik, Z. 1996: Ein spätbronzezeitliches Halbfertigprodukt: Der Gußkuchen. Eine Untersuchung anhand von Funden aus Westungarn. *Archaeologia Austriaca 80*, 165-180.

De Min, M. & A.M. Bietti Sestieri 1984: I ritrovamenti protostorici di Montagnana: elementi di confronto con l'abitato di Frattesina. *Padusa 20*, 397-411.

Dörfler, G., H. Neuninger, R. Pittioni & W. Siegl 1969: Zur Frage des Bleierz-Bergbaues während der jüngeren Urnenfelderkultur in den Ostalpen. *Archaeologia Austriaca 46*, 68-98.

Dular, J. 1994: Beginn der eisenzeitlichen Besiedlung in Zentralslowenien. In: *Festschrift für Otto-Herrman Frey zum 65. Geburtstag* (Marburger Studien zur Vor- und Frühgeschichte 16), 183-195.

Furlani, U. 1996: Depojska najdba iz Šempetra pri Gorici / Il ripostiglio di San Pietro presso Gorizia. In: Teržan 1996, 73-88.

Hänsel, B. 1996: Bronzezeitliche Siedlungssysteme und Gesellschaftsformen in Südosteuropa: vorstädtische Entwicklungen und Ansätze zur Stadtwerdung. In: C. Belardelli & R. Peroni (eds.), *The Bronze Age in Europe and the Mediterranean* (The Colloquia of the XIII International

Congress of Prehistoric and Protohistoric Sciences 11). Forlì, 241-251.

Harding, A.F. 2000: *European Societies in the Bronze Age.* Cambridge.

Jockenhövel, A. 1996: Siedlung, Landschaft und Wirtschaft in Zentralmitteleuropa. In: C. Belardelli & R. Peroni (eds.), *The Bronze Age in Europe and the Mediterranean* (The Colloquia of the XIII International Congress of Prehistoric and Protohistoric Sciences 11). Forlì, 209-222.

Krauß, R. 1998/99: Ein urnenfelderzeitlicher Kupferdepotfund aus Saalfelden-Wiesersberg, Land Salzburg. In: A. Krenn-Leeb & J.-W. Neugebauer (Hrsg.), *Depotfunde der Bronzezeit im mittleren Donauraum* (Archäologie Österreichs 9/10), 115-121.

Mozsolics, A. 1984: Ein Beitrag zum Metallhandwerk der ungarischen Bronzezeit. *65. Bericht der RGK*, 19-72.

Pare, Ch. 1999: Weights and Weighing in Bronze Age Central Europe. In: *Eliten in der Bronzezeit. Ergebnisse zweier Kolloquien in Mainz und Athen* (Monographien der Röm.-Germ. Zentralmuseum 43,2), 421-514.

Salzani, L. 2000: Fratta Polesine. Il ripostiglio di bronzi n. 2 da Frattesina. *Quaderni di archeologia del Veneto 16*, 38-46.

Sperber, L. 2000: Zum Grab eines spätbronzezeitlichen Metallhandwerkers von Lachen-Speyerdorf, Stadt Neustadt a.d. Weinstrasse. *Archäologisches Korrespondenzblatt 30*, 383-402.

Svoljšak, D. 1984: Most na Soči (S. Lucia) e i suoi sistemi di difesa. In: *Preistoria del Caput Adriae. Convegno di studi*, Trieste, 115-118.

Teržan, B. (ed.) 1996: *Depojske in posamezne kovinske najdbe bakrene in bronaste dobe na Slovenskem II / Hoards and Individual Metal Finds from the Eneolithic and Bronze Ages in Slovenia II.* Ljubljana.

Teržan, B. 1999: An Outline of the Urnfield Culture Period in Slovenia. *Arheološki vestnik 50*, 97-143.

Thrane, H. 1996: Bronze Age Settlement in the Nordic Region. In: C. Belardelli & R. Peroni (eds.), *The Bronze Age in Europe and the Mediterranean* (The Colloquia of the XIII International Congress of Prehistoric and Protohistoric Sciences 11). Forlì, 191-199.

Trampuž-Orel, N. & D. J. Heath 1998: Analysis of Heavily Leaded Shaft-Hole Axes. In: B. Hänsel (Hrsg.), *Mensch und Umwelt in der Bronzezeit Europas.* Kiel, 237-248.

Trampuž-Orel, N., D.J. Heath & V. Hudnik 1998: Chemical Analysis of Slovenian Bronzes from the Late Bronze Age. In: C. Mordant, M. Pernot, V. Rychner (éds.), *L'Atelier du bronzier en Europe du XXe au VII- Ie siècle avant notre ère. Actes du colloque international Bronze ,96, Neuchâtel et Dijon I.* Paris, 223-236.

Turk, P. 1997: Das Depot eines Bronzegießers aus Sloweniens – Opfer oder Materiallager? In: A. & B. Hänsel (Hrsg.), *Gaben an die Götter. Schätze der Bronzezeit Europas.* Berlin, 49-52.

Turk, P. 2000: *Depoji pozne bronaste dobe med Panonskim in Apeninskim prostorom (Late Bronze Age Hoards between Pannonia and the Apennines).* Philosophical Faculty, Ljubljana University (unpublished doctoral thesis).

Turk, P. 2001: Some aspects of new Late Bronze Age and Early Iron Age Hoard-finds from Central Slovenia. In: A. Lippert (ed.), *Drau, Mur und Raab Region im 1. vorchristlichen Jahrtausend, Internationales Symposium Bad Radkersburg, 26.-29. 4. 2000* (Universitätforschungen zur prähistorischen Archäologie 78, 155-164).

Vinski Gaparini, K. 1973: *Kultura polja sa žarama u sjevernoj Hrvatskoj / Die Urnenfelderkultur in Nordkroatien.* Zadar.

Vrdoljak, S. 1997: Pokusno sondiranje nalazišta Mačkovac-Crišanj. *Obavijesti HAD-a 29/3,* 61-64.

Vrdoljak, S. & M. Mihaljević 1999: Naselje kasnog brončanog doba na Crišnju kod Mačkovca (Nova Gradiška). *Obavijesti HAD-a 31/2,* 31.

Zannoni, A. 1888: *La fonderia di Bologna. Scoperta e descritta.* Bologna.

Acknowledgements

I would like to thank Bojan Djurić, the head of SAAS, for allowing me to publish the illustration in fig. 1, as well as Miran Erič and Sašo Poglajen for preparing the computerized versions of figs. 1-3, Vesna Svetličič and Ida Murgelj for the drawings in fig. 7 and Aleš Ogorelec for the photo in fig. 4. My special thanks go to Matjaž Novšak, director of Podgorica excavations, for providing me with information and allowing me to publish some of the facts mentioned about this site.

Bronzezeitlicher Landesausbau in der östlichen Adria

Bernhard Hänsel

Die kroatische Küstenregion ist in der Forschung zur prähistorischen Archäologie europäischer Dimension bislang zu wenig zur Kenntnis genommen worden, wenn auch in der jüngeren Vergangenheit bis heute verschiedene international angelegte Forschungsprojekte das Versäumte mit Energie aufzuarbeiten trachten. Darunter befindet sich auch die Kooperation des Archäologischen Museums für Istrien und der Freien Universität in Berlin (Teržan & Mihovilić & Hänsel 1999), über die hier berichtet werden soll. Der Referierende spricht also immer auch zugleich im Namen von Kristina Mihovilić, Archäologisches Museum Pula, und Biba Teržan, Freie Universität Berlin und Universität Ljubljana. Es geht um den bronzezeitlichen Landesausbau in Istrien mit einer kurzen Bemerkung zur Zone weiter südlich und westlich.

Für den gesamten östlichen Adria-Kulturbereich zwischen Albanien und Triest gibt es zwar aus vielen Perioden der vorrömischen Zeiten Fundstoff und Belege für Siedlungstätigkeiten, es kann jedoch nicht behauptet werden, daß ein Überblick über Besiedlungsdichte, Besiedlungsintensität oder gar Besiedlungsformen vorläge. Sämtliche zur Verfügung stehenden oder erstellbaren Kartierungen geben nicht viel mehr als einen beschränkten Forschungsstand mit seinen Zufälligkeiten zur Kenntnis, für Istrien ist es vielleicht ein wenig besser bestellt.

Von allgemeiner Bedeutung sind botanische Untersuchungen in limnischen Ablagerungen auf der Insel Mljet, die einen diachronen Einblick in die Vegetation dieser sehr südlich gelegenen dalmatinischen Insel und wahrscheinlich auch darüber hinaus gewährt haben. Für den Prähistoriker wichtigstes Ergebnis der vor kurzem publizierten Analyse von Jahns & v.d. Bogaard 1998 ist die Feststellung, daß es dort vor einem fortgeschrittenen Stadium der Bronzezeit um etwa 1300 cal. B.C. keine menschliche Beeinflussung der Vegetation gegeben hat. Danach muß wohl vielerorts und vor allem in seewärts exponierten Positionen mit unbesiedelten Zonen bis tief in die Bronzezeit hinein gerechnet werden, auch wenn etwa J. Maran für die Zeit des ausgehenden 3. Jahrtausends v. Chr. mit guten Gründen von einem "adriatisch-ionischen Interaktionsraum" spricht (Maran 1998, Taf. 71A). Mit einem gewissen Recht auf Verallgemeinerung wird man jedoch aufgrund von Befunden, wie sie in ersten Veröffentlichungen über die Forschungen auf der Insel Brač u.a. bekannt geworden sind (Kirigin u.a. 1998; Gaffney u.a. 1997), mit einer tiefgreifenden und flächenwirksamen Aufsiedlung der Insel- und Küstenwelt Dalmatiens erst von der Bronzezeit an zu rechnen haben. Die zahlreich vorhandenen Gradinen oder Castellieri, die mehr oder weniger gut befestigten Bergsiedlungen, werden erst seit dieser Zeit angelegt und bis in die Eisenzeit oder besser bis zur totalen Änderung der Wirtschaftsstruktur Dalmatiens bis Istriens unter römischer Prägung genutzt (Kirigin u.a. 1998 38 Abb. 20). Eine erste auf Brač gefundene, wahrscheinlich mykenische Scherbe (ebenda 39 Abb. 23) kann als Hinweis darauf dienen, daß die konstatierte Siedlungserschließung der Insel- und Küstenwelt auch etwas mit einer von See aus vorangetriebenen wachsenden Prosperität unter der Ägide der kretisch-mykenischen Thalassokratie und der ersten Phase einer "griechischen Kolonisation" zu tun haben dürfte. Schließlich ist auf der italienischen Seite und jetzt verstärkt bis zum Caput Adriae mykenische Keramik in größerem Umfang aufgetaucht (Di Filippo Balestrazzi 2000; Braccesi 2000, Karte S. 33), so daß wir uns die Adria bis zu ihrem Nordende durch Mykener befahren vorzustellen haben. Diese Import-Keramik gehört frühestens in die Palastphase spätmykenischer Zeit und wahrscheinlich sogar noch in die Nachpalastzeit, so daß der nachgewiesene Seeverkehr mit den auf der Insel Mljet gewonnenen ^{14}C-Datum gut zu korrespondieren scheint. Das Anfangsdatum ist damit aber sicher nicht erfaßt, zumal eigentlich gründlichere Erforschungen der Gradinen erst in jüngerer Vergangenheit eingesetzt und dazu neue Fakten geliefert haben. Die Erforschungsgeschichte der Gradinen beginnt vor der Wende zum 20. Jahrhundert (Marchesetti 1903) und führt über Aufarbeitungen verschiedener kleinflächiger Grabungen (Mihovilić 1997; Buršić-Matijašić 1998) zu unseren heutigen Grabungen in der befestigten Bergsiedlung von Monkodonja bei Rovinj in Istrien, von der im folgenden die Rede sein soll.

Zunächst sollte zur Kenntnis genommen werden, daß für den ganzen istrischen Raum trotz einer guten Landeskenntnis der vielen örtlich arbeitenden Archäologen recht wenige Fundstellen aus neolithischer, chalkolithischer und beginnender, sehr früher Bronzezeit bekannt sind. Dabei handelt es sich um Höhlen und wenige Küstenstationen (Mihovilić 1990; Teržan & Mihovilić & Hänsel 1999, 157 Abb. 2). In einem deutlichen Kontrast dazu stehen die zeitlich folgenden Fundstellen, die über das ganze Land in dichten Abständen voneinander verteilt sind (ebenda 158 Abb. 3) und die auch in ihrer Größe als aufwendig gebaute Anlagen bis in den italienischen Raum nördlich von Kroatien und Slowenien (Maselli Scotti 1997; Càssola Guida & Corazza 1999) ein ganz neues Bild einer intensiven Besiedlung des Raumes bieten. Solche bronze- und früheisenzeitlichen Siedlungsanlagen

kann man auf der Grundlage der in Monkodonja gewonnenen Ergebnisse recht gut verstehen. Der Platz im Stadtterritorium von Rovinj, ungefähr 3 km von der Küste entfernt gelegen, bietet für archäologische Untersuchungen in der an Boden- und Schichtenbildungen armen Karstregion den Vorteil, daß er nur innerhalb der älteren bis mittleren Bronzezeit besiedelt war, also nicht allzu stark durch Veränderungen verschiedener Bebauungsperioden verunklärt worden ist. Unmittelbar an der Küste gelegene Gradinen sind zwar auch vorhanden, wie es etwa Funde aus dem Altstadtgebiet der Stadt Rovinj selbst belegen, die Position von Monkodonja inmitten eines ackerbaulich nutzbaren Territoriums ist jedoch typisch für die bronzezeitlichen Siedlungen. Sie haben in Abständen von etwa 6–10 km Entfernung voneinander in Luftlinie in bestimmten Ballungsräumen gelegen (Teržan & Mihovilić & Hänsel 1999, 158 Abb. 3). Was ihre Größe und ihre soziale Bedeutung anbetrifft, dürften sie von gleichrangiger Stellung gewesen sein. Etwa 6 km von Monkodonja entfernt liegt die Altstadt von Rovinj, und von dort aus nach Norden ist es etwa ebensoweit bis zu der in ihren obertägig sichtbaren Befestigungsbauten Monkodonja durchaus vergleichbaren Anlage von Karaštak (Matošević 1998, 12–14). Man kann also ein gewissen Normen folgendes Verteilungsmuster der Plätze erkennen. Thiessen-Polygone zwischen den einzelnen Befestigungen und ihren in der Landschaft durch Hügelregionen recht gut erfahrbaren Grenzen zu zeichnen, sollte man aber besser angesichts mancher Unsicherheiten bei der Datierung der Anlagen unterlassen. Dichter beieinander liegende Plätze sind in der Regel zeitlich unterschiedlich. So ist es sicher nicht zufällig, daß die zwischen Rovinj und Monkodonja gelegene Bergsiedlung Valtida bislang nur Funde geliefert hat, die von der späten Bronzezeit bis in hellenistische Zeit zu datieren sind. Auch der nicht weit vom bronzezeitlichen Karaštak gelegene Castelliere Limska Gradina hat chalkolithische Funde und eine eisenzeitliche Nekropole, nicht aber die für die ältere und mittlere Bronzezeit typischen Lesescherben erbracht (Matošević 1998, 12). Wenn man also beim gegenwärtigen Stand des Wissens ein Modell eines Verteilungsmusters bronzezeitlicher Siedlungen im Gelände Istriens bilden will, so wird dies das Bild nicht immer voll ebenbürtiger, aber auch nicht grundsätzlich im Sinne einer Hierarchie unterschiedlicher im ganzen Land verteilter, jedoch in vielen Ballungszonen beieinander liegender Siedlungen anzunehmen haben. Sicher dürfte es zwischen ihnen Konkurrenzverhältnisse genausogut wie Austausch und Kommunikation gegeben haben, wenn man die beachtlichen Befestigungsbauten der Anlagen berücksichtigt.

Monkodonja

Daß jede dieser Siedlungen für sich genommen einen differenzierten Aufbau aufweist, der sozial gegliedert und wahrscheinlich herrschaftlich organisiert war, haben die ersten Erkenntnisse der Grabungen in Monkodonja ergeben. Man kann hier mit einem gewissen Recht von einer protourbanen oder in ihrem Charakter frühstadtartigen Siedlung sprechen. Die bis 1999 ergrabenen Befunde sind in zwei ausführlichen Vorberichten (Teržan & Mihovilić & Hänsel 2000; Hänsel & Mihovilić & Teržan 1997 [1999]) vorgelegt worden, auf die hier verwiesen sei. Im Jahr 2000 sind manche Ergänzungen hinzugekommen, die aber einen erneuten Zwischenbericht noch nicht rechtfertigen. Die folgenden Zeilen beschränken sich auf Aussagen zur Interpretation des Siedlungsaufbaus, sie verzichten auf ausführliche Befundschilderungen. Die Errichtung der Siedlung insgesamt dürfte als ein kolonisatorischer Akt, nicht als ein allmähliches Wachsen der Anlage aus einem kleineren Kern zu sehen sein. Die Inbesitznahme des Berges begann nämlich mit umfänglichen Steinbrucharbeiten, die Bebauungsebenen in verschiedenen Höhen, in Plateaus und Terrassen schufen und zugleich Steinmaterial für die einzelnen Gebäude und vor allem für die Befestigungsmauern ergaben. Sicher ist, daß für die früheste Bebauung tendenziell gut quaderförmig gebrochene und große Steine zur Verfügung standen. Spätere Bauperioden mußten mehr und mehr mit kleineren und unregelmäßigen Brocken des leicht verwitterbaren weißen Kalksteins vorliebnehmen (Abb. 1). An der ablagerungsreichsten Stelle der Anlage konnten vier Bau- bzw. Umbauphasen erkannt werden. Die Längsausrichtung des durch das Steinebrechen geschaffenen ovalen Bergplateaus beträgt maximal 270 m, die größte Breite 160 m. Die durch die Gründergeneration der Siedlung in einem Arbeitsgang hergerichtete Bebauungsfläche beträgt etwa 2,5–3,0 Hektar. Solch eine Fläche in kürzerer Zeit zu planieren, bedarf eines gewaltigen Einsatzes, der nur von einer großen Menschengruppe unter konkreter gemeinsamer Willensbildung, wahrscheinlich auch nur unter straffer Führung, zu leisten war. Ähnliches gilt

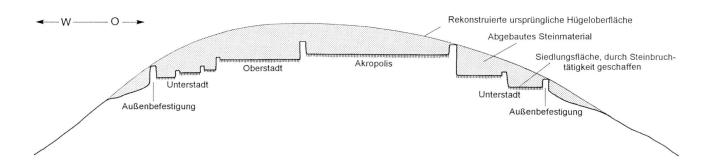

Abb. 1. Schematischer Schnitt durch den Siedlungshügel von Monkodonja. Verdeutlicht werden soll, daß durch den Abtrag des Berges Wohnniveaus hergestellt und zugleich Baumaterial gewonnen werden konnten (Zeichnung P. Kunz).

für die der Planierung folgenden oder gleichzeitig mit ihr vollbrachten Bauleistungen.

Es scheint, als wäre die gesamte Fläche bebaut gewesen. Sicher wird man das niemals feststellen können, weil das Plateau längere Zeit über landwirtschaftlich genutzt wurde und damit stellenweise Siedlungsspuren zerstört worden sind. Nahe der für einen Garten- oder Feldbau besser nutzbaren Flächen fanden sich jedoch stets große Mengen von Lesesteinen, die von bronzezeitlichen Hausbauten stammen und an bestimmten Sammelstellen angehäuft worden waren. Die Mehrzahl der Flächen ist jedoch so steinig, daß dort niemals Pflanzungen stattfinden konnten. Überall dort finden sich bereits oberflächlich erkennbare Bebauungsspuren. Wenn diese Beobachtungen richtig sind, wird man mit einer Einwohnerzahl von 500 bis

Abb. 4. Außenansicht der Akropolismauer mit verlagerten Siedlungsebenen und Anbauten

Abb. 2. Schematischer Plan der Bergsiedlung von Monkodonja (Vermessung Th. Urban)

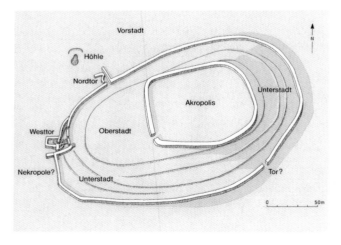

Fig. 3. Schematischer Grundriß der Bergsiedlung von Monkodonja (Zeichnung P. Kunz)

1000 oder mehr zu rechnen haben – selbstverständlich mit der gebotenen breiten Fehlerspanne kalkuliert.

Nicht nur wegen seiner Größe ist der Siedlungsplatz entschieden mehr als ein einfach strukturiertes Dorf. Das ergibt sich aus den Hausformen, der Fundverteilung, den Befestigungsbauten und aus der Topographie des Platzes selbst. Beginnen wir mit letzterem:

Hochwahrscheinlich sind die verschiedenen Ebenen des befestigten Siedlungsplateaus auch von unterschiedlicher Wertigkeit innerhalb der Siedlungshierarchie zu sehen. Das höchstgelegene Plateau hat eine ziemlich regelmäßig rechteckige Form von etwa 100 x 80 m Seitenlänge (Abb. 2–3). Die Fläche ist durch eine besonders mächtige, oft 3,60 m breite Mauer eingefaßt (Abb. 3), die in einer Schalenbautechnik ausgeführt und bis zu 1 m Höhe erhalten ist. Im Westen bildet die Mauer mit gut 5 m Breite eine Art von Podest, auf dem Gebäude errichtet werden konnten. Der stark befestigte Mittelteil der gesamten Siedlung ist also deutlich als selbständiger und prominenter Teil der Siedlung herausgehoben und begrenzt. Seine Befestigung kann nicht ausschließlich fortifikatorischen Zwecken gedient haben, weil ihr außen unmittelbar Gebäude vorgelagert waren (Abb. 4). Diese wären einer militärischen Sicherung im potentiellen Schußfeld eher hinderlich gewesen. Der dem Siedlungsorganismus gliedernde Aspekt

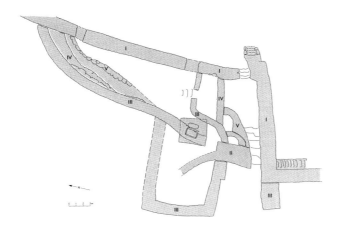

Abb. 5. Schematischer Plan der westlichen Toranlage mit ihren Ausbauphasen I bis V (Zeichnung P. Kunz)

der Befestigung dürfte der wichtigere gewesen sein. Im Zentrum der Anlage befand sich ein baulich abgesetztes, hoch gelegenes Areal, das als Akropolis bezeichnet werden kann.

Die zweithöchste Siedlungsebene, die auf Abb. 2–3 wahrscheinlich treffend als "Oberstadt" bezeichnet worden ist, nimmt etwa zwei Drittel der Fläche der Akropolis ein. Sie ist regelmäßig mit Lesesteinhaufen überzogen. Kaum noch Gebäudestrukturen sind auf

der sehr regelmäßig planen Fläche nachvollziehbar, sie waren jedoch angesichts des reichen Steinmaterials mit Sicherheit vorhanden.

Auch die tiefer gelegenen und randlichen Terrassen waren über weitere Strecken dicht bebaut. Daß sie in der Bedeutung gegenüber der Akropolis abgestuft genutzt worden waren, geht aus den unterschiedlichen Hausformen an beiden Stellen hervor. Dennoch bilden Akropolis, Oberstadt und Terrassen eine Einheit, die durch ein gewaltiges Befestigungswerk als Kernbereich des Platzes zusammengehalten wurde. Außerhalb dieser Ummauerung gibt es diverse Spuren einer randlichen Bergbesiedlung, einer Art von Suburbium, vor allem im Norden des Hügels. Eine durch ein Tor direkt erreichbare, 30 m tiefe Schachthöhle im Nordwesten mit aufwendigen Bauresten in ihrer Umgebung gehört zu den augenfälligsten Spuren der bronzezeitlichen Geländenutzung des Umfeldes der Kernanlage. Grabungen und auch Vermessungsarbeiten konnten in der macchia-überwucherten Zone jedoch noch nicht vorgenommen werden, so daß sich weitergehende Aussagen – auch zur Flächenausdehnung der "Vorstadt" – verbieten. Sie dürfte aber ähnlich groß wie die von der Befestigung eingeschlossenen Fläche gewesen sein.

Abb. 6. Rekonstruktion des westlichen Tores in seiner letzten Ausbauphase (Zeichnung P. Kunz)

Abb. 7. Ansicht des Tores – aus der Siedlung heraus bis zum Meer gesehen.

Die Befestigung selbst hatte ein repräsentatives großes und durch aufwendige Aus- und Umbauten immer stattlicher werdendes Tor, das nach Westen auf den direkten Zugang zum Meer ausgerichtet war. Weitere Tore öffnen sich nach Norden und – in Macchia und in Schutt versteckt – wahrscheinlich auch nach Südwesten. Das Haupttor hat sich aus der einfachen Eckposition in einem Mauerhaken durch immer weitere Zutaten zu einem mehrfach gestaffelten Gebäudekomplex entwickelt, der in fünf Hauptabschnitte gegliedert werden kann (Abb. 5–6). Der aufwendige Ausbau der Toranlage dürfte immer wieder erhebliche Kräfte der Bewohner gebunden und durch wiederholtes gemeinschaftliches Bauen das Zusammengehörigkeitsempfinden der Menschen in Monkodonja gefördert haben (Abb. 7). Eine ausschließlich strategische Bedeutung wird man dem Torbau nicht unterstellen wollen. Repräsentation und ein Zielen auf Wirkung nach außen hin auf den Ankömmling scheinen als Absicht für die Architekten und Bauherren im Vordergrund gestanden zu haben. Die Toranlage bedeckt zur Zeit ihrer größten Ausdehnung etwa 1000 m², obwohl sie an ihrer engsten Stelle kaum mehr als einen Meter geöffnet ist. Ein Reit- und Fahrverkehr ist deshalb auszuschließen,

allenfalls Lasttiere können den schmalen Durchlaß passiert haben. Überhaupt wird man sich in dem karstigen, steinigen Gelände Wagenfuhren schwer vorstellen können.

Die Befestigungsmauer selbst ist grob gerechnet zwischen 2 und 3,2 m mächtig, sie ist in Emplektontechnik gebaut und 650–700 m lang. Heute noch ist sie stellenweise von der Hangseite aus gesehen 3 m hoch und mehr erhalten, ihre ursprüngliche Höhe dürfte dem herumliegenden Schutt nach zu schließen 5 m und mehr gewesen sein. Diese Zahlen sprechen eine deutliche Sprache, was die Gemeinschaftsleistung der Gründergeneration der Siedlung anbetrifft. Die Gruppe der Erbauer der Befestigung kann nicht klein gewesen sein. Sie muß von außen, von wo auch immer, nach Monkodonja gekommen sein, da weit und breit Vorgängersiedlungen bislang nicht entdeckt werden konnten.

Die Formen der Bebauung, die Häuser, zeigen an, daß die verschiedenen herausgehobenen Wohnebenen funktional unterschiedlich genutzt worden sind. Auf der Akropolis wurde in der Nordwestecke ein in sich gegliederter Baukomplex freigelegt, der schematisch rekonstruiert auf Abb. 8,A dargestellt ist: in verschiedene Korridore eingebunden, fand sich ein größerer Raum von etwa 6 x 2,5 m Innenmaßen. Ihm war eine größere Hoffläche vorgelagert, so daß man von einem geschlossenen, multifunktionalen Gebäudekomplex sprechen kann, der um einen zentralen Raum gruppiert ist. Dagegen erscheint das in der Längsausdehnung innen 8,5 m große Haus von der unteren Terrasse am Westtor (Abb. 8,B) gänzlich anders angelegt: Von einer Straße gelangt man in einen kleinen Vorraum, der in das eigentliche Hausinnere führt. Dieses ist in zwei Höhenniveaus – in einer im Karst bis in das 20. Jahrhundert üblichen Weise – gegliedert. In der Mitte findet sich ein großer quadratischer Herd, der von der oberen Wohnfläche ebenerdig, von der unteren aber als Baukörper erhöht zu erreichen war. Eine apsisartige Nische war gegenüber der Eingangsseite am hinteren Ende des Hauses in den Felsen eingearbeitet. Direkt nach Norden und im Süden durch einen extrem schmalen Korridor getrennt, schlossen sich wohl ähnliche Bauten an,

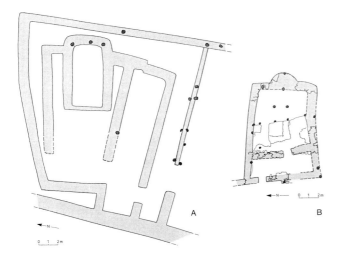

Abb. 8. Vergleich der Haustypen aus der Nordwestecke der Akropolis (A) und der unteren Terrasse/Unterstadt am Westtor (B) (Zeichnung P. Kunz)

so daß eine Art von Reihenhausbebauung vorliegen dürfte – ein deutlich anderes Prinzip als in der Akropolis.

Die Detektorensuche nach Metallen im Oberflächenbereich der ganzen Siedlung hat für eine Areal am südlichen Ende der "Oberstadt" auf einer Fläche von etwa 15 x 25 m eine starke Konzentration von Bronzegußabfällen erbracht. Man sollte davon ausgehen, daß sich hier eine Gießerwerkstatt befunden hat. Wenn dies richtig ist, so gab es innerhalb der Siedlung so etwas wie eine auf eine Handwerkstätigkeit spezialisierte Region, ein Handwerkerviertel. Weiter wurde innerhalb der Akropolis mehr an Metallresten als außerhalb von ihr gefunden. Sollte dies nicht ein Indiz für eine Staffelung des Reichtums sein?

Insgesamt wird man bei dem derzeitigen Forschungsstadium sagen können, daß es hier in Istrien einen dicht besiedelten Platz gegeben hat, der von einer sozial gegliederten Gemeinschaft genutzt worden war. Im engeren Umfeld sind die Voraussetzungen zur Errichtung einer so großen Neuanlage nicht beobachtbar. Von außen dürften die ersten Bewohner gekommen sein. Nach dem Fundstoff zu schließen, dürfte die Siedlung während der Zeitstufe Reinecke Bronzezeit A2 angelegt worden sein. Die Gründe für das Ende der Siedlung lassen sich aus dem Befund selbst nicht ablesen, zu stark hat die Erosion die Oberfläche des Hügels überformt und entstellt. Lediglich durch die Keramik wird man das Ende in die Zeit um Reinecke Bronzezeit D anzusetzen haben. Der Platz ist also etwa vom 19./18. bis zum 14./13. Jahrhundert v. Chr. besiedelt gewesen, also eine recht lange Zeitspanne, jedenfalls wenn man sie mit der Lebensdauer zur gleichen Zeit entstandener Großsiedlungen im Inneren des südosteuropäischen Subkontinents oder Mitteleuropas vergleicht (Nitrianski-Hradok: Točik 1981; Spišsky Štvrtok: Vladár 1973; Barca: Furmánek u.a. 1999, 49–53 u. 114–115; Feudvar: Hänsel & Medović 1991), die allesamt die Frühbronzezeit kaum überdauerte. Offenbar hat doch die Lage am Meer und die damit verbundene große Mobilität und Kommunikation zu Schiff ihren Beitrag zur Lebensfähigkeit geleistet. Sicher war auf dem Wasserwege eine bessere Verbindung zur ägäischen Kulturwelt

Mykenes als über Land zu halten (Braccesi 2000). Dafür spricht aus Istrien ein weiterer Befund von Bedeutung, nämlich ein Kuppelgrab ganz mykenischer Prägung, das bei dem eingangs erwähnten Karaštak auf einem hohen, isoliert in der Landschaft gelegenen Berg angelegt worden ist (Hänsel & Teržan 2000). Ein Kuppelgrab in falscher Gewölbetechnik nach ägäischem Vorbild errichtet, mehrere Tagesreisen zu Schiff von Griechenland entfernt, kann als ein sehr starkes Indiz für die Übernahme mediterraner Repräsentationsbräuche in der Totenverehrung gesehen werden. Kuppelgräber in Griechenland sind herausragende Bestattungsarten für hochgestellte Persönlichkeiten. Eine oder mehrere solcher Herrschergestalten aus dem Territorium der befestigten Siedlung von Karaštak haben sich im Tode präsentieren lassen wie es der griechischen Oberschicht vorbehalten war. Wir nehmen das als ein weiteres Indiz für eine soziale Vertikale in der bronzezeitlichen Gesellschaft Istriens. Diese Oberschicht hatte in ihrer Orientierung an südlicher Lebensweise offenbar wesentlich zur Durchdringung Istriens und zur Erschließung dieses Kulturraumes während der älteren und mittleren Bronzezeit beigetragen.

Literatur

Braccesi, L. 2000: Laguna Greca, nuove scoperte riscrivono la storia di Venezia. *Archeo*, 16,2, 30-35.

Buršić-Matijašić, K. 1998: *Gradina Monkodonja. (Monografije i Katalozi Arheološki Muzej Istre 9)*. Pula.

Càssola Guida, P. & Corazza, S. 1999: *Varianno: Una storia di 3500 anni*. Basilano.

Di Filippo Balestrazzi, E. 2000: Tre Grammenti Micenei da Torcello. *(Hesperia 10, Studi sulla Grecità di Occidente)*. Rom, 203-223.

Furmánek, V., Vehačík, L & Vladár, J. 1999: *Die Bronzezeit im slowakischen Raum. (Prähistorische Archäologie in Südosteuropa 15)*. Rahden.

Gaffney, V. et al. 1997: *The Adriatic Islands Project – Contact, Commerce and Colonialism 6000 BC-AD 600 I. (BAR International Series 660)*.

Hänsel, B. & Medović, P. 1991: Vorbericht über die jugoslawisch-deutschen Ausgrabungen in der Siedlung von Feudvar bei Mošorin (Gem. Titel, Vojvodina) von 1986–1990. *Berichte der Römisch-Germanischen Kommission,* 72, 45-204.

Hänsel, B. & Mihovilić, K. & Teržan, B. 1997: Monkodonja – utvrdjeno protourbano naselje starijeg i srednjeg brončanog doba kod Rovinja u Istri. *Histria Archaeologica,* 28, 1997 (1999) 57-107.

Hänsel, B. & Teržan, B. 2000: Ein bronzezeitliches Kuppelgrab außerhalb der mykenischen Welt im Norden der Adria. *Prähistorische Zeitschrift,* 75, 161-183.

Jahns, S. & v. d. Bogaard, C. 1998: New palynological and tephrostratigraphical investigations of two salt lagoons on the island of Mljet, south Dalmatia, Croatia. *Vegetation History and Archaeobotany,* 7, 1988, 219-234.

Kirigin, B. u.a. 1998: The Island of Brač. In: *2001 Archaeological sites on central Dalmatian islands: what to do with them?* Hvar/Split, 37-41.

Maran, J. 1988: *Kulturwandel auf dem griechischen Festland und den Kykladen im späten 3. Jahrtausend v. Chr. Teil I–II. (Univesitätsforschungen zur prähistorischen Archäologie 53).* Bonn.

Marchesetti, C. 1903: *I castellieri preistorici di Trieste e della regione Giulia.* Trieste (Reprint Trieste 1981).

Masetti Scotti, F. 1997: *Il Civico Museo Archeologico di Muggia.* Commune di Muggia.

Matošević, D. 1998: Kamfanarština u pretpovijesti. In: J. Bratulić (ed.), *Kamfanar i Kamfanarština.* Kamfanar, 9-18.

Mihovilić, K. 1990: Preistoria dell' Istria dal Paleolitico all' età del Ferro. In: *Atti della XXIX riunione scien. Preist. e protost. del Friuli–Venezia Giulia 1990.* Firenze 1994, 101-118.

Mihovilić, K. 1997: Fortifikacija gradine Gradac-Twan iznad Koromačna. (*Izdanja Hrvatsk. Arh. Družestva 18*). Zagreb, 39-59.

Teržan, B. & Mihovilić, K. & Hänsel, B. 1999: Eine protourbane Siedlung der älteren Bronzezeit im istrischen Karst. *Prähistorische Zeitschrift,* 74, 154-193.

Točík, A. 1981: *Nitriansky Hrádok-Zámeček.* Nitra.

Vladár, J. 1973: Osteuropäische und mediterrane Einflüsse im Gebiet der Slowakei während der Bronzezeit. *Slovenská Archeologia,* Bd. 21, 253-357.

Western Europe

Exposing the Gaps in the Long-term History of the Peak District, Derbyshire, England

Mark Edmonds and John Moreland

The growth of interest in long-term landscape histories has been one of the most productive and promising of recent developments in European archaeology. This shift of focus has been driven by several factors, among them the implementation of programmes of extensive surface survey, and a more general shift within the historical disciplines towards regional-level analyses. There have also been important shifts of perspective, in particular, a concern with how patterns of landscape inhabitation are integral to the process of social reproduction (e.g. Ashmore & Knapp 1999; Bender 1993; Ingold 1993; Tilley 1994).

These developments have been very positive. However, even a cursory inspection of many long-term histories reveals common problems. For the most part, relatively few studies deal adequately with the past in the past; with the ways that people at particular points in time lived and worked in relation to the physical traces of the past in their present (Bradley 1987; Gosden & Locke 1998). At the same time, many studies contain lacunae – gaps in the sequence. Usually, these gaps are taken as a manifestation of a real absence in the past. They are seen as the product of the collapse of the structures that bound society together in the previous period, and are almost always equated with a demographic collapse – with population decline and abandonment (Moreland 1993). The model lying (unacknowledged) behind these readings of the evidence is almost ecological – society grows, reaches climax, and then declines.

The process is seen as somehow natural and organic. It is what we expect, and what we find. However, these gaps may often be more apparent than real, and if we shift our focus slightly, some of them actually disappear. In fact, at least some of them are a product of methodologies that are inappropriate to the scales at which human activity unfolded in particular periods in the past.

To some extent at least, these problems also arise because of a more basic conceptual issue; a common failure on our part to discuss what we mean when we use the term *'settlement.'* Preoccupied for some time by more ostentatious monuments, prehistorians, particularly in Britain, have developed a complex and subtle vocabulary for dealing with ritual and ceremonial (Barrett 1994; Bradley 1998). Yet only rarely do they acknowledge the complexity of lifeways bound up in what is often dismissed as routine. In short, many of our models remain far too simplistic. They fail to catch the ways in which different landscapes were occupied in the past; the pattern, character and roll call of tasks as they operated in people's lives. In failing to explore these areas of past experience, we fail to establish important aspects in which specific monuments were set and encountered – a gap which also places limits on interpretation. Not only that, we fail to catch how routine experience – the dull compulsion of day-to-day life – is itself a powerful medium through which concepts of identity, community and even authority are taken on board.

In this short paper, we would like to try and develop these arguments with reference to a long-term landscape project run by the University of Sheffield in the Peak District of Derbyshire. Our aim here is two-fold – to sketch part of the long-term history of the region and to illustrate how we have tried to fill some of the gaps in our evidence. We will begin however, by outlining two techniques which we developed in attempting to write the 'total history' of the region.

Ways of Seeing

The Peak District of Derbyshire lies between the cities of Sheffield and Manchester. It is centred on an area of limestone upland with a topography of rolling ridges, steep sided dales and broader shale-rich valleys. The limestone plateau is surrounded on its eastern, western and northern sides by the edges and higher reaches of the gritstone moors. To the south lie the Trent Valley and the 'champion' country of the English Midlands. So far, our work has concentrated on the limestone, an area where intensive cultivation from the Middle Ages onwards has removed the vast majority of earlier features from the surface. While some of the Peak District is still regularly ploughed (and more of it was in the past), by and large, the limestone is now given over to raising livestock. Under these conditions, surface survey at various scales is an absolute priority; from the analysis of aerial photography and walk-over surveys through to more detailed levels of recording. However, this can only tell us about what is visible on the surface. This means that some periods (indeed much of prehistory) are only represented by a few upstanding monuments – isolated islands in a sea of grass. Our desire to produce a broad based picture of human history across the area meant that we also needed to develop complementary techniques that might create a context for these sites.

Three broad groups of techniques are crucial to the development of research in these sorts of settings. Not surprisingly, palaeoenvironmental data have a critical role to play, but these need to be set alongside

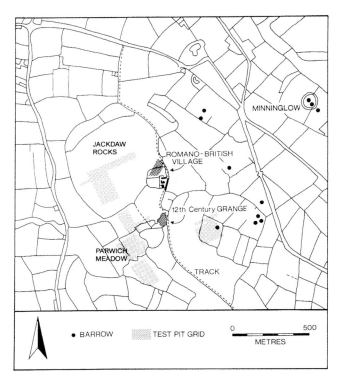

Fig. 1. Map of Roystone Grange study area showing location of multi-period walling systems, barrows and test pit grids (after Hodges 1991, 54).

evidence from other forms of fieldwork. One of the techniques we used to map the pattern of human activity hidden beneath the turf was shovel-testing (also known as test-pitting). This involves digging small rectangular pits (in our work 0.5m x 1m) at regular intervals across the landscape (fig. 1). Though the sample is small, test pitting allows a series of restricted but systematic views into the archaeology of a huge area. It allows you to sample landscape distributions of archaeological material from different periods, as well as providing a window on the nature of soils and sediments in different areas. These data can be drawn upon at a variety of analytical scales; when asking questions about the organisation of activities around known 'sites', or when attempting to chart how the inhabitation of broader landscapes was organised at certain times. Intervals between pits can also be adjusted from intensive (c.5-10m apart) to extensive (50-100m apart) depending upon the specific questions that one is asking. The technique has many advantages, and has recently become a regular component of many projects conducted within the contract archaeology environment. At Roystone we excavated more than 1,000 of these pits by hand.

What other techniques could we employ? One of the most impressive aspects of this part of the region is the way it is criss-crossed in many places by stone walls. As Richard Hodges notes, "walls ... seem a natural part of the landscape – a distinctive feature of the Pennines, in contrast to the hedge country to the south". There is, of course, nothing natural about these features at all. But Hodges' comment is significant because it shows how archaeologists often take walls for granted, sometimes failing to notice them at all. In some places around Roystone, the walls divide the landscape up into strict rectangular boxes. In others, their sinuous curves create fields in the form of a reverse 'S'. Occasionally, they appear as no more than low lines running across the countryside; earthworks being all that remain where older walls have been robbed or otherwise removed. For many of us, this is as far as consideration of walls went. However, Martin Wildgoose, a local farmer, believed that his years of experience of walking over the landscape, observing the way walls were constructed and how they related to each other, allowed him to establish a sequence of building styles.

It had long been understood that the walls which created the large rectangular fields were constructed as part of the system of late eighteenth and early nineteenth century Parliamentary Enclosure; and that most of the reverse 'S' fields were the product of the earlier 'piecemeal' or general enclosure of medieval field systems. Where Martin Wildgoose went further was that he was able to propose that certain types of walls (or remains of walls) were prehistoric, Roman, and medieval in date. We were able to confirm many of these suggestions through selective excavation at critical junctures, and by comparison with the types of walling used in excavated buildings. In effect, we were able to construct a broad 'landscape stratigraphy'. We were able to construct maps of the patterns

of landscape division/articulation, literally, from prehistory to the present. This highly innovative type of landscape survey, combined with test-pitting, excavations, aerial photography, studies of standing buildings and documentary research provided us with an impressive suite of methodologies with which to approach the landscape of this part of Derbyshire.

Roystone Grange

Roystone Grange is situated in what is, in many ways, a valley typical of the White Peak – the limestone heartland of the Peak District National Park (fig. 2). It became the focus of the research activities of the Department of Archaeology in March 1978, and we have been continuously involved with the archaeology of the Peak District ever since. Over four hundred first year students and most members of staff from the Department have participated in the project.

With the main theme of the Aarhus workshop in mind, it is worth presenting a brief summary of the interim results of the test pitting survey. In other parts of Derbyshire, scatters of prehistoric lithic material had been found in ploughed fields (Barnatt & Smith 1991; Garton 1991), but this part of the region (for this period) was, in important respects,

Fig. 2. Roystone Grange Valley in winter, with an ancient field boundary snaking from the foreground towards the line of trees in the middle distance.

an archaeological blank. What the Roystone project demonstrated is that similar evidence for early human occupation could be found in areas given over to pasture.

The first sign of human activity in and around the valley is represented by a 'Creswellian' point (a type of arrowhead) found close to the later Neolithic tomb and barrow complex of Minninglow, which stands on the crest of a ridge above the valley. Dated to between 10,000 and 12,000BC, it was probably lost by one of a group of gatherer/hunters who periodically exploited the region. No other signs of this period were found either in the test-pits or in the many excavations conducted over the years. This absence, at least, is probably a real measure of the intensity of human presence in this land in the early post-glacial period.

Signs of a more significant human presence come in the Mesolithic. The evidence for this comes largely from the test-pits, which located a scatter of late Mesolithic material across an area known as Parwich Meadow. Another test-pit, amongst the crags of Roystone Rocks, produced a late Mesolithic microlith, and subsequent extensions to this pit revealed other flints and signs that this location had also been used in later periods. The topography of Roystone Rocks and the character of the lithics initially prompted the suggestion that this was a hunting stand from which the movement of animals along the valley was monitored. This has its attractions, though perhaps a more honest appraisal would be that we are looking at a location in which activities were both small in scale and of limited duration, at least as far as the working of stone was concerned. The crags do, however, offer a significant contrast to the somewhat less exposed area of Parwich Meadow, where a much wider range of stoneworking tasks are represented. Though direct contemporaneity cannot be assumed, the combination of typochronology and spatial analysis does allow us to start sketching the landscape or 'taskscape' (Ingold 1993) structure of stoneworking traditions at different times.

Though it is hidden when one stands in the lowest parts of the valley, the chambered tomb of Minninglow dominates the Neolithic landscape around

Roystone Grange and is a distinctive landmark for miles around. It is one of around twenty Neolithic tombs in the region. Minninglow has drawn to it generations of antiquarians and archaeologists, much as it drew the mourners/worshippers of the Neolithic and those Bronze Age communities who built smaller barrows in the shadow of what was, for them, an already ancient monument. Until recently, however, it was a monument more or less devoid of contemporary context. Our test pits and excavations have, however, uncovered traces of Neolithic activity widely distributed across the landscape. At Roystone Rocks, Neolithic flint tools and waste material were found in association with Grimston Ware pottery. Perhaps more significantly, these objects were found within a small enclosure formed from long orthostats, which linked up with prominent limestone outcrops to form a bounded area. Sustained, if not settled occupation is further suggested by the small cleared 'fields' which lie down-slope from the enclosure. Test pits revealed that these plots also have a strong association with broadly contemporary flintwork.

This was not the only significant place within the Roystone region. Scatters of Neolithic flint and pottery had also been discovered in test-pits close to the Roman period farms in the valley and in the extensive excavations of the medieval grange. A noteworthy concentration of pottery and some seventy flints (including scrapers, a knife, a blade, and arrowheads) was also found during excavations of a Roman site near Jackdaw Rocks. Much of this material is secondary and tertiary in character, generated at developed stages in particular reduction sequences. Though analyses have some way still to go, this tendency may well indicate that material entered the area in a semi-worked or prepared state – carried perhaps by people who spent some of their time on the move.

Just what forms of occupation these traces relate to is difficult to determine. Recent work suggests that Neolithic activities in some parts of the Peak retained a fluidity and a strongly seasonal character, a pattern to some extent tied to the importance of animal husbandry amongst small, dispersed communities (Edmonds 1999; Whittle 1997). Environmental data, such as they are, provide hints of broad conditions. On parts of the plateau, where limited clearance has been recognised from as early as the fifth millennium, there remained a variety to the conditions that people experienced (Barnatt 1996; Garton 1991; Hicks 1971). Open ground near prominent outcrops and along the spines of major ridges; extensive and varied woodlands running down into upland basins and across perched shelves. Open woodlands of Birch, Hazel and Ash; darker tracts where Lime and Oak predominated. Cereal pollen, present in some areas as early as the fifth millennium, features in a number of sequences. Lower down, clearings, grassland and woodland margins shifted in and out of focus as people and animals tacked back and forth. Darker still were the forests that remained a commonplace in the larger valleys bounding the plateau on all sides.

Under these conditions, it is likely that many places had a season; a good deal of the higher ranges of the plateau witnessing cycles of use for grazing, hunting and the collection of other resources (Barnatt 1996; Edmonds & Seaborne 2001). Accessed from several directions and by different communities, the plateau may have been a part of the region where ranges overlapped and that may be part of the reason why it is here that we find collective/communal monuments such as tombs.

How far these conditions changed during the course of the Bronze Age is a subject of much debate. Environmental evidence for the later third and second millennia certainly points to a patchwork landscape in which stock husbandry, crop cultivation and a range of other activities were a commonplace. However, important questions still remain regarding the scale and duration of settlement and land use around Roystone and across the Peak as a whole (Barnatt & Smith 1991).

Upstanding evidence for the Bronze Age takes a variety of forms, though by far the most common traces are round barrows. A long history of interest in barrows has created a remarkable distribution pattern. More than five hundred barrows have been identified in the Peak, most dating to between 2500 and 1500 BC and thus to both the final stages of the Neolithic and the Earlier Bronze Age. The original figure was surely significantly higher. Records are not always reliable and land use since then has bitten deeply. On the limestone, barrows are relatively rare in areas where the pattern of Medieval strip fields can still be traced, suggesting destruction by the plough from then on. Many have also gone with the advent of more 'industrial' agriculture over the last two centuries, which probably accounts for their relative scarcity in enclosed land on the gritstone. The greatest densities are found on the limestone where barrows occur in a variety of settings, in isolation and in small clusters (Barnatt & Collis 1995).

Above the Roystone valley, a series of barrows have been identified along the ridge to the south and west of Minninglow (fig. 1). One of these, dug in the nineteenth century by Thomas Bateman, revealed the burial of a child and other scattered bones. It also showed evidence of re-use for burial in the Anglo Saxon period. The primary burial in the mound was not recovered until well after Bateman's time; a cist containing cremated human bone and a flaked flint knife. The site is now capped by a wall built in the last few centuries and can be seen in section beneath the lowest courses. Another mound, known now as Lime Kiln Barrow, lies at the southern end of this spread and has also seen excavation, revealing a primary cist burial and the later insertion of other deposits.

The contrast between round barrows and older tombs, in frequency as much as in form, has prompted a variety of interpretations. Some suggest a narrowing of focus and a pulling in of social horizons. Older tombs had brought quite broad communities into focus through complex forms of ancestral ritual. Activities around later round mounds were more overtly concerned with specific genealogies; lines of descent and inheritance that stretched back behind particular families (Barrett 1988; Garwood 1991). This paper is not the place in which to rehearse or explore these arguments in detail. What matters here is that the increased frequency and distribution of round barrows when compared to older tombs has been taken by some as proxy evidence for a process of 'settling down' in traditions of settlement and land use. This is the argument developed by Richard Hodges in his discussion of the barrows on the ridge above Roystone (Hodges 1991). For him, round barrows were the resting places of the dead from small farming families who lived and worked in relatively close proximity.

Hodges' argument is not altogether wrong. But it misses the different scales at which this cluster of barrows may have been perceived. Up close, there is a sense of personal histories and tight genealogies; founding graves and returns with others over time. After the drama of a cremation, the laying to rest of ashes and charred bones with those who shared close ties. That return sometimes meant handling the bones of older kin, or simply remembering the dead whilst looking out, the eye drawn along the ridge, where it fell on other mounds. Though we cannot be certain, the ridge may have been recognised as a small cemetery which extended genealogical time still further. Going perhaps beyond memory, the rhetoric of events at these mounds may have even drawn Minninglow into focus; a Neolithic monument that was perhaps as much a part of myth as it was of history by this time.

More importantly to this discussion, Hodges' argument fails to catch the particular ways that people may have lived and worked across the immediate area in the later third and second millennia. Though most small communities were certainly practicing what we might loosely call 'farming', it is likely that the annual cycle for many still involved a degree of movement and perhaps even longer cycles of fallow and residence relocation. Under these circumstances, barrows may well have had their greatest significance for specific families, but that significance was brought into focus during seasonal visits or even after intervals of a generation or so. It is possible that some barrows were located to draw attention to genealogical ties precisely because people were not always present in the immediate vicinity. Like many others, Hodges does not allow for these sorts of variability in the character of the routine encounter that people may have had with barrows and this limits the interpretation.

There is much that remains unclear on these issues. As John Barnatt has shown for the cairnfields and re-lated evidence of the East Moors, the simple presence of substantial clearance features and building platforms does not necessarily demonstrate continuous and protracted occupation; year in year out and from generation to generation (Barnatt 2000). In fact, the development of more persistent or sustained forms of occupation may well be a process that unfolds over the entire course of the Bronze Age, not something that emerged fully formed the moment that people began to build round mounds to contain their dead. This is one of the issues that we plan to explore through the complete analysis of the test pit data. We will be looking at basic densities of Bronze Age material across the study area, and at possible changes in raw material and technological patterning that may indicate shifts in traditions of movement and settlement. What we cannot assume as a first principle is that we already know what form occupation may have taken at this time.

Problems with determining the character of prehistoric occupation in and around Roystone become even more acute in the first millennium BC. Hodges draws attention to a relative paucity of Later Bronze Age and Iron Age material in the Roystone area: only small quantities of Later Bronze Age pottery found near Jackdaw and Roystone Rocks and in Parwich Meadow. This is taken as evidence for a period of impoverishment and even abandonment of the area throughout much of the first millennium BC. For Hodges, this is a local expression of a general process of abandonment which he suggests can be traced across the Peak as a whole. Pointing to the lack of distinctive ceramics, to well dated settlements or the sorts of material culture found in other regions, he argues that many parts of the region may have been left to their own devices, people retreating back down to the Trent Valley or into what is now South Yorkshire in the face of wetter conditions. Also cited are several late Bronze Age hill-forts in the region. These appear to exist (literally) as high points in an impoverished landscape. Hodges suggests that "competition for local lead needed for making bronze implements may have brought greater strife to the area and led to the construction of communal fortifications. There was certainly a staggering depopulation of the region" (1991: 69). Another 'fact' cited in this argument is the apparent late foundation for many of the settlements associated with the Roman period. Where investigated, many of these farmsteads, terraces and small enclosures reveal evidence for occupation from the first century AD onwards and this is taken to suggest a period of later recolonisation.

Once again, there are a series of problems with this argument, problems of both method and theory. The kind of 'catastrophist' argument offered by Hodges is commonly cited to 'explain' apparent gaps in the archaeological record. But we have to ask, if the area really was so depopulated, who mined the lead ore; who cut down the trees for fuel; who manufactured the implements; and who, in fact, used them? There are material problems too. For example, it is far from clear that we have a particularly well developed knowledge of ceramic sequences for the first millennium BC in the region. Some of the largest assemblages come from the hilltop enclosure of Mam Tor and these are dated only loosely to the Later Bronze Age (Coombs & Thompson 1979). The possibility that similar pottery was being made and used well into the Iron Age is a strong one. The situation is even more problematic for stone. Reflecting trends seen at much broader scales, the later second and first millennia BC see not an abandonment of stone tool use but a collapse of structured routines of procurement and working which undermines the sorts of definition that we normally expect of our typologies (Edmonds 1995; Young and Humphrey 1999). As a consequence, it is currently difficult to recognise assemblages dating to this time. At Roystone, this may mean that material from test pits and excavations does reflect activity of this period but that we simply cannot recognise it yet.

There are also more general problems with the abandonment model as it is currently presented. Pollen cores from various parts of the East Moors point to a strong and persistent presence in the area. Though heather moorland was established on some ground, there was still plenty of maintained grassland and even crop cultivation in the area. There are even

hints of a greater measure of soil loss towards the end of the period; as agricultural regimes finally put paid to extensive tracts of woodland and perhaps gained an intensity not seen before. Given the observations made above, it is quite conceivable that some of the field systems that we see continued in use a good deal of the way through the Iron Age. The historical fact that archaeologists have always referred to this field evidence as "Bronze Age" does not make it a truth. At least some of what we can still see on the surface today may actually be Iron Age in date. Environmental evidence is rather thinner on the ground for the White Peak, but again, what there is does not suggest wholesale abandonment of the form that Hodges suggests.

Beyond the evidence of pollen, it is also likely that work on Roman period settlements of the first few centuries AD has tended to concentrate on specific features from that time, or has been set at a scale inappropriate to identifying just how far the roots of occupation extended back into the past. In other words, where sites have been investigated at all, they have been excavated with questions about the Roman period in mind, not with a view to establishing whether particular locales had histories of use that extended much further back in time. In fact, just such evidence has been found, at sites like Staden, Harborough Rocks and Chee Tor. It is also clear that many of the settlements which survive to be studied today do so because they are now on land that is considered marginal. Their counterparts on ground given different values since the Middle Ages have been all but obliterated by the plough. Coarse handmade pottery seldom survives all that long in such conditions. Beyond all this, it may be unhelpful to see abandonment simply because the Peak lacks the sorts of material culture found in other more extensively studied regions. As Bill Bevan has rightly pointed out, problems of visibility aside, it may well be that things were simply different here, taking another path to that seen in areas like Wessex, East Yorkshire or the Midlands (Bevan 2000).

Given these patterns, it makes little sense to imagine the wholesale abandonment of the region. The mass of farmsteads, 'Brickwork' and other field systems that threaded their way across areas like South Yorkshire at this time might indicate that some people did move. Pushed perhaps by worsening conditions on higher ground or by shifts in the nature of landholding and allegiance. But these areas were not empty either and we should allow that our problem here is also one of recognition. Some land probably did fall out of occupation. Soils on parts of the gritstone became more acid, lost their fertility through overuse, or were washed from the hillsides in greater quantities. Grazing may have persisted even here, just as it does today. It was more that these areas were no longer 'settled' in quite the same way. This was probably not the case across the Peak as a whole. But here, the trail currently runs dry. The communities who probably continued to live and work across the limestone and many of the larger valleys have left little in the way of tracks for us to follow. For the moment we are left with an absence and a series of questions; but most of all, we are left with the need for more focused research at the local and at the regional scale to ascertain if, as has been suggested, the valley of Roystone and the Peak District more generally had reverted to "woodland and scrub … leaving only the hilltops exposed" in the decades preceding the Roman conquest of England.

Discussion

Our purpose in writing this short paper has not been to present the detailed results of a specific landscape study; that would be premature. Instead, we have tried to use the interim results of work at Roystone to raise a series of questions about our methods, and the assumptions that lie behind their application. Our argument is not that abandonment, depopulation, and forest regeneration never happen. However, we should always bear in mind the fact that absence of evidence is not evidence of absence. We simply have to devise methodologies to locate the missing people and the traditions of landscape occupation that they prac-

ticed. When we have exhausted these efforts, then and only then, can we conclude that depopulation was a reality.

By the same token, we have tried to argue that our problems here lie not just with technique but also with the sophistication of our models of routine practice in the past, and of the constitution of the social. Our focus on Hodges' arguments may be a little overstated, but it is clear that we do little justice to our evidence if we assume that the presence or absence of people can be discussed in such a black and white manner. What is needed is an acknowledgement that routine experience is both varied and complex. This, in its turn, is a consequence of the fact that people operate across what Barbara Bender calls 'nested landscapes'; practicing forms of dwelling and interaction that resolve themselves at a variety of scales of spatial and temporal resolution. This is where work like the wall survey undertaken by Martin Wildgoose offers a good deal of potential. The development of landscape stratigraphies establishes something of the changing pattern of activities over time within their local productive context, and gives us a vantage from which to consider developments in and around the valley against evidence from the region as a whole.

There is a good deal of work still to be done in and around Roystone. Work on existing data and the collection of new information. One priority must be to establish far better environmental sequences and correlations with palaeoenvironmental data from a range of sealed contexts. Once again, it is crucial that sampling and analysis is closely tied to appropriate questions and set at appropriate scales. For example, it will be crucial to try and bridge the gap between the more coarse grained environmental sequences and the sorts of seasonal, inter-annual or even generational cycles that operated in the lives of people at different times in the past. We also need to gain a better control of variability at different geographic scales and this can only come through a substantive programme of fieldwork. Beyond this, the work begun at Roystone highlights the fact that if the lives of people operated at a variety of different scales, then our methods have to be in step with that. There is little to be gained from simply taking the details of the history of one little valley and harnessing these to a grand narrative that operates at national or even international scales. What lies between is the region and the more localised historical sequences that are so crucial to interpretation.

Bibliography

Ashmore, W & Knapp, A.B. (eds.)1999: *Archaeologies of Landscape*. Oxford.

Barnatt, J. 1996: Moving between the monuments: Paths and people in the Neolithic landscapes of the Peak District. *Northern Archaeology* 13/14, 45-62.

Barnatt, J. 2000: To each their own: later prehistoric farming communities and their monuments in the Peak. *Derbyshire Archaeological Journal* 120, 1-86.

Barnatt, J. & Smith, K. 1991: The Bronze Age. In: Hodges, R. & Smith, K. (eds) *Recent Developments in the Archaeology of the Peak District*, 22-38. Sheffield.

Barnatt, J. & Collis, J. (eds) 1996: *Barrows in the Peak District: Recent Research*. Sheffield.

Barrett, J.C. 1988: The living, the dead, and the ancestors: Neolithic and Early Bronze Age mortuary practices. In: J.C. Barrett and I.A. Kinnes (eds) *The Archaeology of Context in the Neolithic and Bronze* Age. 30-41. Sheffield.

Barrett, J. C. 1994: *Fragments from Antiquity*. Oxford.

Bender, B, 1993:*Landscape: Politics and perspectives*. Oxford.

Bevan, B. 2000: Peak Practice: Whatever happened to the Iron Age in the southern Pennines? In: Harding, J. & Johnson, R. Pollard, J. (eds.) *Northern Pasts.*, 141-156. Stroud.

Bradley, R 1987: Time regained: the creation of continuity. *Journal of the British Archaeological Association* 140, 1-17.

Bradley, R. 1998: *The Significance of Monuments*. London.

Coombs, D. & Thompson, H. 1979: Excavations of the hillfort of Mam Tor, Derbyshire 1965-1969. *Derbyshire Archaeological Journal* 99, 44-47.

Edmonds, M. 1995: *Stone tools and Society*. London.

Edmonds, M. & Seaborne, T. 2001: *Prehistory in the Peak*. Stroud.

Garton, D. 1991: The Neolithic. In: Hodges, R. & Smith, K. (eds.) *Recent Developments in the Archaeology of the Peak District*. 3-21. Sheffield.

Garwood, P. 1991: Ritual tradition and the reconstruction of society. In: Garwood, P. Skeates, R. & Toms, J. (eds.) *Sacred and Profane*, 10-32. Oxford.

Gosden, C. & Locke, G. (eds.) 1998: *The Past in the Past* (World Archaeology, 30.1).

Hicks, S. P. 1971: Pollen analytical evidence for the effect of prehistoric agriculture on the vegetation of North Derbyshire. *New Phytologist* 70, 647-667.

Hodges, R. 1991: *Wall-to-Wall History*. London.

Ingold, T., 1993: The temporality of landscape. *World Archaeology* 25, 152-74.

Moreland, J. 1993: Wilderness, wasteland, depopulation and the end of the Roman Empire? *Accordia Research Papers* 4, 89-110.

Tilley, C. 1994: *A Phenomenology of Landscape*. Oxford.

Whittle, A.W.R. 1997: Moving on and moving around: neolithic settlement mobility. In: Topping, P. (ed.) *Neolithic Landscapes*. Oxford, 15-22.

The authors

Henrik Thrane
Prehistoric Archeology
Moesgård
DK-8270 Højbjerg
Danmark
farkht@hum.au.dk

Nils Björhem
Malmö Kulturmiljö
Malmö Stad
Box 406
S-201 24 Malmö
Sverige
nils.bjorhem@malmo.se

Jens-Henrik Bech
Museet for Thy og Vester Hanherred
Arkæologisk afdeling
Mellemvej 18, Vang
DK-7700 Thisted
Danmark
jhbthy@post6.tele.dk

Eike Gringmuth-Dallmer
Museum für Vor- und Frühgeschichte
Schloß Scharlottenburg
D-14059 Berlin
Deutschland
mvf@smb.spk-berlin.de

Slawomir Kadrow
Instytut Archeologii i Etnologii
Polska Akademii NAUK
Oddzial w Krakowie
Slawkowska 17
PL-31 016 Kraków
Poland
slawekkadrow@poczta.onet.pl

Jacek Górski
Archaeological Museum in Krakow
Nova Huta Branch
Os. Zielone 7
PL-31-968 Krakow
Poland
igorski@ma.krakow.pl

Václav Furmanek
Archeologický ústav
Slovenskej akademie vied
Akademická 2
SK-949 21 Nitra
Slovakia
nraufurm@sarba.sk

Peter Turk
National Museum of Slovenia
Presernova 20
SI-1000 Ljubljana
Slovenia
peter.turk@narmuz-lj.si

Bernhard Hänsel
Freie Universität Berlin
Institut für Prähistorische Archälogie
Altensteinstraße 15
D-14195 Berlin
Deutschland
free@mail.zedat.fu-berlin.de

Mark Edmonds
Dept. of Archaeology and Prehistory
Northlate House, West Street
GB Sheffield S1 4ET
England
m.edmonds@sheffield.ac.uk

John Moreland
Dept. of Archaeology and Prehistory
Northlate House, West Street
GB Sheffield S1 4ET
England
j.moreland@sheffield.ac.uk